*Thomas Jefferson*

*Draftsman of a Nation*

# Thomas Jefferson

## DRAFTSMAN
### of a NATION

Natalie S. Bober

University of Virginia Press

University of Virginia Press
© 2007 by Natalie S. Bober
All rights reserved
Printed in the United States of America on acid-free paper

*First published 2007*

1 3 5 7 9 8 6 4 2

LIBRARY OF CONGRESS CATALOGING-IN-PUBLICATION DATA

Bober, Natalie.
 Thomas Jefferson : draftsman of a nation / Natalie S. Bober.
  p.    cm.
 Includes bibliographical references and index.
 ISBN 978-0-8139-2632-2 (cloth : alk. paper)
 1. Jefferson, Thomas, 1743–1826—Juvenile literature. 2. Presidents—United
States—Biography—Juvenile literature. 3. United States—Politics and
government—1775–1783—Juvenile literature. 4. United States—Politics and
government—1783–1809—Juvenile literature. 5. Monticello (Va.)—History—
Juvenile literature. 6. Slaves—Virginia—Charlottesville—History—Juvenile
literature. 7. Plantation life—Virginia—Charlottesville—History—Juvenile
literature. I. Title.
 E332.79.B625 2007
 973.4'6092—dc22
 [B]

                                                                2006032722

For Larry,
who least needs reminding
that it is he who makes
it all possible

# Contents

# Chronology

1743: April 13—Thomas Jefferson born at Shadwell, in Virginia.

1757: August 17—TJ's father, Peter Jefferson, dies at age 50.

1760: TJ enters college of William and Mary.
    March 25—King George III of England succeeds George II.

1762: TJ begins legal study with George Wythe.

1764: April 13—TJ turns 21 and inherits his father's estate.

1765: January—Stamp Act passed by Parliament.
    TJ becomes a parish vestryman and justice of the peace.
    TJ organizes Rivanna project.
    July 20—TJ's sister Martha Jefferson marries Jefferson's school
        friend Dabney Carr.
    October 1—TJ's sister Jane Jefferson dies at 25.

1766: Stamp Act repealed.

1767: TJ admitted to bar.
    June 15–July 2—Townshend Acts passed in Parliament.
    Work begins on Monticello.

1768: TJ elected to Virginia House of Burgesses.

1769: Townshend Acts rescinded, except for the tax on tea.

1770: February 1—Shadwell destroyed by fire.

1772: January 1—TJ marries Mrs. Martha Wayles Skelton.
    September 27—daughter Martha "Patsy" Jefferson born.

1773: March 12—TJ and fellow burgesses urge formation of colonial
        Committees of Correspondence.
    April 20—Dabney Carr dies at age 30; TJ takes care of his
        family and affairs.
    May 28—TJ's father-in-law, John Wayles, dies.
    December 16—the Boston Tea Party occurs.

1774:  January—TJ inherits Hemings family of slaves.

February 21—sister Elizabeth Jefferson dies at age 30.

March 31—Parliament reacts to Boston Tea Party by passing the Boston Port Act, closing the port to trade. To be enacted June 1.

April 3—daughter Jane Randolph Jefferson born.

September 5—First Continental Congress meets.

1775:  March 20—Second Virginia Convention meets; Patrick Henry makes speech ("Give me liberty or give me death").

April 18—Battle of Lexington and Concord begins Revolutionary War.

June 8—British governor flees Virginia.

June 22—Second Continental Congress meets.

September—daughter Jane Randolph Jefferson dies at 17 months.

1776:  January 1—British burn Norfolk, Virginia, and Falmouth, Maine.

January 10—Thomas Paine publishes *Common Sense*.

March 31—TJ's mother, Jane Randolph Jefferson, dies.

June 10—TJ elected to write Declaration of Independence.

July 2—colonies vote to declare independence.

July 4—colonies sign Declaration of Independence.

Autumn—TJ and George Wythe begin revision of Virginia law.

1777:  May 28—TJ's son born.

June 14—TJ's son dies at 17 days.

1778:  August 1—daughter Mary ("Polly" or "Maria") Jefferson born.

1779:  TJ succeeds Patrick Henry as governor of Virginia.

1780:  April—capital of Virginia moves to Richmond for safety from Revolutionary War.

November 30—daughter Lucy Elizabeth Jefferson born.

December—Benedict Arnold leads British Army to invade Virginia coast.

1781:  January—Benedict Arnold attacks Virginia; Washington sends the Marquis de Lafayette to defend Virginia.

TJ begins to write *Notes on Virginia*.

April 15—TJ's daughter Lucy Elizabeth Jefferson dies at 5 months.

June 3—Jack Jouett's ride warns TJ of British arrest party.

June—TJ retires from governorship.

1782: May 8—daughter, also named Lucy Elizabeth Jefferson, born.

September 6—TJ's wife, Martha Wayles Skelton Jefferson, dies.

1783: May—TJ's sister Anna Scott Jefferson joins household.

June—TJ elected to Congress. Leaves two younger daughters with his sister-in-law (Martha's half sister, Elizabeth Wayles Eppes) and her husband in Virginia, then takes Patsy to boarding school in Philadelphia before going to take his new seat at Annapolis. In Congress, TJ helps form government of the new nation.

1784: May 7—TJ appointed minister plenipotentiary to France.

July 4—TJ sails for France. Takes Patsy with him, leaving younger girls with Francis and Elizabeth Eppes.

August—TJ and Patsy arrive in Paris.

October 13—TJ's daughter Lucy Elizabeth Jefferson dies at two-and-a-half years old.

1785: May 2—TJ elected to succeed Benjamin Franklin as minister to the French court.

1786: August—TJ meets Maria Cosway.

October 4—Cosways leave Paris.

1787: February 28—TJ leaves for southern France.

December—TJ ends relationship with Maria Cosway.

1788: July—TJ's younger daughter, "Polly," and Sally Hemings arrive in Paris.

1789: April 14—George Washington becomes the first president of the United States.

July 14—Storming of the Bastille in France.

October 8—the Jeffersons begin journey home to Virginia.

1790: February 23—TJ's daughter Martha "Patsy" Jefferson marries Thomas Mann Randolph Jr., a second cousin.

March 21—TJ becomes Washington's secretary of state for term ending December 1793.

1791: January 23—TJ's grandchild Anne Cary Randolph born, the first of Martha's 12 children.

TJ helps Washington plan a capital city.

1792: September—TJ's grandson Thomas Jefferson Randolph born.

1796: TJ elected vice president of the United States.

TJ's granddaughter Ellen Wayles Randolph born.

1797: March 3—TJ inaugurated as president of American Philosophical Society.

March 4—TJ inaugurated as vice president of the United States.

June 18—Alien and Sedition Acts passed.

October 13—TJ's daughter Mary ("Maria" or "Polly") Jefferson marries Jack Eppes, a cousin.

1799: December 31—TJ's grandchild born prematurely to the Eppeses, dies unnamed.

1800: December 3—Thomas Jefferson and Aaron Burr receive equal number of votes for the Presidency.

1801: February 17—Congress elects TJ president of the United States.

TJ's grandson Francis Wayles Eppes born.

1802: Alien and Sedition Acts expire and are abandoned.

1803: Louisiana Purchase enacted.

Lewis and Clark expedition authorized.

1804: TJ's granddaughter Maria Jefferson Eppes born.

April 17—TJ's daughter Mary ("Maria" or "Polly") Jefferson Eppes dies at age 25.

1805: TJ begins second term as president.

1807: TJ's granddaughter Maria Jefferson Eppes dies at 3 years.

1809: TJ returns to Monticello.

1812: June 18—War of 1812 begins.

1814: British burn the Capitol during War of 1812; TJ sells his library to Congress to replace the destroyed volumes.

TJ begins work on Albemarle Academy (later University of Virginia).

1825: March—Lafayette visits TJ as University of Virginia opens.

May 27—TJ's granddaughter Ellen Wayles Randolph marries Joseph Coolidge Jr.

1826: July 4—Thomas Jefferson dies on the fiftieth birthday of the United States.

# Family Tree

Peter Jefferson
(1707–1757)
m.
Jane Randolph
(1720–1776)

- Jane Jefferson
  (1740–1765)

- Mary Jefferson
  (1741–1817)
  m.
  Col. John Bolling

- THOMAS
  JEFFERSON
  (1743–1826)
  m.
  Martha Wayles
  Skelton
  (1748–1782)

  - Martha "Patsy"
    Jefferson
    (1772–1836)
    m.
    Thomas Mann
    Randolph
    (1768–1828)

    - Anne Cary
      Randolph
      (1791–1826)
      m.
      Charles Lewis
      Bankhead

    - Thomas Jefferson
      Randolph
      (1792–1875)
      m.
      Jane Hollins
      Nicholas

    - Ellen Wayles
      Randolph
      (1794–1795)

    - Ellen Wayles
      Randolph
      (1796–1876)
      m.
      Joseph Coolidge

    - Cornelia Jefferson
      Randolph
      (1799–1871)

    - Virginia Jefferson
      Randolph
      (1801–1882)
      m.
      Nicholas Philip
      Trist

    - Mary Jefferson
      Randolph
      (1803–1876)

    - James Madison
      Randolph
      (1806–1834)

    - Benjamin Franklin
      Randolph
      (1808–1871)

    - Meriwether
      Lewis Randolph
      (1810–1837)

    - Septimia Anne
      Randolph
      (1814–1887)

    - George Wythe
      Randolph
      (1818–1867)

  - Jane Randolph
    Jefferson
    (1774–1775)

  - Son (1777)

  - Mary ("Polly"
    or "Maria")
    Jefferson
    (1778–1804)
    m.
    John (Jack)
    Wayles Eppes
    (1773–1823)

    - Infant
      (1800)

    - Francis
      Wayles Eppes
      (1801–1881)

    - Maria
      Jefferson
      Eppes
      (1804–1807)

  - Lucy Elizabeth
    Jefferson
    (1780–1781)

  - Lucy Elizabeth
    Jefferson
    (1782–1784)

- Elizabeth
  Jefferson
  (1744–1774)

- Martha
  Jefferson
  (1746–1811)
  m.
  Dabney
  Carr
  (1743–1773)

  - Jane Barbara
    Carr
    (1766–1840)

  - Lucy Carr
    (1768–1803)

  - Mary Carr
    ("Polly")
    (1768–?)

  - Peter Carr
    (1770–1815)

  - Col. Samuel
    Carr
    (1771–1855)

  - Dabney Carr
    (1773–1837)

- Peter Field
  Jefferson
  (1748–1748)

- Son (1750)

- Lucy Jefferson
  (1752–1784)
  m.
  Charles L. Lewis

- Anna Scott
  Jefferson
  (1755–1802)
  m.
  Hastings Marks

- Randolph
  Jefferson
  (1755–1815)
  m.
  1-Anne Lewis
  2-Mitchie Pryor

*Thomas Jefferson*
*Draftsman of a Nation*

PART I

*Sentimental Revolutionary*

# On the Edge of the Wilderness

IN THE LATE WINTER OF 1760, a tall and lanky young man of sixteen bid his family good-bye, mounted his horse, and set off from a plantation known as Shadwell, situated on the western frontier of the British colony of Virginia, at the foot of the Southwest Mountains. He was headed to the town of Williamsburg, the capital of colonial Virginia, one hundred miles to the southeast.

He had a wide-winged nose, prominent cheekbones, chestnut-red hair, and an abundance of freckles. He wasn't particularly handsome, but there was a kindness apparent in his expression, an intelligence shining in his soft hazel eyes. He was six feet, two and a half inches tall, unusually tall for those days, and he had large hands and feet. He seemed to be growing right out of his clothes. His friends called him "Tall Tom." His name was Thomas Jefferson.

He was strong, and he stood straight as a gun barrel, but his movements were awkward and he was very shy. He was indifferent to clothes and not at all concerned with his appearance. His awkwardness, though, was more than made up for by his bubbling enthusiasm for everything he did. He had taken dancing lessons with his sisters and knew the minuets, reels, and country dances that were popular then. He loved to dance and to play the tunes on his fiddle as well. He carried himself with the bearing of one familiar with a saddle, a gun, a canoe, and a minuet— a country-bred youth who had never been required to till the soil but had the ease and freedom to enjoy country life. Slavery, the "peculiar institution" that enabled this way of life in the South, was an intrinsic part of the culture in the Chesapeake region and made this leisure possible.

As Thomas turned his mare toward Williamsburg, riding along the James River, he was headed toward his first contact with urban life. Williamsburg was a compact, civilized town on the edge of a vast, untamed continent. He had heard stories about it, but until now his world had been rimmed by the horizon of his little mountaintop. He was breaking through that rim, on his first great adventure.

In Williamsburg, Thomas Jefferson would apply for entrance into the College of William and Mary, named for the British king and queen who had chartered it under the auspices of the Church of England. His saddlebags were filled with his books and music. Eager to learn, sensitive, and mature beyond his years, he approached Williamsburg with an excitement and a sense of adventure, a stirring within him of a desire to know, to learn, to become someone, and to make a difference in the world. He already knew the Bible and a few English classics, was well grounded in Greek and Latin, and had perfected his knowledge of French. He had inherited from his father a passion for books and a love of language that would remain with him all his life.

Accompanying him on this journey was another young man, named Jupiter, who, like Jefferson, had been born at Shadwell in 1743. The two had established a friendship as children that would continue into their adult lives. As young boys they had played together on the plantation, had fished and swum in the Rivanna River, and set traplines along its banks. They would travel all over the colony of Virginia together and would eventually find wives on the same plantation.

But Jupiter was not headed for college in Williamsburg. He was accompanying Jefferson as his body servant, to "shave, dress, and follow me on horseback," as Jefferson later described it. Although the two had grown up together, when they turned twenty-one, under Virginia law, Jefferson would own Jupiter, who was part of the property he would inherit. They would become master and slave.[1]

At that time, the Chesapeake region, which consisted of Virginia, Maryland, and North Carolina, was the center of slavery. In 1606 the London Company, a corporation of stockholders residing in and around London, had been granted a charter by King James I to found colonies in America. In 1607 they founded Jamestown, Virginia, the first permanent settlement in America. By 1616, just nine years later, John Rolphe, married to the Indian princess Pocahontas, had perfected methods of raising and curing a pungent weed called tobacco. This process eliminated much of its bitter tang, and smoking tobacco became popular. Soon "tobacco rush" days began as crops were planted wherever they might grow, even in the streets of Jamestown and between the numerous graves in the cemetery.

Growing tobacco required large amounts of land and with that requirement came a demand for slave labor. In 1619, a year before the Pilgrims landed at Plymouth Rock in Massachusetts, the first twenty Africans to arrive in the territory that became known as the thirteen colonies landed at Jamestown and were sold as slaves.

In that same year, representative self-government was also born in Virginia. The London Company authorized the settlers to summon an assembly known as the House of Burgesses, which became the first of many miniature parliaments to mushroom from the soil of America.[2]

By the end of the century, tobacco had become the driving force of the economy in Virginia. As the demand for tobacco increased, so did the demand for slaves to work the plantations. They were the cheapest form of labor, particularly on the large plantations of the southern colonies.[3]

African men, women, and children were being violently seized in Africa by other Africans and delivered to white slave traders. They were then transported to North America as human cargo on what was known as the "Middle Passage,"* a long and treacherous ocean voyage from western Africa to North America. Stripped naked and fearful that the mysterious white people were cannibals, they huddled on board amid unimaginable filth, often shackled to each other or to the deck of the slave ship throughout the voyage. Those who survived could, like other merchandise, be bought and sold throughout the thirteen British colonies that were strung out along the Atlantic coast. African slaves made up nearly one-fifth of the population of Virginia. By the time Thomas Jefferson and Jupiter were born, in 1743, slavery was an integral part of their world. It would shadow and shape their relationship for the rest of their lives.

The Virginia of the eighteenth century was much larger than the state of Virginia as we know it today. The colony stretched from the Atlantic Ocean west to the Mississippi River and north to the Great Lakes. It included what would become the states of West Virginia, Kentucky, Ohio, Illinois, Indiana, Michigan, and Wisconsin. It must have seemed like an empire.

---

*So called because it was the middle leg of the triangular trade route: Europe to Africa, Africa to the Americas, and from the Americas back to Europe.

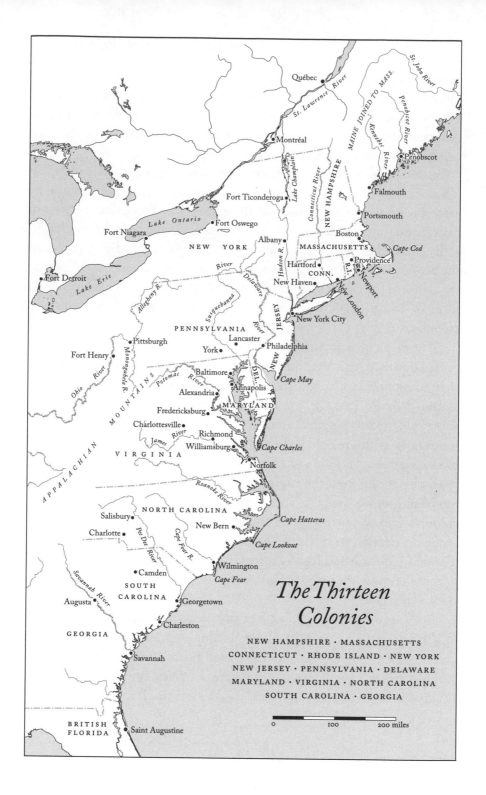

Québec

St. Lawrence River

St. John River

Penobscot River

Montréal

Lake Champlain

Connecticut River

MAINE JOINED TO MASS.

Kennebec River

Penobscot

NEW HAMPSHIRE

Falmouth

Fort Ticonderoga

Portsmouth

Lake Ontario

Fort Oswego

Albany

Boston

Fort Niagara

NEW YORK

MASSACHUSETTS

Cape Cod

Hudson R.

Hartford

Providence

Fort Detroit

Lake Erie

River

CONN.

R.I.

Newport

Allegheny R.

Delaware River

New Haven

New London

Susquehanna River

New York City

Ohio River

Monongahela R.

PENNSYLVANIA

Pittsburgh

Lancaster

Philadelphia

NEW JERSEY

Fort Henry

York

APPALACHIAN MOUNTAINS

Potomac River

Baltimore

DEL.

Cape May

Alexandria

Annapolis

MARYLAND

Fredericksburg

Chárlottesville

James River

Richmond

VIRGINIA

Williamsburg

Cape Charles

Norfolk

Roanoke River

NORTH CAROLINA

Cape Hatteras

Salisbury

New Bern

Charlotte

Pee Dee River

Cape Fear R.

Cape Lookout

Camden

Wilmington

Cape Fear

SOUTH CAROLINA

Savannah River

Georgetown

Augusta

Charleston

GEORGIA

Savannah

# The Thirteen Colonies

NEW HAMPSHIRE · MASSACHUSETTS
CONNECTICUT · RHODE ISLAND · NEW YORK
NEW JERSEY · PENNSYLVANIA · DELAWARE
MARYLAND · VIRGINIA · NORTH CAROLINA
SOUTH CAROLINA · GEORGIA

0      100      200 miles

BRITISH
FLORIDA

Saint Augustine

The Piedmont section, where the Jeffersons made their home, had not been settled until more than a hundred years after the colonization of the eastern seaboard. It was still a vast wilderness, but enterprising young planters were beginning to move west from the crowded and worn-out lands in the east. Situated at the foot of the Blue Ridge Mountains, Piedmont land was fertile, and the air was free of mosquitoes and the diseases they carried. Jefferson's father, Peter Jefferson, was among the earliest settlers of the area. It was a time when large tracts of land, called patents, were readily acquired, and Peter was granted title to his first 322 acres in 1730 in what is now called Albemarle County.

Peter was neither rich nor well born, but he was ambitious and had a fine mind and a pioneering spirit. He was a huge man, freckled, red-haired, and somber. He loved the outdoors and was an expert horseman and hunter and a tireless swimmer. His strength was legendary. While still young, in spite of a meager education, he managed to absorb enough mathematics to learn the art of surveying,* an appropriate profession in a new country where speculators and land-hungry settlers were rapidly pushing into the western part of the colony. He was earning a reputation as a rising young planter and as an explorer and mapmaker.

While living in Fine Creek, on the James River in Goochland County, where he had been born, Peter met William Randolph, a young aristocrat who owned 2,400 acres of adjoining land. They soon became close friends, and it was through this friendship that Peter met William's uncle, Isham Randolph.

Isham was typical of the Virginia planter aristocracy. He was intelligent and well educated, and he lived in a grand house on a large plantation on the James River, staffed by about one hundred slaves. He was also a merchant sea captain who imported slaves and traded with England. He had recently become one of Virginia's leading slaveholders by purchasing part of a consignment of 380 enslaved Africans. Isham and five of his brothers had attended the College of William and Mary. The Randolph family never hesitated to spend its considerable fortune on education.

*A surveyor laid out boundaries of the patented public lands in order that grants and deeds might be obtained.

When William Randolph took his friend Peter Jefferson to visit his Uncle Isham, Peter met Isham's seventeen-year-old daughter Jane. Tall, slender, graceful, and elegant, she had a cheerful disposition and a fine mind. Two years later, on October 19, 1739, she and Peter were married. He was thirty-two; she was nineteen. She brought with her many slaves from her father's plantation. With this union, Peter Jefferson, a man without family prestige or social pretense, became identified with one of the leading families in Virginia. In eighteenth-century Virginia there were two distinct groups: the aristocracy, typified by Isham Randolph; and the yeomanry, who were, for the most part, industrious, belligerently independent, and instinctively democratic. The marriage of Jane Randolph to Peter Jefferson joined the two classes. Of these two strains would come the unique mosaic that was Thomas Jefferson.

In 1735 Peter Jefferson had surveyed and patented for himself one thousand acres of fertile land ideal for tobacco cultivation on the south side of the Anna River, referred to as the Rivanna. Now he had his eye on a choice tract of land across the river as the perfect site on which to build a house. But, he discovered, it had just been purchased by William Randolph.

Randolph, learning of Peter's interest, promptly "sold" his friend four hundred acres in return for the "biggest bowl of arrack punch" that was made by Henry Weatherbourne of the Raleigh Tavern in Williamsburg.

Peter Jefferson immediately began to clear his land and build a house with his own hands. He worked at the task, aided only by an enslaved family, for several years. As he worked, he came to know the Native Americans whose trails passed nearby. A feeling of friendship and mutual trust built up between them, and the American Indians treated him with the respect they were apt to feel for men who never feared and never deceived them.[4]

When his house was finished, sometime before the spring of 1743, Peter Jefferson brought his gentle and well-born wife and their two little daughters, Jane and Mary, to live there. They were eagerly awaiting the birth of their third child.

Peter named the house Shadwell, after the parish in London where his wife had been christened twenty-three years before. It was here at

Shadwell, soon after, that their first son was born.* They named him Thomas, after his paternal grandfather and great-grandfather.

Shadwell was a spacious farmhouse, a story and a half high, with a wide entry and four large rooms on the ground floor and many garret rooms above. Jane's interest in gardening was given free rein here, and soon she was supervising the digging of a terraced garden behind the house and was planting purple hyacinths and yellow narcissus.

The house stood in a clearing on a slight rise of ground, with a view of the hazy Blue Ridge Mountains in the distance. The magic of this beautiful land would have a lasting influence on the mind of the little boy who was born there.

But the family's stay in this idyllic setting was interrupted when he was just two years old. Peter Jefferson's friend William Randolph died, leaving his children orphans. William's wife had died three years earlier, and William's last wish was that Peter, his "dear and loving friend," and family move to the Randolph home, called Tuckahoe, to care for his children—two daughters and one son, also named Thomas—and manage his estate. This unusual request Peter honored as an act of pure friendship. He left his own lands in the care of an overseer.

So it was that Thomas Jefferson's earliest memory was of being handed up to a slave mounted on horseback and cradled on a pillow in his arms for a long distance. While Tuckahoe, situated on the James River, was only about fifty miles from Shadwell, the roads then were hardly more than mud tracks, and the journey took three days.

Jane Jefferson had spent much time in Tuckahoe as a child and felt comfortable there. It was a luxurious house for the times, with a beautifully carved staircase in the entrance hall and magnificent furniture imported from England in its stately parlors. It was staffed by many house servants. According to the terms of William Randolph's will, each of his daughters had three slave girls as her personal attendants. Here, in these

---

*By the calendar then in effect (Old Style, or Julian), he was born on April 2, 1743. The New Style (Gregorian) calendar, adopted by Great Britain and her colonies in 1752, brought the calendar in line with the solar year by adding eleven days. This changed the date to April 13, the date Thomas would celebrate.

opulent surroundings, the Jefferson and Randolph children were brought up together.

Peter Jefferson hired a tutor to teach the three Randolph children and his own two daughters. When his young son turned five, he was allowed to join the older children in the little tree-shaded white frame building that had become their school. Jefferson later called this the "English School" and spoke of it happily. But here he learned one of the harsh lessons of slavery: only white children went to school.

As Thomas Jefferson was growing up, his father and his father's good friend Joshua Fry, who was a professor of mathematics at the College of William and Mary, were often partners on surveying expeditions. When he was six years old the two men were commissioned to find and mark the boundary line between Virginia and North Carolina. They were gone for many weeks. When they returned, the young boy listened wide-eyed as his father told stories of their adventures. As he marveled at his father's courage in fighting wild animals and snakes, he was learning the importance of perseverance in the face of danger.[5]

Peter Jefferson and Joshua Fry were able to use their findings—and their skills—to draw a map of Virginia. The first such map ever attempted was a conjectural sketch made in 1609 by Captain John Smith. Thomas was fascinated as he watched his father and Professor Fry bending over the great table on which their surveys, drafting instruments, and broad sheets were spread out. When the map was completed, they told him, they would send it to London, to Thomas Jeffrys, geographer to the king, to be printed. It would be the first Virginia map to mark the inhabited parts of Virginia, the entire province of Maryland, as well as part of Pennsylvania, New Jersey, and North Carolina. He was still a young boy, but Thomas Jefferson felt some of his father's excitement at what he had accomplished, his pride in what he had taught himself. Peter Jefferson was carving his reputation out of the Virginia wilderness.

When his son was nine, Peter Jefferson decided that the Randolph children were sufficiently grown to allow him to move his family back to their own home at Shadwell. But soon after, he sent Thomas away to study. There were no public schools in eighteenth-century Virginia. Planters' sons received their education by boarding with teachers who were almost always preachers, and the quality of the instruction varied with the quality of the teachers. Thomas attended the Latin School of the Scotsman Rev. William Douglas, minister of St. James Parish, in Northam. Once again, young Jefferson was uprooted from home (the school was fifty miles from Shadwell), this time separated from his entire family, but he tried to console himself with the thought that he would be just five miles from Tuckahoe and his Randolph cousins.

At Rev. Douglas's school the young Jefferson studied the "rudiments" of Greek, Latin, and French. It was here that he seems to have begun to build a library of his own. His father's account book records, in clear and bold handwriting, "Books for my Son £1/10/6,"* a sizable sum of money. He boarded with the Douglas family for the school year and spent summers and holidays at Shadwell. Thomas Jefferson would never again live an entire year with his parents.

During the summers, when he was back at Shadwell, his father found more time to spend with him. He taught his son mathematics, and outdoors he taught him to shoot deer and wild turkey and to paddle a canoe on the Rivanna. He taught him to portage—to carry a canoe overland between two waterways—and when he was satisfied that his son could handle a canoe properly, he gave him one of his own. The young Jefferson learned to watch for logs, rocks, and tree roots in the water and to repair the canoe himself if it needed mending. "Never ask another to do for you what you can do for yourself" was a principle of his father's he never forgot.[6]

When he was ten, his father gave him his own rifle and sent him into the forest alone on a hunting expedition in another attempt to encourage self-reliance. But try as he might, Thomas couldn't shoot anything. Eventually he came upon a wild turkey caught in a pen. Excited, he tied it to a tree with his garter, shot it, and brought it home in triumph. But he never learned to enjoy hunting.

Peter also taught his son to ride and made an expert horseman of him. As Thomas stalked or rode through the Southwest Mountains, or fished on the banks of a stream, he came to know the forest as few did. He grew

*One pound, ten shillings, sixpence (about $2.65 today).

up loving the outdoors, and he became a careful observer of all the plants and animals in the forest. He learned the names and habits of all the birds, and he knew all the insects of the fields.

The strong bond of love and respect for his father was being strengthened daily. As the young Jefferson grew, the physical resemblance between father and son became striking. The son was fast becoming as tall and sinewy as the father.

By this time Peter Jefferson had attained an influential place in the community, accumulating over five thousand acres of land and rising to the rank of colonel in the county militia. In 1754 he was elected to the House of Burgesses.

Peter Jefferson owned about forty books, a sizable library for that place and time; all had been carefully selected. His editions of Shakespeare and the Bible were well worn. In spite of Peter's lack of formal education, he worked hard to educate himself, and he communicated to his first-born son his own love of learning.

Evenings at Shadwell were often spent around the fireplace, where the family gathered to sing together, Jefferson's sister Jane leading the choir. By now there were eight children. Jane, three years older than her brother, was the oldest and his favorite. Then came Mary, Thomas, Elizabeth, Martha, Lucy, and finally the twins, Anna and Randolph, who had been born when their brother was twelve. Two other boys, born at Tuckahoe, had not survived. Thomas was one of ten children born within a period of fifteen years, and the middle child of five born within six years.

His sister Jane could read music and had a good ear for tunes. She encouraged him to learn and helped him with his reading and his music. When Peter realized that his son was interested, he bought him a violin.

A violin, called a fiddle, was almost the only musical instrument known in the back countries of the colonies. Larger instruments like the harpsichord and organ were difficult to ship from Europe and almost impossible to transport overland to the western regions.

During spring holidays, brother and sister often wandered together through the woods near Shadwell. Now and then they stopped to rest for a while on a log. Jane sang folk songs, hymns, or psalm tunes, and her brother accompanied her on his ever-present fiddle. When they returned to Shadwell, their arms were laden with bunches of wildflowers.

In the spirit of Virginia hospitality, Shadwell was open to a constant stream of guests. It was near the main road, called Three-Notched Road for the notches carved in the trees by early trailblazers to prevent travelers from losing their way in the wilderness.[7] Thus it was a stopping-off place for many passersby, including the great Native American chiefs on their journeys to and from Williamsburg. A cordial relationship developed between the Native Americans and the Jefferson family, and young Jefferson spent much time with them. Outacity, the great orator and warrior, and chief of the Cherokee people, was a frequent guest of Peter Jefferson. His son was thrilled when Ontassete, as he called him, made him a beautifully balanced canoe paddle as a gift.

Shortly after the family returned to Shadwell from Tuckahoe, Peter Jefferson began expanding his small farmhouse into a home spacious enough to accommodate his rapidly increasing family. There was always construction going on, and his son grew accustomed to the tumult and the dust constantly swirling around him. Thomas Jefferson probably found the activity exciting.

He loved to stand at the drawing board and watch his father, who, as a surveyor, would have designed the expansion of the main house and laid out the foundations of each of the outbuildings, probably housing for his slaves as well as the kitchen and the privy. John Biswell, a professional builder, worked on the house along with his two slaves. Peter Jefferson's slaves did all the menial household tasks and worked in his tobacco fields as well.

At Shadwell, Thomas watched his father patiently teaching his slaves to be carpenters, millers, wheelwrights, shoemakers, and farmers; and he saw his mother in her sitting room in the morning with her daughters and her servants, busy with household tasks—one spinning, one basting, another winding yarn. A plantation had to be almost completely self-sustaining. Young Thomas had yet to comprehend slavery's bitter realities.

Growing up in a comfortable society created by planters who cultivated tobacco and relied on slave labor, he experienced no physical hardships and no financial worries. His family was the center of his life. The freedom, openness, and simplicity of up-country life were subtly coloring his values.

But in June of 1757, when he was just fourteen years old, his father suddenly became ill. The efforts of his physician and good friend Dr. Thomas Walker were in vain. Peter Jefferson died on August 17. He was forty-nine years old. His young wife was only thirty-seven.

Jefferson was devastated. In the frightening confusion that ensued at home, he felt helpless and abandoned. He wandered off to seek solace in his mountains—the mountains he had climbed with his father, the mountains he had come to know and to love even as he loved and revered his father. He was overwhelmed by a sense of sadness and of loss. Now he was the only male, except for a two-year-old brother, among his mother and six sisters.

Peter took care of his son in death as in life. Before his death he had made known his wishes for his eldest son. His dying instruction was that his son should receive a "thorough classical education" and the "exercise requisite for his bodie's development." Physical exercise was as important as mental stimulation.

Several months before his death, Peter Jefferson had made careful provision in a detailed will for the welfare of his wife and his children. He did not weigh the scales heavily in favor of his elder son in spite of primogeniture, the English tradition of the right of the eldest son to inherit the entire estate of his parents.

He left a large estate, including sixty slaves, two hundred hogs, seventy cows and steers, eleven sheep, and twenty-five horses. To his son Thomas he left "my mulatto fellow Tawney, my books, mathematical instruments, and my cherry tree desk and bookcase" and "either my lands on the Rivanna River and its branches, or my lands on the Fluvanna in Albemarle County . . . which of the two he shall choose" when he reached the age of twenty-one. Thomas's younger brother, Randolph, would inherit the other. In the meantime, his land would be held in trust for him by his mother, who for the next seven years would control every aspect of his life at home. Shadwell, on four hundred acres, was left to her for her lifetime. It was filled with fine furniture and silver.

Peter Jefferson had been an example of industry and responsibility, but it was his love of learning more than anything else that was his legacy to his son. The only thing Thomas Jefferson wrote about his father—almost sixty-four years later, when he was seventy-seven—reveals what was most important to him throughout his life: ". . . being of strong mind, sound judgment, and eager after information, he read much and improved himself." Books would become for his son the means to "improve himself," the keys to unlock the mystery of any subject he wanted to learn. Books would become the passion that ruled and shaped his life.

In deference to his father's wishes, Jefferson's guardians decided that he should study with one of the most scholarly and prominent clergymen in the colony, the Reverend James Maury. Rev. Maury's home was fourteen miles from Shadwell, in the shadow of what was referred to as "Peter's Mountain." Jefferson lived with Maury during the week and returned home on Saturdays. James Madison (cousin of the future president), James Maury Jr., John Walker, and a boy from nearby Louisa County named Dabney Carr were also students there. The four boys, all between the ages of fourteen and sixteen, soon became close friends. But Jefferson's special friend was Dabney Carr. They were the same age and very much alike in temperament and personality. Dabney often went home with Jefferson on weekends.

Sometimes they rode the several miles to what they called "Tom's Mountain," an 850-foot peak that soared above the broad Piedmont valley, climbed a tree there, and looked out at the vast panorama spread out beneath them. To the south and east they could see the heavily wooded forests of the Piedmont with its countless varieties of trees and flowering shrubs. To the west the tiny village of Charlottesville lay between the mountains. North was Peter's Mountain, higher than Tom's, and beyond it, the Southwest Range. Young Jefferson thought this had to be the most beautiful place on earth.

At Rev. Maury's Latin School the boys all had horses. They rode every day, following mountain trails. Jefferson became a fearless rider. But he loved to walk, too—this was his favorite exercise—and he often tramped through the woods, alone or with a friend.

Rev. Maury taught the boys well, and it was here that the world of books was fully opened to Jefferson. Maury had a library such as his young student had never seen: over four hundred volumes. He wrote forceful and elegant English prose and taught his students to do the same. Maury helped Jefferson develop a classical prose style reminiscent of the concise elegance and simplicity of the writing of the Roman patriot Cicero. In fact, Jefferson was learning to read Cicero and the Roman poet Horace in Latin, Homer and Plato in Greek, and modern French literature in the original. He often read the Greek poet Homer on his canoe trips down the Rivanna, or the great Roman poet Virgil when he stretched out on the grass in the shade of an oak tree. But he turned to Cicero when he was trying to suppress his grief over his father's death. It was Cicero's peaceful, accepting philosophy that he returned to again and again.

In Maury's classes, as Jefferson learned what he called a "correct" knowledge of Greek and Latin, he developed an appreciation for languages as tools of communication and as a pathway into history and mythology. He came to regard Greek as the perfect language, and carried his Greek grammar book in his pocket even as he played with his friends.

He listened when Rev. Maury recommended to his own son that he "reflect and remark on and digest what you read, to enter into the spirit and design of your author, to observe every step he takes to accomplish his end, and to dwell on any remarkable beauties of diction, justness or sublimity of sentiment or masterly strokes of true wit which may occur in the course of your reading."[8]

Now Jefferson began to keep his own Literary Commonplace Book, a notebook or personal journal into which he copied passages of the literature he was reading that resonated with him. Much of what he copied was poetry. Some passages reflected the turmoil going on inside him. Perhaps they reflected his anger at losing his father, and his defiance and rebellion against his mother's control as he tried to assert his own identity:

> The fiery Seeds of Wrath are in my Temper,
> And may be blown up to so fierce a Blaze
> As Wisdom cannot rule.

But Jefferson would soon learn to control his temper. "This firm grip on even his deepest emotions would characterize his personality for the rest of his life."[9]

The years he spent at Maury's were happy ones. "Reviewing the course of a long and sufficiently successful life, I find no portion of it happier moments than these were," he would write when he was sixty-nine years old. He always acknowledged his "deep and lasting" debt to Maury's scholarship. The Reverend Maury became the surrogate father that Thomas Jefferson needed for the two emotionally painful years after his father's death.[10]

At Christmastime in the year 1759, the last year of the reign of George II of England, Jefferson accepted an invitation to a party at the home of Colonel Nathaniel West Dandridge, whose son and daughter were close to his age. As he sat easily astride his spirited mare, a fiddle in a light case hung around his neck and a roll of minuets newly arrived from London in his saddlebag—Jupiter riding just behind him, as befitted a wealthy young squire—he was a little apprehensive about what he would find at the party. But humming as he rode along, he told himself not to worry because he danced well, and the girls seemed to like him. When he arrived, he was immediately welcomed into the large merry group of young people who had assembled for the festivities, and all his fears dissolved. There was a frankness, an earnestness about him, a friendliness in his tone, that immediately attracted people to him. Besides, he knew all the country fiddle tunes of the day. He kept his friends entertained for hours, although some of the girls would have preferred that he dance with them rather than play the fiddle all evening.

The next morning another guest who lived nearby arrived. Shabbily dressed in coarse hunting clothes, he seemed older than most of the young people there. Jefferson learned that he was almost twenty-four, and he was married. He appeared to be popular with the others, though, and was greeted joyously. His name was Patrick Henry.

Jefferson was immediately drawn to Henry and discovered that he fiddled also. Patrick Henry didn't know the classical music that Jefferson did, but he had a keen ear and could follow any tune that Jefferson played. They made music together all evening.

Christmas then was still enthusiastically observed in the old English style as a season, not just a day, and Virginians celebrated it from Christmas Eve until Twelfth Night* with joyful abandon. Fall plowing had been done, and the harvests of tobacco had been gathered. Hogs had been slaughtered and butchered, and sportsmen had brought in abundant supplies of wild game and occasional deer or even black bear from the swamps. Barrels of oysters were in the cellars.

Every house was an open house, and no invitations were necessary. Hosts never knew in advance how many guests would share their dinner or sleep in their beds. The numerous slaves on the plantation attended to that.

The young people remained at Colonel Dandridge's for two weeks— occasionally moving to a neighboring plantation and then returning— all the while dancing, singing, feasting, flirting, and drinking toasts to King George II.

During these weeks a warm friendship began between Thomas Jefferson and Patrick Henry. Henry had a gaiety that was contagious. He was a favorite of all the young people. They loved his stories, his practical jokes, and his infectious good humor. Jefferson saw Henry simply as a fun-loving young man. Patrick Henry probably didn't recognize in this shy, redheaded boy a future political leader. Neither could imagine that a partnership would develop in which Thomas Jefferson would be called the pen of a revolution, and Patrick Henry its tongue.

When the festivities at Colonel Dandridge's ended, Jefferson began the leisurely ride home. But he felt restless. He had a vague feeling that he was wasting time. He realized that he had been attending parties for almost two weeks, and that when he returned to Shadwell he would be caught up in yet another round of parties, since his sister Mary was to be married on January 24. Again time would be taken away from his studies, and the expenses incurred on the estate would be considerable.

As he and Jupiter rode home through the Virginia hills, he began to ponder the alternatives. At Colonel Dandridge's he had heard talk of the College of William and Mary, and he began to think of the possibility of attending the college himself. So on New Year's Day, 1760, he visited the most influential of his guardians and his mother's cousin,

*The evening before January 6, the twelfth day after Christmas.

Peter Randolph. Together they agreed that he should attend William and Mary. Two weeks later, he summoned all his courage and wrote a letter to another guardian, John Harvie, who was the manager of his business affairs, requesting permission to attend college:

> Sir,
>
> I was at Colo. Peter Randolph's about a fortnight ago & my Schooling falling into Discourse, he said he thought it would be to my advantage to go to the college, & was desirous I should go, as indeed I am myself for several reasons. In the first place as long as I stay at the Mountains the Loss of one fourth of my Time is inevitable, by company's coming here & detaining me from school. And likewise my Absence will in a great Measure put a stop to so much Company, & by the Means lessen the expenses of the Estate in Housekeeping. And on the other Hand by going to the College I shall get more universal Acquaintance, which may hereafter be serviceable to me; & I suppose I can pursue my Studies in the Greek and Latin as well there as here, & likewise learn something of the Mathematics. I shall be glad of your opinion.[11]

It was an awkward letter, with no hint of the graceful prose that would later win Thomas Jefferson such wide acclaim, but it set down the reasons that were important to him then and would remain so throughout his life. It must have made its point to Harvie. Thomas Jefferson was on his way to Williamsburg.

❧ 2 ☙

# Discovering Devilsburg

A S JEFFERSON AND JUPITER approached Williamsburg, they were startled by what they saw. It was cooler than usual, and the early spring flowers were covered with snow. Students from the college, in their black gowns and tricornered hats, were everywhere.

Williamsburg, the capital of Britain's largest colony in North America, was a carefully planned town with what some considered the handsomest public buildings to be found in the English colonies. But later Jefferson described them as "rude, misshapen piles which, but that they have roofs, would be taken for brick kilns."[1] While Williamsburg was little more than a village, it had many metropolitan attractions similar to those found in New York, Philadelphia, and Boston. The first theater in America was built in Williamsburg, and it was here that Jefferson saw his first play. From then on, he rarely missed an opportunity to attend the theater. And it was in Williamsburg that he found the intellectual companionship that he craved, as well as the books and bookstores to satisfy him. Dixon and Hunter, a Williamsburg bookseller, had more than three hundred titles in stock.

The main street, named for the Duke of Gloucester, stretched for nearly a mile, with the College of William and Mary at one end and the Capitol at the other. Public buildings lined the street in between. The Governor's Palace, at the end of the wide, tree-lined Palace Green, was the official residence for the governor, appointed by the king. It was a handsome and imposing brick building, a symbol of the power and prestige of the Crown in colonial Virginia.

Jupiter frequently found himself walking down Duke of Gloucester Street to purchase books, fiddle strings, and wig powder, and to pay the bills of the baker, shoemaker, and washerwoman for his master. Occasionally, Jupiter had to lend his master money for tips for the slaves who were his friends' servants.[2]

The principal function of Williamsburg was government. Its ties with England were perhaps closer than those of any other colonial capital. The aristocracy of the Tidewater section of Virginia liked to think that going to Williamsburg was like going to court in London. The young men who were students at William and Mary were privileged to listen at the doors to the House of Burgesses, although they were not allowed inside. But as they watched the leaders of the province in action, several of whom were relatives of Jane Jefferson, they came to know and respect them and, unconsciously, to absorb valuable training in the operation of government. The college became the training ground for some of the greatest minds of the next generation.

At the college Jefferson met John Page, a nephew of the wife of his father's friend William Randolph. John lived at Rosewell, a magnificent three-storied mansion in Gloucester County that had been built by his grandfather and was said to contain thirty-five rooms. Jefferson and Page were in the same class and had many of the same interests. They became good friends. Jefferson began to spend weekends with Page at Rosewell and eventually came to love him like a brother. They spent many happy evenings together on Rosewell's great lead rooftop, absorbed in their shared enjoyment of astronomy.

Page quickly became Jefferson's guide to the Williamsburg social scene. Jefferson made friends easily and went to horse races and fox hunts with them, joined a secret society that later came to be called the Flat Hat Club—the first college fraternity in British America devoted entirely to fun—played chess, attended plays, dined with relatives, and danced at balls at the Raleigh Tavern. He became conscious of all the

Jefferson met John Page at the College of William and Mary. They remained close friends for fifty years. By John Wollaston, ca. 1758. (Courtesy of the Muscarelle Museum of Art, College of William and Mary)

pretty girls around him, and he began to spend money on his clothes. He was a much-sought-after young man and a leader among the young people. Often they would all gather at the home of their friends Anne and Betsy Blair on Duke of Gloucester Street to sit on the steps and sing in the dusk of a warm evening. They were a close-knit group, all of whom loved the gossip, the whirl of social life, the excitement that was "Devilsburg," their nickname for the town.

All of this left Jefferson little time for his studies. It was only after he had finished his first term at the college that he suddenly realized how much time he had wasted. Now he resolved to change his ways. He vowed to behave in a manner that would have made his father proud.

~~ 3 ~~

# "Bold in the Pursuit of Knowledge"

WHEN JEFFERSON RETURNED to William and Mary for his second year, Dabney Carr went with him. That year he found the *only* man of knowledge and ability at the college, the one skillful and sympathetic teacher, and the one member of the faculty who was not an Anglican clergyman, Dr. William Small. It was Dr. Small, a Scotsman, who set him on a course of inquiry and learning that would stay with him always.

The two were immediately drawn to one another, the older man (Small was thirty-one) recognizing in the eager eighteen-year-old a curiosity and a thirst for learning equal to his own. The young Jefferson found in Dr. Small a teacher, a friend, and a surrogate father. Unmarried and lonely, Small made Jefferson his daily companion. The two often went for long walks together. Small had a logical mind, and he loved to talk—and to watch the enthusiasm with which his young student absorbed the ideas he put forth.

In the time he spent at William and Mary, William Small did much to liberalize the college. He made a drastic departure from the teaching methods of the day by abandoning the ancient practice of compelling students to memorize lessons, instituting instead the modern lecture system. Small talked to a small group of students, then asked that later, in their rooms, they write out what they remembered and understood of what he had said. Some days Thomas Jefferson wrote for hours.

He was excited by all he was learning, and he found that Dr. Small had awakened in him the love for mathematics that his father had initiated so many years before. It would remain his favorite subject, and he would use it as a familiar, obedient servant. From that time on, whenever he went on a journey, he carried a box of mathematical instruments and a book of logarithms, and he always had a ruler in his pocket. "We have no theories here," he said of math; "no uncertainties remain on the mind; all is demonstration and satisfaction."

Jefferson's friend John Page, another extraordinary student, called Dr. Small his "ever to be beloved professor" and credited him with inspiring his own abiding interest in all branches of math. But years later Page would say, "I never thought . . . that I had made any great proficiency in any study, for I was too sociable, and fond of the conversation of my friends, to study as Mr. Jefferson did, who could tear himself away from his dearest friends, and fly to his studies."[1]

Dr. Small also taught Jefferson to observe objects with a scientist's eye. But what he learned most from his teacher was delight in the exercise of the mind and in the world of ideas. Small was one of those rare teachers who spark the imagination of their students and forge new paths of learning for them. Thomas Jefferson said later of this unusual man that William Small had "probably fixed the destinies of his life." Small showed him what the mind can do.[2]

But William Small did more than just introduce young Jefferson to the world of ideas. Perhaps equally important, he introduced him to a small brilliant group of people and a way of life he had never known. It was a world of taste, refinement, and scholarship that existed beyond the boundaries of Virginia.

First among these new acquaintances was George Wythe,* at thirty-four a thoughtful and distinguished lawyer and one of the most learned men in Virginia. Wythe, in turn, introduced Jefferson to Francis Fauquier,

---

*Pronounced to rhyme with Smith.

governor of the Colony of Virginia, and to the extraordinary circle that surrounded him.

Fauquier, who had come to Virginia in 1758, when he was almost sixty years old, was a country gentleman from Hertfordshire, England, and a Fellow of the Royal Society, a philosophical society in London. Charming and gracious, Fauquier was an excellent musician and linguist and had traveled all through Europe. According to rumor, he had lost his entire inheritance to Lord Anson, a famous admiral, in a single night of gambling. Anson, out of compassion for Fauquier, saw to it that he was given an appointment as a governor in the New World. All who knew Fauquier knew he was a man of high personal and official honor.

When Fauquier first arrived in Williamsburg, he was astonished to see a hailstorm in July that broke every window on the north side of the palace and left enough ice on the ground for him to cool his wine and freeze cream the following day. He measured the hailstones and thereafter kept a daily record of the Williamsburg weather. Thomas Jefferson would eventually do the same at Monticello and in Washington.

George Wythe, Jefferson's "faithful and beloved mentor in youth and most affectionate friend through life." By Trumbull. (Courtesy of the Print and Picture Collection, The Free Library of Philadelphia)

Governor Fauquier, historians tell us, "left an impression of taste, refinement, and erudition on the character of the colony,"[3] and certainly on the redheaded youth whom he made his companion. Impressed by the brilliant, soft-spoken young man, by his open mind and his willingness to consider both sides of a question, Fauquier invited the student to the palace for dinner with Dr. Small and Mr. Wythe. At this table Jefferson was privileged to hear stimulating conversations and exciting new ideas. The governor was also a lover of good music and held a weekly amateur chamber concert at the palace. When he learned that Jefferson could fiddle, he asked him to join their musical group. Jefferson was delighted.

So it was that once a week he and Small would be joined by the slender but erect and vigorous Wythe, always meticulously dressed, his dark eyes glowing with warmth and intelligence, in a stroll to the palace. There, in the parlor, while Wythe and Small listened, the young man and the governor of Virginia would tune up their fiddles, and in the candlelight that illuminated the room, with portraits of the king and queen of England gazing down on them from the wall, they would play some of the music recently arrived from Europe.

There were others in the group also. Jefferson, not yet proficient enough to play first violin, played second; occasionally he played the cello. His cousin John Randolph played first violin. Robert Carter, a close friend of the governor, lived near the palace and often played the harpsichord or the German flute. At times, John Page was invited to join the group, possibly playing the violin. He and Jefferson frequently practiced together on weekends at Rosewell.

Jefferson had loved music since he was a young boy, but it was probably during these years in Williamsburg that music became for him "the favorite passion" of his soul. No doubt it was the first time in his life that he heard music performed in concert.

It was after dinner at the palace, as they sat around the table and drank port wine, that he absorbed more than any student at William and Mary had ever learned at college. It was the governor's conversation that did the most to form his mind. Governor Fauquier, whom Jefferson would later call "a compleat gentleman" and "the ablest man who ever filled the office," was a man of the world and a scholar, an open-hearted and open-minded eighteenth-century gentleman interested in new ideas and good talk. At the governor's table the young Jefferson, shy but eager to learn, heard talk of the theaters of old London, of works of art, of the governor's colleagues at the Royal Society. He heard discussions of the problems of taxation and of recent meteorological phenomena. He heard the literary gossip of London, and he heard of strange lands that existed far beyond Virginia. He was learning to judge things by other than Virginia standards—to see the world in perspective.[4]

As he listened with wonder to their conversations, he was quick to absorb all that these accomplished men had to offer. He recognized even then the rare privilege that was being afforded him. In later life he recalled that at those dinners he had "heard more good sense, more rational and philosophical conversations, than in all my life besides." This table, he knew, was truly his university.

The eighteenth century is often referred to as the Age of Enlightenment, the great intellectual flowering that was transforming Europe in the 1700s. It was a time when new ideas and new approaches to old institutions were being discussed, setting the stage for revolutions to come, particularly in France and America. Enlightenment philosophers believed that the present was better than the past, and that one could best understand nature and man through the use of one's own mental faculties. They believed that human reason could be used to combat ignorance, superstition, and tyranny. Their principal targets were an intolerant church and the domination of society by a hereditary aristocracy.

It was necessary to use reason in order to appreciate man, society, and the universe, and through reason improve human circumstances and build a better world. They viewed the ability to reason as the distinguishing mark of human beings—the only authority in determining one's opinions or course of action. Reason would aid human development by helping humans to explore, understand, and shape their environment. They preached freedom of the mind. For Thomas Jefferson, the enlightened philosophes of Europe laid the foundation for his own belief in the power of human intelligence.[5]

It was from Dr. Small that Thomas Jefferson first became familiar with the major ideas of the Enlightenment. Small introduced

John Locke (1632–1704) was a British philosopher and Oxford academic revered by Jefferson. Much of his work is characterized by opposition to authoritarianism. He advocated the use of reason to search for truth. (Courtesy of the Library of Congress)

him to the work of Isaac Newton, the English mathematician and astronomer who had defined the laws of gravity and had been a friend of Fauquier's father; to the works of Francis Bacon, the brilliant English statesman, essayist, and philosopher who believed that knowledge is power; and to the writings of John Locke, many of whose ideas were being discussed in Williamsburg then. In fact, Locke's scientific and political views were revolutionizing the thinking of the English-speaking world.[6]

In his *Second Treatise on Civil Government,* Locke had put forth the revolutionary ideas that "since reason is the only sure guide which God has given to man, reason is the only foundation of a just government," and "since governments exist for men, not men for governments, all governments derive their just powers from the consent of the governed." Locke had also written: "The state of nature has a law to govern it, which obliges everyone; reason, which is that law, teaches all mankind . . . that being all equal and independent, no one ought to harm another in his Life, Health, Liberty, or Possessions."[7]

By stating "All Men by Nature are equal," Locke was affirming the God-given equality of *all* human beings. Thomas Jefferson considered this simply common sense. For the rest of his life, he would refer to

Newton, Bacon, and Locke as his "trinity of immortals." He revered them as the three greatest men the world had yet produced.

Jefferson also came to admire the brilliant English statesman and philosopher Henry Saint-John Bolingbroke and copied into his Commonplace Book many selections from Bolingbroke's *Essays and Fragments*. Bolingbroke, one of the century's giants, became one of Jefferson's favorite writers of prose.

Known as an eloquent speaker and critic of orthodox religion, Bolingbroke had argued that Christianity relied on miracles and superstition, rather than on reason or experience. It was Bolingbroke whose "uncompromising commitment to *reason* as the final arbiter of knowledge and validity" convinced Jefferson that there should be no authority over—or restraints upon—individual reason in any field, including religion. Jefferson's readings of Bolingbroke, when he was only about twenty-two or twenty-three, awakened in him a belief in Deism (a system of thought that upholds the existence of a God or supreme being but denies revealed religion) and made a lasting impression on his consciousness.[8]

Years later he would write to his grandson that Bolingbroke's writings, written with "the lofty, rhythmical, full-flowing eloquence of Cicero," prove him "a stronger advocate for liberty than any of his countrymen." They should be read by those "who are not afraid to trust their reason with discussions of right and wrong."[9]

In the spring of 1762, just before Jefferson's nineteenth birthday, Dabney Carr told him that that evening the great Cherokee chief Outacity would speak to his people, who were camped just outside the town. Outacity was about to journey across the sea to put his people's needs before the king of Great Britain.

Jefferson had always had an interest in the Cherokee Nation and particularly admired Outacity. He still cherished the canoe paddle the chief had made as a gift for him when he was a young teenager. He was curious about the Cherokee culture and eager to learn more about it.

That night he and Dabney Carr walked to the campsite together and, in the splendor of a full moon, listened spellbound as the great warrior and orator bid his people good-bye. Describing it fifty years later, Jefferson said the scene "filled me with awe and veneration, although I did not understand a word he uttered." There was a magic in the air that night. As he stood listening, he could feel his own father's presence. He never forgot it.

In April, shortly after he heard Outacity speak, and just two years after he arrived at William and Mary, Jefferson left the college. He continued to study privately with Dr. Small until Small returned to England later that year.

At that time, young men interested in pursuing a career in law "read" law under the direction of an established attorney. When Dr. Small suggested that Jefferson study law, the young man readily agreed. It was a profession that would challenge his mind, supplement his income, and render him useful to society. George Wythe was happy to take him on as a student.[10]

Wythe was a kindly man. Considered one of the most learned men in Virginia, he had read widely in English and Roman law, he was a distinguished classical scholar, and he loved to teach.

Wythe's first, and most significant, assignment to his student was to study Littleton's *English Law with [Sir Edward] Coke's Commentaries.* He referred to it as the "lawyer's primer." He also recommended that Jefferson attend the General Court when it was in session, and the House of Burgesses, and record his impressions of what he heard there. And he advised him to continue his study of the classics and philosophy, impressing on him the importance to a lawyer of general knowledge. Jefferson heeded all Wythe's advice. He particularly enjoyed listening at the door of the General Court to the battles of wit being waged inside.

Deciding that a "great inequality is observable in the vigor of the mind at different periods of the day," Jefferson divided his day into five parts: "rise at 5 a.m.; read til 8: books on agriculture, botany, zoology, chemistry, anatomy, religion; 8–12: read Coke and Littleton; 12–1: read politics; afternoon: read history, then run a mile into the country and back, because 'my father believed that running keeps a man fit.' And in the evenings read rhetoric, oratory, literature and language." Later, he squeezed in the study of Anglo-Saxon, since English law came from the Saxons. He didn't realize that he had neglected to plan time for meals. But Jupiter saw to that. He put meals in front of his master and hovered until he ate. "I was bold in the pursuit of knowledge," Jefferson explained to a friend years later, "never fearing to follow truth and reason to whatever results they led, and bearding every authority which stood in their way."[11]

Jefferson continued to study intensely for five years—at a time when one could enter the practice of law with just a meager understanding of it. But he was not in a hurry. "For with slight efforts how should one obtain great results? It is foolish even to desire it," he copied from the Greek playwright Euripides into the Literary Commonplace Book he had begun to keep at the Reverend Maury's school.

In the fall of 1762, when Jefferson was nineteen, he met Rebecca Burwell, a coquettish young lady of sixteen, and immediately fancied himself in love with her. Rebecca, who had been orphaned at the age of ten, was living with her aunt and uncle, the William Nelsons of Yorktown, good friends of the Pages.

Over the course of the next year Jefferson seems to have carried on a love affair with her, albeit mostly in his imagination. Although he saw Rebecca several times over the next few months, he never made his feelings known to her, and at the end of December he decided to go home to Shadwell. He remained there for nine months, even as he fretted over his inability to win Rebecca's heart. During that time, he wrote long letters to John Page in which he poured out his heart and asked for advice about Rebecca. In one letter he beseeched Page to approach "Belinda" for him and intercede on his behalf. He often referred to Rebecca as "Belinda" or "Adnileb" (Belinda spelled backward) and sometimes as "Campana in die" (which means "bell in day" in Latin) in order to disguise her name in case others should read his letters. Rebecca knew nothing of his turmoil.

At Shadwell he worked on his land, and he continued to read. Dabney Carr had also returned home from Williamsburg, and many days he and Dabney, their books under their arms, tramped across the fields and up the hill to their special spot on "Tom's Mountain," stretched out on the grass under their favorite oak tree, and read aloud in the shade of its branches. Here they could look out on the world as they discussed the contents of their books, talking about government, politics, philosophy, and literature, and sharing their thoughts and ideas. And here one day they made a pledge that whoever should die first would be buried beneath this tree.

When Carr left to take a job in a law office in Charlottesville, Jefferson continued to read and to wrestle with "Old Coke." He was "tired of . . . [the] old dull scoundrel," he wrote to "Dear Page," as he always addressed him.[12] Nonetheless, he filled his Commonplace Book with notes on the law. He was beginning to think of the law as something that lives and moves. He continued to read Coke and ultimately developed an admiration for him that the years did not erase. His efforts would be rewarded, for it was Sir Edward Coke who had challenged the royal prerogative* in Britain, just as Jefferson would do years later, "with the same arguments for the rights of freeborn Englishmen," in the colonies of North America.[13]

Most days at Shadwell Jefferson arose in the morning when the hands of the clock on the mantelpiece in his room could be distinguished in the gray light of early dawn, and he read until sunrise. Then he crossed the Rivanna in his little canoe and walked up to the summit of his beloved mountain. He began to think of someday building a house there.

October 1763 found Jefferson back in Williamsburg. He had gone there to attend a ball at the Apollo Room of the Raleigh Tavern. There he would finally see Rebecca again, after almost a year. And there, he vowed, he would finally express his feelings to her.

In colonial America the tavern was the heart of the community, and the Raleigh Tavern, built in 1735, was the most famous in Virginia. It was the center of political and social activity, for it was here that many of the distinguished lawyers who came to Williamsburg to attend court and the legislators who came to attend sessions of the House of Burgesses stayed while in the capital. In addition to the rooms in which the men lodged, the tavern contained the post office where the burgesses could pick up their mail, meeting rooms, a bar, and game rooms. Advertisements of all kinds were posted on its walls. It was a hub of activity.

*Coke, as chief justice of the Court of Common Pleas (1606–16), had ruled that the common law is supreme law, even when the Crown disagrees.

Here, the wisest men of the day drank with the abandon of the times. And here in the Apollo Room, ablaze with candlelight, musicians on the balcony played flutes, fifes, and fiddles as the young people danced quadrilles, minuets, and the Virginia reel. At these times, the room echoed with laughter and song.

But when Thomas and Rebecca danced together that evening, in spite of all his preparations—he had rehearsed in his mind exactly what he would say to her—he found himself completely tongue-tied. The young lady made no attempt to ease his embarrassment. Later, when he described the scene in a letter to Page, who had not yet arrived back in Williamsburg, his despair and shame were palpable. "For God's sake, COME," he ended the letter.[14] Beneath the mask of a charming, aristocratic bachelor lurked a sensitive and shy young man. Within six months Rebecca was engaged to be married to Jacquelin Ambler, who was somewhat older than Jefferson and had really made up his mind.

For the next few years, Jefferson continued to study independently at Shadwell, returning to Williamsburg periodically to consult with Mr. Wythe, to attend sessions of the General Court, to buy books, and, during the winter months, to attend the functions given by the gentry there.

## 4

## Rhetoric of Revolution

ON FEBRUARY 20, 1763, when the Treaty of Paris was signed, there was great rejoicing in the colonies and in England. The war between England and France, begun in 1756 and known throughout Europe as the Seven Years' War and in the colonies as the French and Indian War, had ended. Before the start of the war France had held most of North America. She had claimed Canada and New France—the stretch of land following the Mississippi River all the way to Louisiana, which included the Great Lakes and the Ohio River valley.

A strong bond of protection against the common enemy, France, had bound the colonies to the mother country. But when the French flag was lowered throughout the North American continent and Canada became British, this bond was snapped. There were even some who speculated that once the threat of France was removed from North America, the colonists would "strike off their chains."

Britain had not only defeated France (and Spain) but had won a dominant position in Europe's trade with Africa and Asia and had taken firm control of much of India. She became the financial heart of the world, and her navy rode triumphant on the seas. It was, for her, a golden age.

But if Britain was victorious, she was also exhausted. She now possessed, along with one of the largest empires in the world, the largest debt—£140 million, half of which had been incurred defending the American colonies from French and Indian attacks. Great Britain was close to bankruptcy.

In London, George Grenville, newly named chancellor of the exchequer (sometimes referred to as first lord of the treasury) and leader of the House of Commons, decided that the American colonists should help pay for the general welfare of the entire empire. Thus, on March 22, 1765, he initiated the Stamp Act, a bold and fateful policy to raise money from the colonists. The Stamp Act established the right of the British Parliament to lay an internal tax* on the American colonies for the single purpose of revenue. Scheduled to take effect in November, it would be the first *direct* tax Britain had imposed on Americans.

The Stamp Act required placing a stamp that certified payment of a tax on all legal and commercial documents, including birth certificates, marriage licenses, death certificates, wills, diplomas, pamphlets, freight bills, and even newspapers and playing cards. All official documents would have to be stamped with an ink stamp similar to a postal cancellation. Printed revenue stamps could be purchased at a stamp office. Documents without stamps would be considered illegal. The Stamp Act would reach into the pockets of every citizen throughout the country. It affected every court of law, every ship, every school.

---

*As opposed to an external tax, such as customs duties paid at the port of entry for the regulation of trade.

The colonists were enraged. Since they were without legal representation in the British Parliament, they felt that taxes in any form would change them from free subjects into slaves and destroy their right to govern and tax themselves. They believed strongly that only colonial assemblies could tax Americans; Parliament could not. They called it taxation without representation and charged that the Stamp Act was an attempt to impose on America the tyrannical system from which their forefathers had fled. The Stamp Act set in motion a series of events that would precipitate a violent response.

As the colonists were speaking out for freedom from parliamentary taxes and deploring the English tyranny that was attempting to "enslave" them, some began to recognize the contradiction in the fact that they themselves owned enslaved Africans. Now as crowds shouted "Liberty and no stamps," they began to worry that their slaves would hear the call for liberty and rebel.[1]

It was at this time that Patrick Henry was elected to the House of Burgesses. One of the members of the Virginia assembly had resigned his seat to allow room for Henry because of his "audacity, his tempestuous eloquence, his fighting spirit."[2]

Henry dominated the scene in Williamsburg from the first moment of his arrival there. In spite of his appearance—his clothes were coarse and worn—his eloquence when speaking about the rights of man soon changed the opinions of the assembly from contempt to admiration. He quickly became "Mr. Henry" to all of Williamsburg, an indication of respect and honor.

May 1765 found Mr. Henry in Williamsburg to take his seat at the spring session of the assembly. Sentiment was running high against the Stamp Act, but no one knew quite what to do. There was no thought of formal resistance. Henry sat in the assembly day after day, waiting for one of the older members to open the subject. Only three days of the session remained.

Then, on Thursday morning, May 29, 1765, Patrick Henry and Thomas Jefferson walked to the Capitol together. They were a study in contrasts as they made their way along Duke of Gloucester Street. Jefferson was dressed in the height of fashion in a coat of elegant red fabric, its large cuffs trimmed with braid and buttons, a tight-fitting waistcoat, and breeches that stopped at the knee. The buckles on his shoes had been polished till they shone. Henry was wearing plain hunting clothes. He carried an old copy of *Coke upon Littleton*, borrowed from Jefferson, under his arm. Jefferson had noticed his friend hastily scribbling on the flyleaf of the book earlier that morning.

When they reached the Capitol, Henry proceeded to his seat in the House of Burgesses, and Jefferson, with his younger friend John Tyler, who was also studying law, took his place at the open door to the Assembly Room. They often stood here, listening to the stormy debates taking place inside. They were not yet eligible to enter.

Shortly after the meeting was called to order, with an unfailing instinct for choosing the right psychological moment, Patrick Henry rose slowly from his seat and began to speak haltingly in a flat, quiet voice. Only his eyes revealed his passion. Jefferson and Tyler could sense the tension in the air.

Then Henry began to read the resolutions against the Stamp Act that he had scribbled on the flyleaf of Jefferson's book. As he spoke, he seemed to gain confidence. Gradually, he straightened his shoulders and stood erect, his voice picked up, and soon his words rang through the room. People were hearing for the first time words that they had thought but had been too afraid even to whisper to themselves. "Old Coke's" comments on the Magna Carta, the Great Charter of English liberties,* were suddenly being transformed from dead law into living truths.

Jefferson stood spellbound as he heard Henry thunder, "Caesar had his Brutus, Charles the First his Cromwell and [pausing] George the Third . . ."

"Treason!" cried John Robinson, the Speaker, at this list of rulers and their assassins. "Treason! Treason!" echoed from every part of the House.

But with amazing presence of mind, and not hesitating for an instant, Henry calmly concluded, ". . . may profit from their examples. Sir, if this be treason, make the most of it."[3]

With this speech Patrick Henry issued a challenge to the ruling class

---

*The Magna Carta was issued by King John at Runnymede in June 1215. It has been regarded by Englishmen, and all who have adopted English laws, as their chief constitutional defense against arbitrary or unjust rule.

in the colony. He became the spokesman for the common people, the champion of colonial liberty. Virginia was divided into two groups: the Whigs, or Patriots; and the Tories, those who remained loyal to Great Britain. Here for the first time was the rhetoric of revolution against the king of England. Virginia, Jefferson suddenly realized, was on the road to separation from the mother country.

Not long after Patrick Henry spoke out for colonial liberty, he began to wonder how "a country [Virginia] above all others fond of liberty" could practice such a cancerous evil as slavery. "A time will come when an opportunity will be offered to abolish this lamentable evil," he said. But Henry explained that he was "drawn along by the general inconvenience of living without [slaves]." The best he could do at the moment was to "treat the unhappy victims with lenity." Thus did many of Virginia's slave owners rationalize what they instinctively knew in their hearts to be wrong.[4]

⟋⟋⟍ 5 ⟍⟋⟋

# The Spirit of the Law

JUST TWO MONTHS after Henry's speech, in July 1765, Thomas Jefferson set aside his studies and his concern about the growing political tensions in the colony and went home to Shadwell for a happy celebration. His sister Martha, then nineteen, was about to marry Dabney Carr.

From the time that Carr had first come home from the Reverend Maury's school to spend vacations with Jefferson at Shadwell, the two young men and Jefferson's sisters Jane and Martha had spent much time together on "Tom's Mountain." Now Carr would be his brother-in-law as well as his friend.

Soon after the wedding Dabney and Martha moved to a small house in nearby Charlottesville, where Dabney opened his own office and began to practice law.

News of the colonies' hostile reception of the Stamp Act was arriving regularly in England. British authorities found it impossible to land the hated stamps in America, and British merchants could not receive payments for goods shipped to the colonies without the proper stamps. British merchants were also suffering because American merchants from Boston to Charleston had stopped buying English goods. Americans objected not only to the tax but to the principle behind it—to the *right* of the British Parliament to raise taxes on Americans. By the end of 1765 it was obvious that the Stamp Act could be carried out only by military force. On March 28, 1766, it was repealed.

About that time Thomas Jefferson began to collect a library of the best books in every branch of human knowledge. In the eighteenth century a well-educated man was expected to be interested in many things. In this respect, Jefferson was typical of his generation. The difference lay in degree: he simply went further. He remained a lifelong student, and he would eventually become one of the most widely read Americans of his day. He studied because he liked to. "Nature intended me for the tranquil pursuits of science* by rendering them my supreme delight," he would say later.

Although he spent much time reading, he also loved the fine arts, practiced his violin three hours a day, and often danced away the evenings or spent them with friends at backgammon or chess. He managed to find time for everything.

His friendships with Dabney Carr and John Page intensified, and he copied into his Commonplace Book another passage from Euripides: "Nothing is better than a reliable friend, not riches, nor absolute sovereignty. Nay more, the crowd is not to be reckoned with, in exchange for a noble friend."[1] Indeed, their letters to one another reveal undisguised affection and mutual respect.

That he treasured his friendships throughout his life is abundantly clear. He wrote to John Page, when he had known him for more than forty years, "But friends we have, if we have merited them. Those of our earliest years stand nearest in our affections."[2]

He continued to read the Greek classics for their practical value and

---

*"Science" meant *all* knowledge.

in order to derive from them moral lessons. He learned from Homer and Euripides to look at life with courage, and that a man could never justify his existence unless he lived for others as much as for himself.

In later life Jefferson often expressed his indebtedness to his father for his classical learning: "I thank on my knees him who directed my early education for having put into my possession this rich source of delight; and I would not exchange it for any thing."[3] Many years later, his great-granddaughter Sarah Randolph would recall that "he used to say, that had he to decide between the pleasure derived from the classical education which his father had given him and the estate he had left him, he would decide in favor of the former."

Jefferson particularly admired the political and moral essays written by David Hume and Francis Hutcheson, two of the major philosophers of the Scottish Enlightenment, and throughout his life he would remain influenced by them. Hutcheson, founder of the Scottish school of thought, taught that humans have an innate "moral sense" that enables them instantly to detect good and right actions. Out of this came Hutcheson's belief that "the height of virtue was achieving the greatest good for the greatest number." Jefferson agreed with Hutcheson that man possessed an innate "moral sense." "The moral sense, or conscience, is as much a part of man as his leg or arm," he would tell his nephew Peter Carr many years later.[4]

This concept of a universal moral sense within human beings became extremely important to Jefferson and made his democratic optimism possible.[5]

Another recent purchase of Jefferson's was the French philosopher Charles de Secondat Montesquieu's *De l'esprit des lois* (*The Spirit of Laws*), published in France in 1748. In it, Montesquieu stressed that "every government should provide that its energetic principle should be the object of the education of its youth."[6] Perhaps even more importantly, he believed in justice and the rule of law, and he was one of the first philosophers to advocate the abolition of slavery. "In a true state of nature," he wrote, "all men are born equal, but they cannot continue in this equality. Society makes them lose it, and they recover it only by the protection of laws."[7]

To the restless minds of Jefferson and his friends, minds that refused to accept the principle of authority, these classical and Enlightenment authors offered new and practical views that they were ready to accept. These early readings provided models that would shape their development. And as they absorbed the philosophy of the Roman poets, who stressed the need to work for the future without thought of present or personal reward, they were, unknowingly, preparing themselves for the roles they would play in the coming fight for freedom.

## 6

## Zeal to Improve the World

"PURPLE HYACINTHS BEGIN to bloom." With this prosaic entry Thomas Jefferson began his Garden Book on March 30, 1766, when he was twenty-three years old. He would keep it for more than half a century, making an enormous number of entries, a testament to his love of observing nature. No doubt, though, making this entry was a poignant reminder of the sudden death just six months before, of his favorite sister, Jane.

Jane, three years older than her brother, had been his equal in intelligence. Her mind and her spirit were in tune with his, and the depth of her understanding, the earnestness and simplicity of her nature, had endeared her to him. He had talked to her about the Stamp Act, about the colonies' worsening relations with England, and about conversations he had overheard in the Raleigh Tavern in Williamsburg. And he had shared with her a dream that was beginning to take shape in his mind to someday build a home on his mountain. Together they had pored over the plans and descriptions of gardens in a book he had recently purchased, *The Theory and Practice of Gardening*. He would never fully recover from the loss of Jane. Half a century later he would speak of her to his grandchildren as though she had died only recently.

From childhood, when he had first wandered in the woods with Jane or hunted and fished with his father, Jefferson's love of nature had been so intense that his attentive eye saw everything and forgot nothing. As he matured, he had continued to observe, to ask questions, to study, to collect. And he had kept careful notes on everything. Although his Garden Book began simply as a diary of his garden, it became over the years a written repository for his many varied interests.

Jefferson had begun keeping detailed records in various books two years before, in April 1764, on his twenty-first birthday, when he came into his inheritance from his father's estate. At that time he declared himself financially independent of his mother and began to pay rent to her for the four hundred acres at Shadwell and the five slaves who became his. While the guardians appointed by his father remained legally responsible for his younger siblings, Thomas Jefferson assumed his place as head of the family and manager of its business affairs. He now kept pocket account books as well as records of important dates and incidents in his life.

When he recorded that he had sowed a bed of peas, his favorite vegetable, he couldn't resist noting that "500 of these weighed 3 oz—18 dwt about 2500. fill a pint." Such detailed descriptions of garden activities not only delighted him but would later allow him to make "a comparative study of the blooming, the fruiting, the time the different articles came to the table, and their disappearance."[1]

Throughout his life Jefferson continued to exhibit an extraordinary attention to detail, indeed, a fondness for minute detail that never ended. He explained it simply by stating that "a patient pursuit of facts, and cautious combination and comparison of them, is the drudgery to which man is subjected by his Maker, if he wishes to attain sure knowledge."[2] And Thomas Jefferson hungered after knowledge.

His passion was diffusing that knowledge by putting it to work to make the world a better place. He called it his "zeal for improving the condition of human life." His aim was "to promote the general good of mankind by an interchange of useful things."[3] He considered the human mind an instrument to be used in the cause of progress, and found "infinite delight" in his lifelong quest for knowledge. In fact, knowledge was the only power he really craved. But knowledge was to be valued not for itself but rather as a means to some end, as an instrument of reason.

It was this belief that inspired him, when he was just twenty-one, to initiate a plan that would ultimately improve navigation of the river that flowed through his lands—the Rivanna, or the north branch of the James River. As far as he knew, no tobacco had ever been transported to Richmond via the Rivanna. Passage on the river was obstructed by rocks and fallen trees. Everything grown at Shadwell, therefore, had to be hauled to Richmond overland by wagon, a tedious and expensive job. Jefferson explored the river on his own by canoe, paddling as far as he could. When his progress was stopped by rocks, he waded into the stream and attempted to dislodge some of them. When these moved easily, he realized that the stream could be made navigable.

He immediately began to raise money for the project and interested his neighbor Dr. Thomas Walker, a member of the House of Burgesses, in it. By the next summer a channel in the river was opened, and the harvests were floated to market on rafts. This was Jefferson's first official involvement in a local project, his first collaboration between the public and private sectors, and he was proud of it.

It was this same desire to use knowledge to make the world a better place that motivated him to be inoculated against smallpox two years later. There was much heated debate at the time about the safety of the crude method of vaccination being used. It was a simple yet dangerous procedure: a physician made a small slit in the arm, inserted a drop of pus taken from an infected person, and closed the incision with a bandage. This was intended to build up resistance to the disease in the blood. Still, the patient was being infected with the great killer disease of the age. Results, Jefferson knew, could range from the complete absence of any signs of smallpox to serious disfigurement from eruptions on the skin, or even death. The procedure was against the law in New York and was performed only rarely in Virginia. In fact, when it was first introduced in America in 1721, Bostonians rioted against it, despite the fact that prominent clergymen and physicians had endorsed it. In Norfolk County in Virginia, two doctors who performed the inoculation were indicted by the county court. When one doctor scheduled inoculations to be performed at his plantation three miles outside of town, an organized mob attacked his house and set it on fire.

But Jefferson's interest in science far outweighed any fear of danger, and he decided to run the risk. So, on May 11, 1766, he set out on his first journey outside Virginia. Jupiter went with him, driving the carriage. The day dawned bright and clear, and Jefferson's spirits were high. Filled with excitement and anticipation, he was not prepared for the mishaps that beset him. On the very first day, he told John Page in a letter, his horse ran away with him twice, and he feared his neck would be broken. On the next day, as he rode over the vast countryside in his open carriage, there was a sudden torrential downpour, and not a single house in sight at which to stop and ask for shelter. The rivers swelled from the heavy rains, and on the third day, as he crossed the unfamiliar Pamunkey River, he went through water so deep it flowed over the cushion he was sitting on. A wheel of his carriage hit a submerged rock with such force that he was almost catapulted into the stream. But the rain stopped, the weather cleared, and the sun came out to dry him.

From then on, Jefferson had a leisurely trip through the lovely Virginia spring, stopping along the way, as was the custom, to visit friends. When he arrived in Annapolis, the capital of Maryland, he found the people in the midst of rejoicing over the repeal of the Stamp Act. It had taken months for the news to travel to Annapolis. Other than newspaper reports, this may have been the first sign that Jefferson had of a common interest among the colonies.

From Annapolis, he rode north through Delaware and on to Pennsylvania, where he saw beautifully cultivated fields of grain, clover, and flax, and "luxuriant orchards." Years later he would remember this and encourage the growth of crops like these in Albemarle.

When he finally reached the city of Philadelphia, Jefferson was introduced to the celebrated Dr. William Shippen, a specialist in this new form of medicine. Dr. Shippen performed the vaccination procedure, and with it began a lifelong friendship between the two men.

After a period of quarantine, and when Jefferson was well enough to travel again, he and Jupiter continued their journey to New York. This was the first time that Jefferson had seen the large cities of the New World, and he was particularly fascinated by the richness of detail and design in the architecture. But the trip north by horse and carriage had been a difficult one, so he decided to sail home. He went by boat from New York City to Norfolk, Virginia, while Jupiter rode south with the horses. He met Jupiter in Norfolk, and from there they drove home to Shadwell.

Jefferson's "zeal for improving the condition of human life" would continue throughout the years and would manifest itself in many ways. Perhaps the most significant would be his revolutionary proposal for the establishment of a system of free public education for all free citizens. Jefferson looked on intelligence as the most precious gift of nature, and he wanted to see it nurtured and developed in all children. Ignorance, to Jefferson, was the root of all evil, and he believed that the only secure basis for republican government was in a "diffusion" of knowledge for the mass of free men and women.

He would fight against the privilege of wealth and station, providing for an informed, educated electorate—an aristocracy of learning and intelligence. His vision of a "natural aristocracy" of talent and virtue was to replace the "artificial aristocracy" of wealth and birth. And, he insisted, rich and poor must be educated together and matched against each other in academic competition. Only in that way, he believed, would the best students rise to the top and be eligible to advance to further public-supported education. Public education must be based on academic merit.[4] But in making this proposal, he would gain for himself the hostility of wealthy aristocrats, some of whom would hate him for the rest of his life.

Patrick Henry had been admitted to the bar after three months of preparation. It took Thomas Jefferson five years from the time he began to "read" with Mr. Wythe to consider himself ready. Early in 1767, shortly before his twenty-fourth birthday, he took the necessary examinations and was admitted to the bar of the General Court by George Wythe, his "faithful and beloved mentor in youth and most affectionate friend through life."[5]

The cases he handled were, for the most part, typical of an agrarian community. They involved problems of land ownership: boundaries, partitions, sales, and inheritance.

During the next five years that he practiced law, he traveled frequently to the county courts and to Williamsburg, where he maintained an office. On court days, when farmers came to the various county seats to buy and sell lands and slaves, Jefferson had an opportunity to get to know "ordinary citizens" and gained an invaluable insight into their thoughts. Generally, he went on horseback or in a one-horse carriage. Jupiter, who by now had been his companion for more than ten years, accompanied him. Jefferson trusted him with everything. Jupiter carried his luggage, paid the saddler and the ferryman, bought bread and candles, and continued to lend his master money when he ran out.

As a lawyer, Mr. Jefferson, as he was called now, was very different from Patrick Henry. Henry, all fire, was more advocate than lawyer, seeking to win his case by passionate oratory. Jefferson was cool, unemotional, and always prepared. He had all the facts meticulously researched and carefully and systematically written down before he began. He knew the law thoroughly, and he stated the issues clearly and concisely. He spoke softly, with ease and elegance. It was impossible for him to shout. If he raised his voice, it soon grew husky.

He was aware of his own limitations. He didn't attempt what he knew he could not do. Rather, he used the talents he possessed to become a legal counselor and office lawyer. He was liked and trusted. When there was a case to be tried before a jury, he sometimes asked Dabney Carr or Patrick Henry to argue it for him. His own joy derived from digging into the case and discovering evidence for them to present.

## ◦﹏ 7 ﹏◦

# First Assignment, First Failure

D URING THE TWO YEARS following the repeal of the Stamp Act the people appeared to Jefferson to have fallen "into a state of insensibility to our situation."[1] The furor over the Stamp Act had subsided, yet the colonies were moving quietly but steadily toward a crisis. They were, in fact, being pulled by two powerful, opposing tides: one, stability represented by the Old World; the other, the opportunity and openness of the New.

In England, King George III, who had ascended the throne in 1760 at the age of only twenty-two, had learned from the failure of the Stamp Act that he could not raise revenue that way. He decided, at the suggestion of his new flamboyant chancellor of the exchequer, Charles Townshend, known in the London coffeehouses as "Champagne Charley," to raise revenue from the colonies in a different manner—one he hoped they wouldn't notice.

In the summer of 1767, Townshend convinced Parliament to pass the famous acts that bear his name, the Townshend Acts of Trade and Revenue. The most important of these imposed a small import duty on glass, white lead, printer's paper, and paint, items that the colonies were required to import from Great Britain, and tea, which was brought to England by the powerful East India Company and then reexported in large quantities to the colonies. Unlike the Stamp Act, this tax was an *indirect* customs duty payable at American ports. Since the colonists had objected to internal taxes, Townshend thought he could accomplish his purpose by imposing external taxes.

The Virginians were not pleased. In their eyes the Townshend Acts threatened the authority and even the very existence of the colonial governments. This new tax on tea was particularly annoying because it affected so many. About one million people drank tea twice a day.

Once more, a wave of protest swept through the colonies. The colonists were quick to recognize that the Townshend duties were simply new revenue taxes. They had nothing to do with regulation of trade, as England had implied, but everything to do with Parliament's raising revenues without the colonists' consent.

In March 1768 a seemingly unrelated event gave impetus to the growing dissatisfaction over the Townshend Acts. To Thomas Jefferson's deep sorrow, Governor Fauquier died after a long and difficult illness. In the absence of a royal governor, the colonists could give free expression to their feelings: that no power on earth has a right to impose taxes on the people, or take the smallest portion of their property, without their consent given by their representatives. At a meeting of the House of Burgesses, Patrick Henry vehemently denounced the acts: "Parliament has enslaved us," he thundered. "Oppose them with steadfastness and they will be repealed. . . . We shall not yield our God-given right to tax ourselves."[2]

That spring, a messenger rode into Williamsburg carrying a letter from the Massachusetts assembly to the House of Burgesses. It announced that Massachusetts intended to resist the Townshend duties by all constitutional means and asked Virginia to do the same. The messenger had already stopped in the middle colonies on his way down the coast. He then continued south to deliver copies of the letter to the Carolinas and Georgia. The letter urged all the colonial legislatures to unite with Massachusetts to inform King George of their collective hostility to the new duties.

Thomas Jefferson's cousin Peyton Randolph, who had been unanimously elected Speaker of the Virginia House of Burgesses, sent word to the Speaker of the Massachusetts house that the Virginia representatives "could not but applaud them for their attention to American liberty." He went on to say that they were in full agreement with Massachusetts and would support them.[3] A network was forming that would make communication among all the colonies easier.

Some months later, on October 21, the Right Honorable Norborne Berkeley, baron de Botetourt, arrived in Williamsburg from England to become the new governor of Virginia. Jefferson and some of his friends were among the throngs lining Duke of Gloucester Street at sunset to witness his procession to the palace. Botetourt came with all the pomp of royalty: a large retinue of servants and baggage and a magnificent coach drawn by six white horses. Botetourt was loyal to his king, but he was honorable and friendly, and the people soon grew to love him.

As was the custom on the arrival of a new governor, the House of Burgesses was dismissed and writs issued for the election of a new assembly. Thomas Jefferson was named a candidate for the county of Albemarle. He won the election easily.

At ten o'clock on the bright, sunny morning of May 8, 1769, when the House bell sounded, Mr. Jefferson entered the chamber and joined the nearly one hundred assembled burgesses being sworn in that day.

Among them was a young colonel and planter named George Washington. George Wythe, as clerk of the House of Burgesses, was present to see his young friend Thomas Jefferson sworn in.

It was the custom to assign some formal duty to new members in order to introduce them to public business and to afford them an opportunity to display their talents. Accordingly, the task of drafting a response to the governor's speech of welcome, in the form of resolutions, was assigned to the freshman member from Albemarle, Mr. Jefferson.

Jefferson completed his task in the courtly style of the day, combining loyalty with firmness, and stating that he hoped that any question affecting Great Britain would be resolved in light of the principle that "her interests, and ours, are inseparably the same." He prayed that "Providence, and the royal pleasure, may long continue his Lordship the happy ruler of a free and happy people."

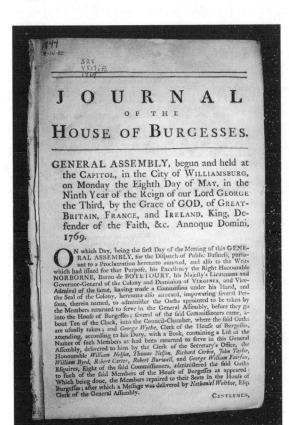

The pages of the *Journal of the House of Burgesses* for May 8, 1769, the day on which Thomas Jefferson was sworn in as a member of the House. (Photo courtesy of L. H. Bober)

Jefferson was then asked to prepare the address to the governor based on these resolutions, which he did simply and concisely. But some of the older members of the House were not satisfied. They wanted a fuller discussion. One of these members, Robert Carter Nicholas, then rewrote Jefferson's address. The young and sensitive new member was humiliated. He was convinced that he was beginning his political career with a failure.

Jefferson was appointed to other committees during the session, but he remained a silent member, expressing his views quietly to just one or a few people at a time. But he was learning a great deal.

Britain had reacted angrily to the letter circulated by Massachusetts and ordered the colony to rescind it. Massachusetts refused. Parliament then threatened to dissolve the Massachusetts legislature. It also threatened to revive an old statute dating back to Henry VIII that allowed the government to call to England for trial persons accused of treason outside the kingdom. The threat was specifically directed against the "traitors" in Massachusetts, but the law could have applied to Patrick Henry and Peyton Randolph as well.

The Virginia burgesses denounced Britain's right to impose taxes on *any* colony and to destroy the colonial jury system. In a "humble address" they declared that they, and not Parliament, had the right to levy taxes on the colonies; that it was their privilege to petition the king directly for a redress of grievances and to join with other colonies in doing so; and that all trials for treason should be held within the colony, and not removed to British courts. Finally, they resolved that these resolutions would be circulated to the assemblies of the other colonies.

They were openly defying the British government. At the same time, though, they assured the king that they were "ready at any time to sacrifice our lives and fortunes in defense of your Majesty's sacred person and government."[4]

Governor Botetourt responded by dissolving the House of Burgesses. The governor might dissolve the House, but he could not dampen its spirit. The burgesses conferred hurriedly, then "with the greatest order and decorum" went immediately to the home of one of the members. There they elected Peyton Randolph moderator and decided to meet as an unofficial body in the Apollo Room of the Raleigh Tavern, where so many of them had only recently danced the minuet.

Early the next morning, May 18, 1769, Thomas Jefferson signed his first significant public paper, a nonimportation, nonconsumption agreement called the Virginia Association. It asserted that the colonists would not import or purchase any goods that were taxed by act of Parliament for the purpose of raising revenue in America. The document was drafted by George Mason and signed by George Washington, Patrick Henry, and Richard Henry Lee, among others.

The list of contraband goods was enormous. Designed to stop all trade with the mother country, it included such items as meat, butter, cheese, sugar, oil, fruit, wine, paper, clothing material, and leather. Members of the association agreed to inform their correspondents in England not to send them anything until Parliament had repealed the acts to which they objected. This was the first time a colonial legislature had *officially* engaged in an act of rebellion.[5]

Women, accustomed at that time to remaining in the background, became ardent supporters. Upper-class ladies dressed in "Virginia cloth," or homespun, instead of the beautiful silks and laces they had previously imported from England for their ball gowns. Since cloth was Britain's major industry, the boycott of textiles was the most important weapon the colonists could use against the mother country. Spinning and weaving their own cloth became a patriotic activity. By reducing the American market for English cloth, American women were engaging in economic warfare. Their spinning wheels became their weapons. Many gave up drinking tea as well.[6]

On November 7, 1769, word arrived from London that, except for the tax on tea, the Townshend Acts would be repealed by Parliament the following March, and no further taxes would be levied against the Americans for the purpose of raising revenues. In Jefferson's opinion nothing had been settled. He considered the tax on tea an affront to the American principle, and the main issue with Parliament no closer to resolution than at the start of the controversy. He thought of himself as a loyal subject of the king, but he was firm in his belief in colonial "rights."

The spirit of discontent that had been simmering in the colonies over the past few years was beginning to boil over. The "ball of revolution" was starting to roll, and young Thomas Jefferson was ready to keep it moving.

## 8

# Essay in Architecture

JUST A FEW MONTHS after he was admitted to the bar, on August 3, 1767, Thomas Jefferson had entered in his Garden Book: "inoculated common cherry buds into stocks of large kind at Monticello."[1] He had planted an orchard and begun to graft cherry trees on the hillside just below the site he had chosen for his home. He had some years before resolved to build a house atop "his" mountain, and had confided his dream to his sister Jane and to his friend Dabney Carr. When he and Dabney had studied together under the old oak tree, he had known that this was where he would live. In those days, when he contemplated life as a bachelor, he had thought he might name his house The Hermitage, but now he decided to call it Monticello, from the Italian for "little mountain," pronouncing it the Italian way, *Montichel'lo.* It had a more romantic sound to him.

There was no precedent in America or England then for the romantic, impractical spot on which Jefferson chose to build. It took an imaginative leap to plan a house high on a hilltop, on the edge of a wilderness. But the site commanded a majestic panorama of the surrounding countryside, and the misty Blue Ridge Mountains he loved were visible in the distance. His eye, like his mind, seemed to be searching for this broad view, this view of beauty, and for a new horizon beyond the mountains.

He knew that what he planned appeared foolish and impractical. Most of the great Virginia manor houses were built along the rivers. In addition to providing an ample water supply, the rivers were roadways for transporting commercial products and made it relatively easy to visit neighboring plantations by small boat. Even the exact location of the house on the mountain went against tradition. Jefferson's house was to face southwest, in order to catch the best view of the mountains.

In order for him to build on his mountain, timber would have to be cleared from the summit and the stubborn soil of the building site leveled. Long, steep roadways would have to be built up the mountain and maintained. He knew there was a severe water shortage on the mountain, and water would have to be carried from a great distance. But Thomas Jefferson was a "romantic" architect: he had found the one spot on his land that he loved and where he might study and enjoy nature, and he had made up his mind to build there. He believed that he could use his imagination to solve the problems, and he resolved to go ahead with his project. He never regretted his decision.

The first plans he drew for Monticello are the earliest working drawings for a Virginia house that have survived.

The study of architecture as a profession did not exist in the colonies at that time, so when Jefferson decided that he wanted to build his own house, he did what was most characteristic of him: he turned to books to learn how. He understood that there were rules in architecture as in nature. A house had to have harmony and symmetry.

He began to teach himself mechanical drawing, and he became a competent, though limited, draftsman. He never simply sketched to convey an idea. He always solved a problem by first working out the proportions mathematically. His mind was mechanical and precise, and he always drew with ink, not pencil.

It was during his student days at William and Mary that Jefferson had bought his first book on architecture from an old cabinetmaker who lived near the college gate. He probably acquired additional books on the subject from Richard Taliaferro (pronounced *Tolliver*), George Wythe's father-in-law, who had studied architecture in England and with whom Jefferson often discussed the subject. These books were the beginning of a collection that would be considered among the most important of its kind in America.

Now Jefferson turned to the writing of the famous Italian architect Andrea Palladio, who, next to Michelangelo, was considered the most important architect of the sixteenth century. Palladio believed that architecture must be governed by certain universal rules that he recognized in some of the ancient Roman ruins.

Jefferson felt himself drawn to the classical proportions of the buildings Palladio had designed. When he began to think about the shape Monticello should take, he knew that he wanted a simple, classic design with clean lines and carefully planned symmetry. He thought about the Georgian manor houses that he was familiar with, such as Tuckahoe, Carter Hall, and Rosewell, but this was not what he wanted. He liked their grand scale but not their style. He was unconsciously searching for an architectural style that represented a break with the English architecture of the day, one that incorporated the principles of Roman design into a "new creation" that reflected America.

Perhaps, also, living on the edge of the frontier and knowing that his father and others like him had carved a home out of the wilderness, he needed a different kind of environment for himself—a house that would become an oasis of order amid the chaos that attended the birth of a new nation.

One month after his twenty-fifth birthday, on May 15, 1768, Jefferson made an agreement "with Mr. Moore that he shall level 250 f. square at the top of the mountain at the N. E. end by Christmas, for which I am to give 180 bushels of wheat, and 24 bushels of corn, 12 of which are not to be paid till corn comes in. If there should be any solid rock to dig we will leave it to indifferent men to settle that part between us."[2]

On Friday, July 14, a Mr. Dudley began making bricks for the house. Jefferson had decided to use brick even though most houses at that time were built of wood. Frame houses, he felt, were too susceptible to fire. He wanted a durable material. He determined that the bricks would be seven and a half inches by two and a half inches and that they would be made in kilns at the top of the mountain. In this way he would not have to purchase the bricks, nor would they have to be hauled up the mountain. But he noted in his Garden Book that it required six hogsheads (barrels) of water to make two thousand bricks. And he calculated the exact number of bricks that he would need. Nails and wooden trim were fashioned on the mountain also, but the windows and "a small parcel of spare glass to mend breaks" were ordered from England.[3]

The design Jefferson decided on was a practical one. It called for a two-story central house with two one-story cottages, called wings, on either side of the mountain, spread over a vast area and situated so as to take full advantage of all the spectacular views. Two L-shaped terraces would run from the main house to the cottages. The house would be simple yet dignified, solid but beautiful.

He decided, also, that instead of the ordinary rectangular rooms found in most colonial Virginia houses, his rooms would be polygonal— or many-sided. Once again, Jefferson was moving away from traditional ideas and using his imagination to develop an architectural style that was uniquely his own.

So it was that on a cold, snowy day late in 1768, Jefferson, with a mixture of pride and pleasure, watched as some of his slaves, "four good fellows, a lad, and two girls of abt. 16," began to dig a cellar in the stiff mountain clay. But it would take six months of hard labor for them to dig and then cart away the top of the hill before any building could begin.

Less than a year later, the first structure was completed, and Jefferson

Jefferson's freehand ink sketch of his first plan for Monticello, ca. 1768. (Courtesy of Monticello/Thomas Jefferson Foundation, Inc.)

was able to move into his mountaintop "laboratory." A simple eighteen-by-eighteen-foot brick building, it was the cottage that came to be known as the South Pavilion.

The building contained just one room with two windows, a door, and a fireplace. A kitchen below was equipped with a fireplace and an oven. But it provided Jefferson with the solitude he craved to write letters or to read, away from the distractions and pressures of daily life—"the business of society," as he called it.

In February 1771 he wrote to a friend in London: "I have lately removed to the mountain from whence this is dated. . . . I have here but one room, which like the cobbler's, serves me for parlour, for kitchen and hall. I may add, for bedchamber and study too. My friends sometimes take a temperate dinner with me and then retire to look for beds elsewhere. I have hopes of getting more elbow room this summer."[4]

This was the beginning. Monticello would be shaped and reshaped over a period of forty years, almost the rest of Jefferson's life, for in his mind it would never be finished. He was making a home, and a home would have to change to accommodate changing family needs. It would become, too, a laboratory in which he could experiment with fresh new architectural ideas. He would refer to it as his "essay in architecture."[5]

The South Pavilion, or "Honeymoon" Cottage, was the first building to be completed at Monticello. Begun as a bachelor's retreat, this tiny cottage (18 feet by 18 feet) became the home to which Thomas Jefferson brought his new bride. (Courtesy of L. H. Bober)

For the rest of his life, no matter where in the world he was, his heart would be on his mountaintop.

## ᴄᴆᴖ 9 ᴆᴖᴄ

## All Men Are Born Free

ON FEBRUARY I, 1770, after a quiet dinner with his family at Shadwell, Jefferson left for Charlottesville, three miles away, to attend to some business. Shortly after he arrived there, a slave arrived and breathlessly told him that Shadwell had burned to the ground. Fire, whipped by the winter winds, had raged through the house and swiftly destroyed it.

After making certain that no one had been injured, Jefferson immediately inquired if anyone had saved his books and papers. "No, Master," was the reply, "but we saved the fiddle!"[1] The fiddle had cost five pounds in Williamsburg the year before. Except for a few books, including his Account Books, his Garden Book, and his Commonplace Books, which were at Monticello, all that he valued most in the world—his books and his papers, both private and legal—were gone. Jefferson was distraught. He wrote to John Page:

> My late loss may perhaps have reached you by this time; I mean the loss of my mother's house by fire, and in it of every paper I had in the world, and almost every book. On a reasonable estimate I calculate the cost of the books burned to have been 200 pounds sterling. Would to God it had been the money, *then* it had never cost me a sigh! To make the loss more sensible it fell principally on my books of common law, of which I have but one left, at that time lent out. Of papers too of every kind I am utterly destitute. All of these, whether public or private, of business or amusement, have perished in the flames. I had made some progress in preparing for the succeeding General Court, and having, as was my custom, thrown my thoughts into the form of notes, I troubled my head no more with them.

These are gone, and like the baseless fabric of a vision, leave not a trace behind. The records also, and other papers which furnished me with states of several cases, having shared the same fate, I have no foundation whereon to set out anew.[2]

For this compulsive letter writer and record keeper who learned through the eye rather than the ear, and who could not speak without notes in front of him, the loss of every record and note he had composed until the age of twenty-seven was devastating.

His letter makes no mention of the emotional loss of the home in which he had been born, nor of the devastating loss to his mother of the home her husband had built for her and with it all the priceless Randolph family heirlooms. Jane Jefferson and her children crowded into one of the outbuildings that had survived the fire, seeking shelter from the harshness of a mountain winter.[3] Shadwell was never rebuilt.

"The letters of a person, especially of one whose business has been chiefly transacted by letters, form the only full and genuine journal of his life," Jefferson would write years later. Indeed, the burning of Shadwell became what one historian has called "one of the great blows to American scholarship."[4]

Jefferson's friends reacted as though there had been a death in the family. When Jefferson sent a letter to his friend Thomas Nelson Jr., enclosing a list of the books he needed most, Nelson immediately replied that he had forwarded a copy of the list ("for fear the original should miscarry") to his book dealer. Nelson went on to assure his friend that his father, who was secretary of the Colonial Council of Virginia, would ask the courts to "indulge you with a continuance of your causes [i.e., postpone his cases] . . . as the court has frequently done it where there have been good reasons for it." Thomas Nelson Sr. himself wrote: "I was extremely concerned to hear of your loss. . . . As I have a pretty good collection of books, it will give me pleasure to have it in my power to furnish you with any you may want."[5]

John Page also sent condolences, and George Wythe sent his young friend some grafts of nectarines and apricots and some grapevines. He wrote: "You bear your misfortune so becomingly that, as I am convinced you will surmount the difficulties it has plunged you into, so I foresee you will hereafter reap advantage from it several ways."[6]

❧ Jefferson wasted no time in beginning to rebuild his library. He sent to Philadelphia for books and frequented the bookstores in Williamsburg whenever he was there. He also found constant stimulation in the college library at William and Mary. But he recognized that the majority of books would have to be ordered from London.

As he began to draw up lists of the titles he wanted, he realized that many were books that dealt with theories of government. Some of the important ones that he had purchased in 1769 and now had to reorder were John Locke's *On Government* and Montesquieu's *L'esprit des lois.* The more of Montesquieu he read, the more excited he became, for he realized that this French philosopher was expressing many of the ideas that he had been pondering himself these last months. Montesquieu's freshness and originality, his theory of liberty, his desire for reform and for the betterment of the human condition were qualities that spoke to this young idealist.

Jefferson borrowed one hundred pounds from Dabney Carr to buy books. Within three years he owned more volumes than he had lost. By 1773 he had 1,256 volumes in his library. He may have spent as much as one quarter of his income annually on books. But he did more than simply collect them. He read and reread them, his mind eagerly absorbing the information and the new ideas he encountered. He would be well prepared for the difficult tasks that lay ahead.

❧ Even as he pondered the problems of government, Jefferson was fighting against the injustices of slavery. In 1769, when he was just twenty-six, he drafted—and asked Richard Bland, a more commanding figure, to introduce—a bill in the Virginia House of Burgesses allowing owners the right to manumit (or free) their slaves without first getting legislative approval. Approval was necessary in Virginia at that time, although not in every southern colony. His bill was swiftly defeated. A year later, he refused to defend a white man who had whipped a black woman to death.

Another case, referred to as *Howell vs. Netherland,* testifies to his recognition of the injustices of slavery. In 1705 a white woman had given birth to a baby girl by a black slave. The existing law condemned the mulatto (mixed-race) girl to slavery until she reached the age of thirty-one. During the years of her servitude the girl gave birth to a daughter, who in turn gave birth to a son. The son, Samuel Howell, was sold into slavery by the slave owner to whom the grandmother was bound, and the new owner claimed his service until he reached the age of thirty-one.

In 1769 Samuel Howell, "a pauper," as Jefferson described him, asked Jefferson to help him win his freedom. Jefferson agreed and wrote in his memorandum book, "Charge no fee." On December 15, he took out a writ at his own expense. *Howell vs. Netherland* came to trial in April 1770.

When Jefferson rose before the General Court, he acknowledged the legality of the grandmother's servitude. He further recognized that the law extended the sentence to her children. But, he pleaded, there was no law that reached to the grandson. "It remains for some future generation, if any should be found wicked enough, to extend [slavery] to the grandchildren and other issue more remote," he argued. "Under the law of nature all men are born free, everyone comes into the world with a right to his own person, which includes the liberty of moving and using it at his own will. This is what is called personal liberty, and is given him by the author of nature."[7]

The court was shocked. Never before had they heard opinions such as these expressed publicly. What did he mean by "all men are born free," "the law of nature," "personal liberty"? When George Wythe, attorney for the owner, rose to reply to Jefferson's argument, the judge pounded his gavel and cut him off. Motioning him to his seat, he gave judgment in favor of Wythe's client. The boy went into slavery.

Jefferson had lost the case, but his deep feelings about human rights had come to the surface. He was finally articulating ideas that had been silently taking shape in his mind as he continued to read the works of John Locke. Locke had written that all men are "naturally" in a state of perfect freedom and equality "within the bounds of the law of nature."[8] The members of the court had not yet begun to think this way.

## 10

## "Worthy of the Lady"

B Y THE FALL OF 1770, Jefferson realized that most of his friends were already married, and he was beginning to feel that he was missing something as a bachelor. Certainly, he was beginning to muse about the joys of married life. He had stopped copying into his Commonplace Book passages from the poets that disparaged women. He was copying instead lines from Milton's *Paradise Lost* celebrating the joy of marriage:

> Nor gentle purpose, nor endearing smiles
> Wanted, nor youthful dalliance as beseems
> Fair couple, linkt in happy nuptial league,
> Alone as they.[1]

And he was writing to John Page of their friend Dabney Carr, whom he refers to as Currus: "He speaks, thinks, and dreams of nothing but his young son. This friend of ours, Page, in a very small house, with a table, half a dozen chairs, and one or two servants, is the happiest man in the universe. Every incident in life he so takes as to render it a source of pleasure."[2]

Suddenly Jupiter found himself kept very busy buying hair powder and buckles as well as theater tickets for his master to go courting. The social season in Williamsburg had just begun, and Thomas Jefferson had met Martha Wayles Skelton. Martha was a bright and beautiful young woman, at just twenty-two a mother and a widow. Jefferson, five and a half years older, fell quickly, and deeply, in love.

Martha had been married to Bathurst Skelton (whom Jefferson had known at the College of William and Mary) at the age of eighteen. She became a mother at nineteen and a widow before she turned twenty. Distraught, she took her baby, John, and returned to The Forest, her father's home in Charles City County, west of Williamsburg.

When the prescribed period of mourning was over, Martha found she had many suitors, among them an eager Thomas Jefferson. Martha delighted in Jefferson's intelligence and in their shared love of music. In Williamsburg, Jefferson had taken violin lessons from Francis Alberti, an Italian living in the city, who had also taught Martha to play the harpsichord. Often, when Jefferson visited her at her father's home, the two made music together. On occasion, he sang to her accompaniment.

The story is told that one day, when he was visiting her, two of his rivals happened to meet on her doorstep. They were shown into a room from which they heard her harpsichord and her voice, accompanied by Jefferson's voice and violin, in the passages of a love song. Whether it was something in the words or in the tones of the singers is not known, but the two men took their hats and left and never again pursued their suits.

Jefferson was very different now from the young boy who had danced with Rebecca in the Apollo Room of the Raleigh Tavern seven years before. He seems to have grown better looking as he grew older, and he had matured from a shy, bashful student into a successful lawyer and member of the House of Burgesses.

He made regular visits to The Forest, riding his horse from Williamsburg, his violin tucked under his arm. Jupiter always went with him. Jupiter, too, was pursuing a suit: he had met and fallen in love with Suck, the young cook in the Wayles home.

Martha was the daughter of John Wayles, a successful lawyer who was also actively engaged in the transatlantic slave trade. Indeed, as late as 1772 native-born Africans were still forced to endure the Middle Passage, and when the *Prince of Wales* sailed up the James River that year, its human cargo was consigned to John Wayles's trading firm.[3]

Agreeable, pleasant, and good-humored, Wayles had arrived in Virginia alone, and settled into the populated area of the Tidewater. As an industrious and practical lawyer, he spent years on horseback, traveling from plantation to plantation earning a living from his conscientious preparation of legal documents for men of property in the region. Long journeys and hard work made it possible for him ultimately to buy or patent several thousand acres of land. Since most of the desirable land along the James River had been taken, Wayles went to Charles City County. He had come from Lancaster, England, known then as the home of royal forests. Thus he was proud to call his own land in the New World "The Forest."

In 1746 John Wayles married Martha Eppes of the prominent Eppes family of the plantation known as Bermuda Hundred. Because her husband had no family in Virginia, Martha's family took precautions to ensure that she would always be protected. They saw to it that she would inherit land and certain of their slaves as well as the future children of those slaves. Among them was "A Negro girl named Bettey," a bright eleven-year-old mulatto born of a full-blooded African woman and an English sea captain. When Betty was eighteen, she was claimed by a sailor and, during the next eight years, she gave birth to four children, Mary, Martin, Bett, and Nance. Title to these slaves was to go, ultimately, to the future children of Martha Eppes Wayles.

Martha and John Wayles had twins who died in infancy. Their daughter, named Martha for her mother, was born in October 1748, but just weeks after her baby's birth, Martha Eppes Wayles died suddenly. A year later, in 1749, John Wayles married Tabitha Cocke. Three daughters were born of this marriage: Elizabeth, Tabitha, and Anne. Elizabeth, the eldest, would become the special friend of her half sister Martha and would marry Francis Eppes, Martha's first cousin. When Anne, the youngest of the girls, was only four years old, their mother died, and in 1760 John Wayles, anxious to provide a mother for his four daughters, married for a third time. But this wife died just one year later.

Heeding his oldest daughter's plea that she not have another stepmother, John Wayles now took the "Negro girl named Bettey" (Betty Hemings) as his concubine. Betty had probably been serving as the girls' "mammy," or nurse, since 1748, when Wayles's first wife died. Betty's children fathered by Wayles were half sisters to Wayles's other four daughters. This relationship between John Wayles and Betty Hemings would later knot the lives of three generations of blacks and whites into a tangled web.

Martha Wayles Skelton was petite (an old slave called her "low") and lovely. No pictures of her exist, but she is described as having been very beautiful. Her complexion was radiant, her hazel eyes large and expressive, and her thick hair a beautiful shade of auburn. She was a graceful rider and dancer, and enjoyed long walks. She was lively and impulsive, and at times may have had a fiery temper. But she was gentle and warm-hearted as well.[4]

Martha had a fine mind and was better educated than the average Virginia belle of the day. She read more widely than most and could discuss books with intelligence. But nothing appealed to Jefferson more than her love of music. They seemed to be unusually well matched. For the first time since his sister Jane had died, Thomas Jefferson had found a woman who could play music, sing, and talk on topics that interested him. Her gay spirit offset his characteristic seriousness. In her presence he could unbend, and he found himself drawn to her.

Jefferson spent much time visiting Martha (whom her father and sisters called Patty) at The Forest, where he was always welcome. Even the servants looked forward to his coming and to his generous and welcome tips. He enjoyed conversations with Martha's father, and he loved to play with little John. When Martha consented to marry him, he looked forward to having John as a stepson and set up an account for him, with himself as guardian. But this was not to be. The little boy died suddenly on June 10, 1771, not quite four years old. He had probably developed one of the infections common at that time that the doctors were helpless to diagnose or to treat. This was an era when two out of every three children failed to survive childhood diseases.

By the summer of 1771, Jefferson was still unable to convince John Wayles to consent to the marriage. Wayles wanted something better for his favorite daughter. With Shadwell in ashes and his own house at the very beginnings of being built, Jefferson did not have the proper house to which to bring a beautiful and wealthy wife. Work needed to be speeded up on Monticello.

In spite of this, he ordered a wedding gift for Martha. In June he wrote to his British agent requesting that he send "a Forte-piano. . . . let the case be of fine mahogany, solid, not veneered, the compass from Double G. to F. in alt, a plenty of spare strings; and the workmanship of the whole very handsome and worthy the acceptance of a lady for whom I intend it."[5]

Jefferson probably drove a carriage similar to this one. (Photo courtesy of L. H. Bober)

When John Wayles finally gave his consent to the marriage on November 11, 1771, the wedding date was set for New Year's Day 1772. A jubilant Jefferson tipped the servants at The Forest with abandon, then bounded off on his horse with Jupiter trailing behind. He would go to court in Williamsburg, then return home for his reelection to the House of Burgesses and to prepare for his marriage.

Thomas Jefferson and Martha Wayles were married at The Forest on New Year's Day. The house was filled with guests, and the festivities lasted for days. It was not until January 18 that the newlyweds set out in a phaeton* for Monticello, more than a hundred miles away. Jupiter and some other servants had been sent on ahead.

The phaeton, which had been mended once before they began their journey, needed further repair after they left The Forest, so they stopped at Tuckahoe, where Jefferson had lived when he was a young boy. They spent a few days with "Tuckahoe Tom," as his cousin Thomas was called. They did not reach Monticello until January 26. The trip had not been easy.

In Virginia there is often no serious winter until after the New Year, when all at once it comes rushing down from the north in a torrent of wind and snow. There was some snow on the ground when they left Tuckahoe, but it grew deeper as they neared the mountains. Finally, it became too deep for their carriage. But they managed to push on through three feet of snow, the deepest Albemarle had ever known,

*A light, open, four-wheeled carriage usually drawn by two horses.

until they reached their friend Edward Carter's Blenheim Plantation. Here they abandoned the phaeton. Then, just at sunset, they mounted their horses and rode the remaining eight miles over a rough mountain track.

When they finally arrived at the small clearing at the top of their mountain, Martha had her first view of her new home. Dark and deserted, the little brick house clung to the side of the steep slope. There was no light to greet them, no voice to welcome them, no fire to warm them. The servants, who had waited until after dark for their master and their new mistress, had decided that the snow was too deep for travel and the hour too late for them to arrive. So they had put out the fires and returned to their own houses for the night.

Jefferson would not disturb them. He stabled the horses himself, then took his new bride into their home.

As Martha shivered inside her long wool cloak, her husband lit a fire in the fireplace, then suddenly remembered a hidden treasure. With a shout of pleasure, he jubilantly pulled out from behind a shelf of books a half bottle of wine. It would serve them for warmth and for supper. Soon the snug little cottage, 580 feet above the world, with the village of Charlottesville, the blackened ruins of Shadwell, and the wild and romantic Rivanna River below them, but with three feet of snow to block out any intruders, was lit up with the laughter of sheer happiness and with song. As they stood before the fire, wrapped in each other's arms, the warmth of the fire, of the wine, and of their happiness and their love seemed to spread through the house.

The honeymoon lasted until April, for not until then did the Jeffersons come down from their mountain. Jefferson did not attend the meeting of the House of Burgesses in February, nor did he take care of any legal business in Williamsburg until the spring. Martha had her husband completely to herself. The year 1772, the first year of his married life, was probably the happiest he was ever to know. He and his Patty could look forward with hope to a long and sunny life together.

A lull in the political storm gave Jefferson an interval of peace. The General Court called him to Williamsburg in April and October, but for most of the year he remained on his mountain, with a ruler in his pocket and his case of instruments near at hand, watching every operation. As he rode or walked about his plantation, he could always be heard singing or humming to himself. He had a fine, clear voice and usually sang the minuets that were the popular music of the day. As he supervised the laying out of his grounds and the cutting of roads and paths through the woods, and as he planned parts of his house and watched the garden and ever-widening farms develop, he kept brief, exact records of whatever he did, saw, or learned.

When Jefferson first brought Martha to live at Monticello, work on the main house was well under way. The foundations and the basement were finished, but the house itself was not livable. The northwest, or dining-room wing, was the first part completed, and it may have been enclosed, if not finished, that first winter.

In April Martha accompanied her husband to Williamsburg. They stayed for two months and were part of the spring social season there. They went to dances and to the theater. They rode out to Rosewell to visit the Pages. And they made visits to dentist Baker and Dr. Brown, who confirmed their hopes that Martha was pregnant.

At the end of May they went to The Forest for a month, to visit Martha's father, then returned to Monticello at the end of June. Jefferson spent the summer overseeing the progress of the mansion. For Monticello continued to grow like a tree—slowly, steadily, gracefully.

On September 27, 1772, at one o'clock in the morning, Martha gave birth prematurely to their first child, a daughter whom they named Martha, but who would be known to the family as Patsy. She was a sickly baby, and for six months they were fearful that she might not live. Then she "recovered almost instantaneously by a good breast of milk," provided by a black wet nurse who had just become a part of the Jefferson "family."

Jefferson had purchased her and her two sons, fourteen-year-old George and five-year-old Bagwell, at an auction because his wife was "very desirous to get a favorite house woman of the name of Ursula." Very soon after, at Ursula's request, Jefferson purchased her husband, George, from another plantation owner. This family would fill some of the most important positions at Monticello for the next twenty-five years.

# PART II

# Pen of a Revolution

# "Young Hot-Heads"

L ATE IN 1772 Bostonians learned that the British government intended to pay the salaries of the governor, lieutenant governor,
superior court judges, and other legal officials in the colony from the revenues collected by the American commissioners of customs. This meant
that these officials would no longer be subject to legislative control in
Massachusetts. Sam Adams, a zealous patriot and master politician in
Boston, warned that the mother country was destroying the checks and
balances in the Massachusetts constitution.

In fact, Adams saw evidence of what he—and many colonists—
feared was a conspiracy against liberty. They were becoming more and
more certain that there was a deliberate plan afoot to destroy the British
constitution with all the rights and privileges it guaranteed, not only in
England but in the colonies as well. Sam Adams met this crisis by organizing the Boston Committee of Correspondence, which would link
all the towns of Massachusetts.[1]

When the Virginia assembly, which was by now the southern focus of
resistance to Parliament, met in Williamsburg in March of 1773, the
members, too, were disturbed by the news of how Massachusetts government salaries would be paid. They also learned that a special court of
inquiry had been established that had the power to send colonists to England for trial. What happened in New England might happen to them.

But Jefferson worried that the older, more conservative leaders might
not be willing to take action. So he, Patrick Henry, Francis Lightfoot
Lee and his brother Richard Henry Lee, and Dabney Carr met one
evening in a private room of the Raleigh Tavern. They knew that they
were already being branded by the more conservative members of the
House as "young hot-heads."

They came to the conclusion, as Sam Adams had in Massachusetts,
that it was urgent for all the colonies to band together. They must act as
a united group. To accomplish this they proposed forming intercolonial

"committees of correspondence" through which each colony could exchange ideas and information with other colonies.

Richard Henry Lee proposed the appointment of a "Standing Committee of Correspondence and Inquiry." At the direction of the assembly, the committee would communicate to the assemblies of the other colonies the Virginians' anxieties about the reported threats to their ancient legal and constitutional rights, and suggest that the other assemblies appoint similar committees. The men then drew up resolutions to be presented to the burgesses on the following day.

On the morning of March 12, when the burgesses took their seats, all Williamsburg was tense. Students at William and Mary had learned what was happening and crowded the Capitol.

Mr. Jefferson had been urged to move the resolutions, but had declined in favor of Dabney Carr, "my friend and brother-in-law, then a new member, to whom I wished an opportunity should be given of making known to the House his great worth and talents."[2]

Dabney Carr's speech supporting these resolutions has been called "a happy blending of boldness, prudence, and courtesy."[3] The resolutions were carried, and Jefferson was exhilarated by what Carr had done. He was certain that his friend was destined for a brilliant career in politics. These committees of correspondence were instrumental in stimulating sentiment in favor of united action among all the colonies in opposition to British policy, and evolved directly into the first American Congress.

The two young men rode home together at the close of the session. Early in April, Jefferson had to leave again for Williamsburg to attend the April term of the General Court. Dabney Carr had cases to plead in the county court in Charlottesville. Dabney had been happily married for eight years now, and he and his Martha had six children. The youngest, Dabney Jr., was an infant.

Soon after he reached Charlottesville, however, Dabney was suddenly stricken with a malignant case of typhoid fever. Its course was so rapid that he died before anything could be done for him. He was twenty-nine years old.

Dabney was buried at Shadwell before Jefferson even knew of his death, for he was still in Williamsburg. When he returned, remembering their boyhood pledge that whoever should die first would be buried beneath their favorite oak tree on the southwestern slope of Tom's Mountain, Jefferson had his friend's body moved to this spot.

The inscription he wrote for Dabney's tombstone and nailed temporarily on their tree, to be engraved on a plate of copper, attests to his strong feeling for this special friend. It ends: "To his Virtue, Good sense, learning, and Friendship, this stone is dedicated by Thomas Jefferson, who of all men living loved him most."

Yet Jefferson was able to note with cool precision in his Garden Book, under the date May 22, 1773, that the graveyard he had planned years before was on this day begun as a resting place for his friend. He noted that "2 hands grubbed the graveyard 80 feet square = $1/7$ of an acre in $3^{1}/2$ hours, so that one would have done it in 7 hours, and would grub an acre in 49 hours = 4 days," and that the first peas had come to the table. Never one to give outward expression to his private emotions, he turned for relief to figures, to garden peas and the weather, to the ordinary affairs of every day.

Jefferson and Martha immediately invited the entire Carr family to live with them at Monticello, although there was hardly room for them at the house then. The family eventually went to live there permanently in 1781.

Jefferson cared for his sister, took charge of his friend's legal affairs, and raised and educated his children, particularly Peter, the eldest, as though they were his own.

Work was moving forward on Monticello. Bricks were still being molded on the mountaintop, and construction on the mansion was in progress.

Jefferson was constantly experimenting in his garden. He planted an extraordinary variety of trees, shrubs, grasses, grains, vegetables, bulbs, fruits, and nuts. He tried chestnuts from France, alpine strawberries, and melons and grapes from Italy. He was helped in these endeavors by a new friend and neighbor, Philip Mazzei, who had come to Virginia from Italy to plant vineyards. Jefferson was interested in Mazzei's desire to introduce the cultivation of the grape and the olive into the colony, so he invited Mazzei to remain as a guest at Monticello until his own house was built. When a dozen workmen arrived from Tuscany to assist Mazzei, they were delighted that their tall, friendly host spoke to them in Tuscan, which he had picked up by himself.

In the spring of 1774, soon after the peaches had come into full bloom, Jefferson laid out a permanent vegetable garden. He gave some of the vegetables Italian names, in honor of his friend Philip Mazzei.

His tobacco fields continued to earn him a good living. This was important because tobacco was the only crop that could be marketed for cash or sent to London to be exchanged for books, furniture, fine clothes, musical instruments, and choice wines. Jefferson was always adding to his library and his wine cellar.

He spent most of his time on his mountain, partly to work on his farm, and partly because Martha was expecting their second child in April. Pregnancy for Martha was an emotional as well as a physical crisis. Her own mother had died soon after childbirth, and that knowledge hung over her as a constant threat. And childbearing seemed to be particularly difficult for her physically as well.

But her fragility seemed to make her all the more special to her husband. He loved her even more, fussed over her, cared for her, stayed close to her, and considered himself the happiest of men.

Jane Randolph Jefferson, named for her grandmother, arrived at eleven o'clock in the morning on April 3, 1774. Her older sister, Martha, called Patsy, was an eighteen-month-old toddler. Jefferson was delighted with his second little girl and relieved that Martha had come through the ordeal so well. He would willingly have spent the rest of his life in the idyllic setting on his mountain, reluctantly going to Williamsburg to sit in the House of Burgesses twice a year. But events would not let this happen.

Three and a half months before Jane was born, on December 16, 1773, the Boston Tea Party had taken place. In protest against the hated tax on tea that the British had imposed on the colonies by the Tea Act of 1773, 342 chests of tea, worth about ten thousand pounds, had been broken open and their contents dumped into Boston Harbor. A silent crowd watched approvingly from the darkness of the shore as salty tea was brewed for the fish.

Outraged, Parliament retaliated with measures that would brew a revolution. The most drastic of these, the Boston Port Act, threatened to close the tea-stained harbor.

Jefferson, in Williamsburg for the spring session of the assembly, heard of these happenings when dust-covered express riders from Boston came pounding into the capital with news of this retaliation and a plea for help from Virginia. He was incensed at the British threat against Boston. He feared it would cause the "utter ruin" of a prosperous commercial city.

There was much excitement and heated debate in the assembly as the members argued over which side to take. They were split into two groups: the Tories, sympathetic to the British, and the Whigs, who were committed to the precept that people have a right to have a say in choosing who will govern them. The older and more cautious among both the Tories and the Whigs sought to resolve the issue without resorting to war. They still hoped to preserve their allegiance to the king. The younger Whigs were more aggressive and defiant. Jefferson, among this group, was frustrated as he heard his friend George Wythe try to quiet the tumult. Jefferson knew that Wythe had the best interests of the colony at heart, but he felt that Wythe and most of the older members of the assembly were clinging to the futile hope that they could gain colonial rights by more petitions to the king. He began to realize that, much as he respected these men, leadership could no longer be left in their hands. They moved too slowly. They were fearful of change.

"We must boldly take an unequivocal stand in the line with Massachusetts," Thomas Jefferson said. "An attack on any one colony should be considered an attack on the whole."[4] The aristocratic young lawyer from Albemarle was becoming a revolutionary.

Poring over journals and books, searching for a precedent, an idea to apply to this situation, Jefferson finally found what he was looking for: In 1746 the Puritans in Massachusetts had resorted to fasting and prayer for deliverance from the French during the war between France and Great Britain known as King George's War (1744–48). He would do the same. He proposed a day of fasting, humiliation, and prayer to signal the closing of the port of Boston. It would focus attention on this affront to colonial liberty, "inspire us with firmness in support of our rights, and . . . turn the hearts of the King & parliament to moderation & justice," he said.

Who could object to their praying for the people of Boston? And gentlemen who kneel together side by side in prayer might suddenly find themselves on the same side in the controversy.[5]

The plot that Jefferson and some of his young friends (Patrick Henry, Richard Henry Lee, and Francis Lightfoot Lee, among them) had "cooked up" (as he later described it) did not spring from a deep religious feeling. But these young men recognized the power of the church over the people and knew how strong its influence could be. They would give a religious appearance to a political maneuver.

⤨ 12 ⤪

# The Rights of British America

O N THE FIRST DAY of June in 1774, the air in Williamsburg was warm and thick, heavy with the scent of the linden tree. Early in the morning, the townspeople began to emerge from their houses and gather together for the short walk to Bruton Parish Church. Humble townspeople and elegantly clad ladies and gentlemen mingled together as they walked behind the Speaker of the House of Burgesses along Duke of Gloucester Street. This was the day on which the closing of the port of Boston was scheduled to take place. The people were about to observe the day of fasting and prayer that Jefferson had proposed to mark it. They would congregate at the church and pray to heaven to avert the evils of civil war.

In fact, all across the colony of Virginia, people were answering the call to prayer. They thronged to their parish churches, anxiety and alarm evident on their faces. Thomas Jefferson, at home with his family, attended a service at his parish in Albemarle. "The effect of the day was like a shock of electricity, arousing every man, and placing him erect and solidly on his center," Jefferson described it. Virginians were deeply moved by compassion for the people of Boston and were fearful that they might be next to feel the wrath of King George III.

Obviously, Lord North, prime minister of England, had made a mistake. The Port Act, instead of isolating Boston, seemed to be "the very means to perfect *that union* in America, which it was intended to destroy, and finally restore the excellent constitution even of the mother country itself."[1] All up and down the seaboard men were coming to the conclusion that they must band together. "The whole continent seems inspired by one soul, and that soul a vigorous and determined one," reported the *Boston Gazette.*

On July 26, 1774, in all the counties throughout Virginia, the freeholders reelected every member of the original Virginia assembly to act as deputies at the Virginia Convention, scheduled to be held in Williamsburg on August 1. Fairfax County reelected George Washington, and Louisa County returned Patrick Henry. Thomas Jefferson and his friend John Walker were reelected in Albemarle.

Soon plans were underway for a "general congress" of all the thirteen colonies. Representatives would meet in Philadelphia, the largest city and geographic midpoint, on September 5, 1774. This association would be known as the Continental Congress. Thomas Jefferson realized that the delegates to this congress would need formal and exact instructions about how to proceed. He would draft those instructions.

As he pondered the problem, he looked, once again, for a historical precedent for the freedom he was so certain was right. Jefferson thought back to the reading he had done when he first began to practice law. He had returned to early British sources and traced the origin of the common law of England to the Angles and the Saxons. As he reread the notes he had taken as a young law student, his great respect for King Alfred's common law was renewed. When he read that, more than a thousand years before, the Anglo-Saxons in England had lived under customs and unwritten laws based on the natural rights of man, he concluded that these customs and laws had permitted individuals to develop freely, normally, and happily.[2]

Now he adapted Saxon history and law to serve the interests of the colonists. As he traced the settlement of England from the first incursion of Saxons from Germany and Angles from Denmark through the final invasion of the Danes in the tenth century, he decided that what the Saxons had done in England and were allowed to do by their mother country, the colonists had a right to do in America and should be allowed to do by *their* mother country. The Saxons, he concluded, had established and governed themselves by their own laws after their arrival in England. This Saxon law, he believed, was the origin of English common law.[3]

This would become the basis for the resolutions he would draft. He hoped they would be adopted as the instructions to Virginia's delegates to the Continental Congress. He hoped, too, that they would be incorporated into an address to the king, setting before him the grievances of all the colonies. But, Jefferson cautioned, Congress should address the king so that he understood that the colonists were asking not for favors but for rights:

> Our ancestors, before their emigration to America, were the free inhabitants of the British dominions in Europe, and possessed a right, which nature has given to all men, of departing from the country in which chance, not choice has placed them, of going in quest of new habitations, and of there establishing new societies, under such laws and regulations as to them shall seem most likely to promote public happiness.[4]

The theory of natural rights was taking a dominant place in his thinking; and with the concept of happiness as the object of government, he was sounding a new note.

He went on to say that the wilds of the American continent were settled at great sacrifice by the colonists. "Their own blood was spilt . . . their own fortunes expended . . . for themselves they fought, for themselves they conquered, and for themselves alone they have right to hold."[5] The fierce determination of his pioneer spirit was surfacing. No longer was he the shy and timid new member of the House of Burgesses whose first assignment had been rejected. Now he was directly, publicly, and fearlessly criticizing King George III.

Kings, he boldly informed George III (in an age when kings were approached with reverence), are the servants, not the proprietors of the people. "Open your breast, Sire, to liberal and expanded thought," he lectured him. "Let not the name of George the third be a blot on the page of history. . . . The whole art of government consists in the art of being honest." Men were born to freedom, not to slavery, Jefferson continued. He had said this publicly four years before, when, as a young lawyer, he had tried to win freedom for a young slave. Now he was saying that the colonists were independent of the British government. They were subject to no laws except those they had freely adopted when they had consented to a new compact and formed a new society. Parliament had no right whatsoever to exercise authority over the colonies. Self-government, Jefferson knew, was right: "The God who gave us life, gave us liberty at the same time: the hand of force may destroy, but cannot disjoin them."[6]

He had studied, he had thought carefully, and he had come to the conclusion that the only solution was rebellion. He wrote with a "freedom of language and sentiment which becomes a free people claiming their rights, as derived from the laws of nature, and not as the gift of their chief magistrate."[7] He was an idealistic young man, fired with the passion of separating right from wrong. His words would set aflame the imagination of the people and become their battle cry.

Unfortunately, on his way to Williamsburg to attend the convention, Jefferson suddenly fell ill with a severe case of dysentery and knew he had to return home. He gave the two copies of the resolutions he had prepared to Jupiter—who, as always, was accompanying his master—and instructed him to deliver one copy to his friend Patrick Henry, who he hoped would read it aloud, and the other to his cousin Peyton Randolph, who he was certain would be elected chairman of the Virginia Convention. He assured Jupiter that he could get home alone. Thus Jupiter carried to Williamsburg the words, "The abolition of domestic slavery is the great object of desire in those colonies, where it was unhappily introduced in their infant state. . . . the rights of human nature [are] deeply wounded by this infamous practice."[8] We can only wonder whether Thomas Jefferson recognized the irony in the situation.

In the end it was Peyton Randolph, who had indeed been elected to preside over the Virginia Convention, who read his copy aloud to a large group of delegates assembled at his house. The younger men present were wildly enthusiastic, but the older, more conservative members shifted uncomfortably in their chairs as they pondered Jefferson's bold statements. They were hearing for the first time a categorical denial of Parliament's authority over the colonial legislatures. The resolutions were not adopted.

"The leap I proposed was too long, as yet, for the mass of our citizens," Jefferson explained later. Mr. Jefferson was wont "to run before the times in which he lived," was his cousin Edmund Randolph's accurate appraisal.[9]

But some of Jefferson's friends, inspired by his daring ideas, had the resolutions, titled *A Summary View of the Rights of British America,* printed by Clementina Rind, Williamsburg's only woman printer, without asking his permission. Among the first to purchase a copy was George Washington, who noted in his diary that it had cost him three shillings nine pence.

The pamphlet was reprinted in newspapers throughout the colonies. Eventually it found its way to England. Jefferson learned that when it was read in Parliament by Edmund Burke, as he pleaded the case of the colonies, the name Thomas Jefferson was added to the rapidly growing list of "outlaws" to be brought to England for trial.[10]

*A Summary View* became the first sustained piece of American political writing that subjected the king's conduct to direct and pointed criticism. At age thirty-one, Thomas Jefferson was establishing his reputation as a serious political thinker.[11]

## ᕦ 13 ᕤ

# A Masterly Pen

JEFFERSON SPENT THE END of 1774 and early 1775 on his mountaintop, watching as Monticello was taking shape. But there were problems he had not anticipated. Bricks that had been molded and fired on the mountaintop were stacked alongside lumber and building rubble, and scaffolding was left in place on unfinished walls from one season to the next. Fifty thousand bricks were fired in 1774 alone, and by the end of the year, what Jefferson called "the middle building" was completed. It contained the parlor, library, and drawing room, with a bedroom above. It wasn't until fifteen months after he had ordered them from England that fourteen pairs of sash windows arrived. Only then was this building completely enclosed from the weather. Martha, with two small children to look after, had to contend with all the hazards and inconveniences of construction.

As Jefferson continued to read and to ponder the problems facing the colonies, he began to realize that he was devoting less and less time to his law practice. Politics was claiming all his energy. He had been trained from youth to assume responsibility for many people, and he found now that to serve the people was what he really loved best.

He was a wealthy man, he reasoned, and he didn't need the income from his law practice. He could earn enough as a planter. And now he had additional income. Martha's father, John Wayles, had died suddenly on May 28, 1773, leaving Jefferson with an inheritance that "was about equal to my own patrimony, and consequently doubled the ease of our circumstances."[1]

But Thomas Jefferson inherited more than money. He inherited 135 slaves, including the entire Hemings family. Half-white Betty Hemings, who had become John Wayles's mistress after the death of his third wife, had six children fathered by Wayles: Robert, James, Thenia, Critta, Peter, and Sally, the youngest, just two years old when Wayles died.

These six children, with a half-white mother and a white father, were extremely light-skinned. When the family was brought to Monticello, they were given jobs inside the house. Betty, along with her older children, immediately took charge of the entire domestic staff. Members of the Hemings family were always treated with exceptional kindness and were never sent to work in the fields. The Monticello overseer, Edmund Bacon, "was instructed to take no control of them," which "was a source of bitter jealousy to the other slaves," Jefferson's grandson would say many years later. But Betty Hemings had been the one constant maternal presence in Martha Jefferson's life as she was growing up at The Forest, and Martha was delighted to have her at Monticello now.[2]

What Jefferson didn't recognize at the time were the complicated financial transactions that would accompany this inheritance. Along with 11,000 acres of land, John Wayles left a heavy debt to an English mercantile firm. In order to pay his share of the debt, Jefferson sold 6,000 acres, for which he was paid in promissory notes, not cash. The maker of the notes would ultimately fail to redeem them, and Jefferson would be left with the original debt to be paid a second time.

Now Jefferson decided to turn his law practice over to his young cousin, Edmund Randolph, the son of John Randolph, attorney general of Virginia. Edmund was fast becoming one of the outstanding lawyers in the colony.

Although he himself was a fine and successful lawyer, Jefferson never thought highly of lawyers as a group. "The lawyers' trade is to question everything, yield nothing, and talk by the hour," he said. Years later, he would write to a friend: "I was bred to the law, and that gave me a view of the dark side of humanity. Then I read poetry to qualify it with a gaze upon its bright side."[3]

Jefferson never returned to the practice of law, but he never regretted his training. "[H]e who knows nothing of [the laws of the land] will always be perplexed, and often foiled by adversaries having the advantage of that knowledge over him," he would write to his son-in-law Thomas Mann Randolph Jr. many years later.[4] It was the *power* of knowledge that was important to him. Although he never appeared in court after August 1774, the honing of his legal and writing skills had set the stage for his public career. In his most important state papers he became the advocate pleading a cause and buttressing it with precedents. His legal practice became a "crucial link between his adolescent reading and his adult writing."[5]

For the rest of his life Jefferson would turn to his law books at critical moments to pursue what he considered to be justice. In his quiet, determined way, he would contest colonial, state, and federal judges, using his legal knowledge and experience to reform and reshape the law.[6]

By early 1775, committees of safety were being formed throughout Virginia to serve as governing bodies and to enforce the Virginia Association of 1769, the ban on the importation and exportation of British goods. Jefferson was elected to head the Committee of Safety of Albe-marle County. Soon after, he and John Walker were elected to represent their county at the second Virginia Convention. It was held in Rich-mond on March 20, at St. John's Church, a simple white wooden build-ing with about fifty to sixty pews, the only place in that city large enough to hold the delegates.

As Jefferson sat with George Washington and Richard Henry Lee, thoughtfully listening to the conciliatory resolutions being read, Patrick Henry suddenly jumped to his feet and called for a militia to be formed for the defense of the country.

Pandemonium broke loose. The members were not prepared for such a radical step. The conservative members opposed the resolution. They cautioned against armed resistance, fearing that military threats might hinder their progress.

Then Henry, with his perfect sense of timing, once again rose from his seat, this time solemnly and majestically. He was recognized by

St. John's Church, Rich-mond, where, on March 20, 1775, the second Virginia Convention was held. Here Patrick Henry electrified the members when he cried out, "Give me liberty or give me death!" (Courtesy of L. H. Bober)

Patrick Henry was a member of the Virginia assembly. His "audacity [and] eloquence" caught the admiration of the whole assembly. By Thomas Sully, 1815. (Courtesy of the Colonial Williamsburg Foundation)

Speaker Peyton Randolph. "We have done everything that could be done to avert the storm which is now coming on," he cried. "There is no longer room for hope. If we wish to be free . . . we must fight! I repeat, Sir, we must fight!" His voice fell to a whisper as he continued. Then, eyes blazing, it rose to a thundering challenge and rang like an anvil through the timbers in the little church: "Is life so dear, or peace so sweet, as to be purchased at the price of chains and slavery? Forbid it, Almighty God! I know not what course others may take; but as for me . . . give me liberty or give me death!"[7]

Not a sound was heard as he finished and sank into his seat. The men sat stunned and silent. Then, with his "usual elegance," Richard Henry Lee rose and supported Mr. Henry. Everyone started to talk at once, and above the din of voices could be heard such words as "liberty" and "freedom."

Suddenly, Thomas Jefferson asked to be heard. His friends were amazed. Never before had he participated in public debate. He spoke too softly to be heard, and sometimes stammered. Now, overcoming his shyness, he argued "closely, profoundly, and warmly" in support of Patrick Henry and Richard Henry Lee.[8]

Captivated by his charm, his ability to speak, and "the exact conformity of our political opinions,"⁹ Jefferson and his radical friends vehemently supported Patrick Henry. But George Washington remained silent, deep in thought.

The resolutions passed with a vote of 65 to 60, an example of "the inequality of pace with which we moved, and the prudence required to keep front and rear together," Jefferson wrote later. "We often wished to have gone faster, but we slackened our pace, that our less ardent colleagues might keep up with us; and they, on their part, differing nothing from us in principle, quickened their gait somewhat."¹⁰

Jefferson continued, as was his practice, to work behind the scenes, talking and planning in small groups. Good-natured, mild mannered, never aggressive, he managed to instill his ideas into others so subtly that they came to believe that it was they who had originated them. He had a genius for friendship and a shy warmth that always attracted people to him. It proved extremely helpful now. But he continued to wish that war could be avoided. It was not what he wanted.

Peyton Randolph had been chosen to be the delegate to the Second Continental Congress, scheduled to be held in Philadelphia in May 1775. But if the new royal governor, Lord Dunmore—who had arrived in Williamsburg from England in October 1771 following the sudden death of Lord Botetourt—should call a meeting of the House of Burgesses, he would not be able to attend. Before the members of the Virginia Convention adjourned, they elected Thomas Jefferson as an alternate to take Randolph's place.

But when the burgesses were, in fact, summoned by Lord Dunmore to consider a conciliatory proposition put forward early in 1775 by the British prime minister, Lord North, Randolph prevailed upon Jefferson to postpone his journey to Philadelphia and come to Williamsburg to prepare the reply. By this time, the name of Thomas Jefferson was frequently on the lips of the people of Virginia, and Randolph was convinced that there was no more effective writer in America. He chose him over all the older and respected veterans of the House of Burgesses. Jefferson was only thirty-two.

He wrote the reply with characteristic simplicity and forthrightness. It concluded:

These, my Lord, are our sentiments on this important subject. . . . For ourselves we have exhausted every mode of application which our invention could suggest as proper and promising. We have decently remonstrated with Parliament, they have added new injuries to the old: we have wearied our King with supplications, he has not deigned to answer us; we have appealed to the native honour and justice of the British nation, their efforts in our favor have hitherto been ineffectual. What then remains to be done? That we commit our injuries to the even-handed justice of that Being who doth no wrong; earnestly beseeching him to illuminate the councils, and prosper the endeavors of those to whom America hath confided her hopes; that through their wise direction, we may again see, reunited, the blessing of liberty and property, and the most permanent harmony with Great Britain.[11]

By this time, "the shot heard round the world"* had been fired in Massachusetts on April 19, 1775. Ten days later Virginians learned that British soldiers in Boston had marched to Lexington, Massachusetts, where they tried, unsuccessfully, to capture Sam Adams and John Hancock, two of the leading patriots there. Then they fired without orders, killing eight militiamen and wounding ten others. A young man in his teens, Isaac Muzzy, died at his father's feet. Jonathan Harrington, hit in the chest, crawled to the doorstep of his house and died there, before the horrified eyes of his wife and son. Paul Revere, attempting to save a trunk of John Hancock's papers from falling into British hands, carried it through the militia on the Lexington green, where musket balls were "flying thick around him."

The British then moved on to Concord, where they planned to seize the ammunition stored there. This encounter, Jefferson wrote, "has cut off our last hopes of reconciliation and a phrenzy of revenge seems to have seized all ranks of people."[12]

By the close of the day, a change had taken place in the colonists. From Englishmen rebelling against the unjust laws of their king, they had become Americans fighting for their freedom.

In another show of British strength, the impetuous and self-important

---

*This famous phrase is from Ralph Waldo Emerson's "Concord Hymn."

Lord Dunmore had secretly removed fifteen barrels of gunpowder stored in the magazine—or storehouse—at Williamsburg and had them taken to a warship lying at anchor in the York River. The colonists were furious. "The . . . bloodshed at Lexington . . . ," Edmund Randolph wrote, "had in Virginia changed the figure of Great Britain from an unrelenting parent into that of a merciless enemy." The Revolutionary War had begun.[13]

The following week, on June 8, the governor and his family fled the palace in the middle of the night. British rule in Virginia had come to an end.

Suddenly, the Continental Congress meeting in Philadelphia became very important, and Thomas Jefferson was eager to be there. Peyton Randolph remained in Williamsburg.

Jefferson finally arrived in Philadelphia on June 20, 1775, a hot and humid day. His journey from Williamsburg, more than 250 miles over roads that were little more than trails through the wilderness, had taken ten days.

Philadelphia in 1775 was a large city, teeming with life. Its broad straight avenues were paved with cobblestones or brick, unlike the dirt roads that turned to mud in the rain in other cities. It had a greater population (about 40,000) than any other city in the colonies. Jefferson saw people from all walks of life on its streets. Fashionably dressed ladies in elegant silks mingled with plain, simply dressed Quakers and militiamen in their rough uniforms. Messenger boys hurried along, jostling each other as they ran to deliver letters and important documents. Fashionable shops lined the streets. Jefferson's observant eye missed nothing.

He found rooms with a cabinetmaker named Benjamin Randolph, whom he paid for "a fort-night's [two weeks] lodging for self and servant 3-15." His horses were more expensive. He paid three pounds ten shillings a week for their care.[14]

Congress sat in the redbrick colonial State House (which would later come to be known as Independence Hall) on Chestnut Street. The Pennsylvania Assembly had lent Congress its room on the ground floor, a large, beautiful white-paneled chamber with high windows lining two sides. A lovely glass prism chandelier hung in the center.

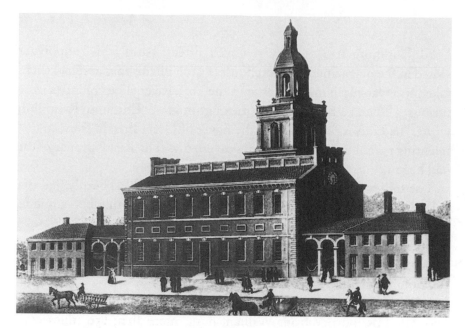

The redbrick Pennsylvania State House, which later came to be known as
Independence Hall, where Thomas Jefferson first met John Adams and Benjamin
Franklin. It was here that the delegates to the Second Continental Congress met to
decide to fight for "independency." (Courtesy of the National Archives)

The Second Continental Congress met in the simple, yet elegant and inspiring
Assembly Room in the Pennsylvania State House. (Courtesy of Independence
National Historical Park)

Crowds had already gathered outside in the yard to watch the Philadelphia Associators, a militia company, drilling their newly formed battalions of soldiers when Jefferson arrived at the State House on the morning of June 22. A feeling of war was in the air.

Inside, to ensure secrecy, the delegates, wiping damp and dripping brows, locked the doors and opened the high windows just a crack from the top in spite of the sweltering heat. Insects buzzed and banged against the panes.

When the tall, thin, redheaded new member from Virginia presented his credentials to Congress, he was greeted warmly, and his concern about participating in this august group of men was quickly allayed. The other Virginia delegates had boasted about him, and the members were eager to meet this young man who wrote such eloquent prose about liberty and freedom.

Unbeknownst to Jefferson, he had already established the reputation of "a masterly pen . . . , in consequence of a very handsome public paper which he had written for the House of Burgesses, which had given him the character of a fine writer," according to John Adams, one of the Massachusetts delegates at the Congress.[15] And Samuel Ward, another delegate, said of Jefferson, "I have not been in Company with him yet, [but] he looks like a very sensible spirited, fine Fellow and by the Pamphlet which he wrote last Summer he certainly is one."

Jefferson himself was particularly drawn to two men: Benjamin Franklin, at sixty-nine America's most experienced statesman as well as a philosopher and scientist of world renown; and John Adams of Massachusetts, the brilliant lawyer and leader of the radicals whose political opinions, Jefferson had heard, were exactly the same as his. Indeed, the unlikely friendship between the tall, angular, and reserved Jefferson and the chubby, rotund, and outspoken Adams, who had a "heart formed for friendship," would span the first half century of the Republic and would come to be considered one of the great friendships of all time.

"He soon seized upon my heart," John Adams wrote to his wife, Abigail, and remarked to a friend that Jefferson was "the greatest rubber-off-of-dust." Jefferson had not been in Congress more than a few weeks when his quick, commanding way in committee became evident to all

John Adams was one of the most persistent and convincing voices at the Second Continental Congress. His extraordinary friendship with Thomas Jefferson withstood a break over politics and resumed after both had retired. (Courtesy of the National Archives)

who worked with him. "He was prompt, frank, explicit, decisive," John Adams described his new young friend. "He will be given work at once."[16]

Mr. Jefferson was quickly invited to join a group of delegates who dined together at the City Tavern, a new and fashionable inn, at the conclusion of the session every day. And he was just as quickly given an assignment, as John Adams had predicted. He was appointed to a committee to draw up a Declaration of the Causes and Necessity for Taking Up Arms. It would be presented by General Washington to his troops. John Adams had persuaded Congress to form a Continental army made up of American volunteers, and to appoint George Washington commander-in-chief. In his new uniform—a blue and buff coat with rich gold epaulets, a small, elegant sword at his side, and a black cockade in his hat, Washington was a quiet reminder of where they might be heading.

Now Washington was preparing to leave to join the army near Cambridge, Massachusetts. The delegates felt that the soldiers should understand recent political happenings to justify the steps that were being taken toward war.

John Dickinson, a conservative delegate from Pennsylvania who still hoped for reconciliation with England, wrote the first part of the paper. Of Jefferson's paper, only the final four and a half paragraphs were included. Jefferson recognized that the moderates still shied away from independence, so he understood that he must move slowly and quietly. The colonies must be united in taking the final step. He did not want to instigate civil war. His stirring words, read aloud by Washington to his men, echoed through the colonies and brought the people closer to the side of the radicals:

> We fight not for glory or for conquest. We exhibit to mankind the remarkable spectacle of a people attacked by unprovoked enemies, without any imputation, or even suspicion of offence. . . . In our native land, in defense of the freedom that is our birthright, and which we ever enjoyed until the late violation of it; for the protection of our property, acquired solely by the honest industry of our forefathers and ourselves, against violence actually offered, we have taken up arms. . . .[17]

Finally, on November 7, 1775, Lord Dunmore brought on the most dreaded event of all for white Virginians: an uprising of slaves against their masters. He issued a proclamation to the people of his "rebellious colony" in which he declared martial law and demanded that all able-bodied citizens of Virginia capable of bearing arms report "to his Majesty's STANDARD, or be looked upon as traitors." He then shocked most white Virginians by offering freedom to slaves "appertaining [belonging] to Rebels" who would be willing and able to bear arms for the king "for the more speedily reducing this Colony to a proper Sense of their Duty." Thousands of slaves responded. They immediately fled to British lines, where hundreds joined the newly created Royal Ethiopian Regiment, under the command of British officers. Many wore shirts with the motto "Liberty to Slaves" stitched across the front, mocking the rebels' badges imprinted with "Liberty or Death."[18]

In December the representatives of the fourth Virginia Convention responded to Dunmore's proclamation with "A Declaration." The document proclaimed that "all slaves who have been, or shall be, seduced by his lordship's proclamation . . . to desert their masters' service and take up arms against the inhabitants of this colony . . . may return in safety to their duty, and escape the punishment due their crimes." They would be pardoned but not freed.[19]

Lord Dunmore had miscalculated. Moderate burgesses who had been unwilling to fight the British and who had been acting as a brake on their more radical compatriots suddenly realized that the time had come to act. They viewed Dunmore's offer of freedom to their slaves as one more attack on their private property, and they worried about the inability of their plantations to function without slave labor, not to mention their fear for their own safety. White Virginians had long been haunted by the terror of a slave uprising. No issue could have solidified them more.

"If [Dunmore] is not crushed before spring," George Washington predicted, "he will become the most formidable enemy America has. His strength will increase as a snowball."[20]

The time had come to join the radicals.

## ❧ 14 ❧

# "An Expression of the American Mind"

THE YEAR 1776 began in Virginia with the senseless ravaging of a peaceful seaport town, an event that gave the final impetus to the push for independence. Norfolk was burned to the ground by the British on the first day of the new year. The war had reached Virginia.

Then, on January 10, a pamphlet called *Common Sense* was published, and people all up and down the seaboard began to talk of independence. *Common Sense* was written by Thomas Paine, an Englishman who had recently immigrated to America. In it, Paine, a gifted political propagandist, pleaded the case of the colonies in simple language: "nothing more than simple facts, plain arguments and common sense." It was "absurd," he said, "for a continent to be perpetually governed by an island." The people were ready to hear what he had to say. Paine made people think, and his words were soon on everyone's lips. Eventually, over 100,000 copies of *Common Sense* were sold. "The period of debate is closed," the pamphlet said. "Now is the seed time of continental union, faith and honour."[1]

Jefferson, reading and rereading *Common Sense* at home on his mountaintop, thought it contained sound doctrine and logical reasoning. When he rode through the area to sound out the people in the nearby local counties, he concluded that nine-tenths of them agreed with Paine and favored independence.

Early in September 1775 Jefferson and Martha had lost their seventeen-month-old baby daughter, Jane, and six months later, early in the morning on the last day of March 1776, his mother suffered a stroke and died within an hour. She was fifty-seven years old. Jefferson recorded this loss tersely in his little pocket account book in a simple

With his pamphlet *Common Sense*, published January 10, 1776, Thomas Paine paved the way for the decision to declare independence taken by Congress in July. (Courtesy of the National Archives)

unemotional statement that was consistent with his reticence on all personal matters.

Very little is known about Jefferson's relationship with his mother, for nowhere is there any indication of how he felt about her. But immediately after her death, following quickly after the death of his little daughter, in spite of his seeming lack of emotion, he suddenly became ill himself. An intense pain throbbed through his head for weeks. He called it "the head ach." He seems to have been suffering from what is now referred to as a migraine, the result, no doubt, of the terrible personal strain under which he was living. It kept him at Monticello for an additional six weeks.

On a lovely morning early in May, when he finally took leave of his delicate wife, who was not yet strong enough to accompany him on the long journey to Philadelphia, he tried hard to keep his emotions in check and to hide his disappointment—and his uneasiness—at leaving her behind. He was beginning to worry more and more about Martha's health. She seemed unusually frail to him. Both childbearing and the loss of her baby had worn her out physically and emotionally, and she was sinking into a state of depression.

Jefferson tried, also, to allay her fears for him and her fears of a revolution. He was torn by his desire to remain on his mountaintop with the woman he adored and who needed him, and with his cheerful little three-year-old daughter, Patsy, in whom he delighted and who was growing up so quickly. But he understood that his country was calling, and it was his duty to answer the call.

Thomas Jefferson finally arrived in Philadelphia to attend the Second Continental Congress on May 14, 1776. He had as his only companion his slave Bob Hemings, the slim, light-skinned, fourteen-year-old son of his late father-in-law, John Wayles, and Betty Hemings. Bob had replaced Jupiter as Jefferson's body servant soon after the Hemings family came to Monticello in 1774. Jupiter had assumed new duties as Jefferson's coachman and had been given charge of the Monticello stables, which included caring for the carriages, harness, and, most importantly, his master's valuable horses. It is possible that Jupiter requested this change, perhaps to have more time at Monticello. He and the Jeffersons' new cook, sixteen-year-old Suck, whom Jupiter had first met in the kitchen at The Forest and who had come to Monticello as part of the Wayles inheritance, were now husband and wife. She was "the first to connect the Wayles and Jefferson enslaved populations through marriage."[2]

Jefferson found lodgings once again with Benjamin Randolph on Chestnut Street, then went to take his seat in Congress, where he found waiting for him a month-old letter from John Page, who was now a member of the Board of Visitors of William and Mary and a representative to the House of Burgesses. "For God's sake declare the colonies independent and save us from ruin," his friend had written from Williamsburg. But Jefferson knew that he himself was only a delegate to the Congress. He had to wait for instructions from the Virginia Convention, then meeting in Williamsburg.

The atmosphere in Congress was extremely tense when Jefferson arrived. John Adams described the long hours of debate and the overwhelming sense of responsibility as "drudgery of the most wasting, exhausting, consuming kind," concerned with measures that will affect "the lives and liberties of millions yet unborn." Indeed, "every post and every day rolls in upon us independence like a torrent," he wrote to his friend James Warren.[3]

On May 15, at Adams's suggestion, Congress had recommended that each of the colonies form new governments to meet their needs. Jefferson would have much preferred to be in Williamsburg to take part in helping to formulate "a plan of government" for Virginia. He was already more concerned with what would follow a formal separation from England than with the action itself. He was anxious to see his ideas about human rights actually carried out.

In one form or another, the problem of how Americans should govern themselves would preoccupy him all his life. On May 16, he wrote to Thomas Nelson of his desire to be in Virginia to help in drafting its constitution: "It is a work of the most interesting nature and such as every individual would wish to have his voice in. . . . In truth, it is the whole object of the present controversy; for should a bad government be instituted for us in future it had been as well to have accepted at first the bad one offered to us from beyond the water without the risk and expence of contest."[4]

What Jefferson didn't know was that just the day before, on May 15, the Virginia Convention, meeting at the Raleigh Tavern in Williamsburg, had unanimously approved resolutions, offered by his friend Thomas Nelson, instructing its delegates in the Continental Congress to move at once for "independency." It would take twelve days for the instructions to arrive in Philadelphia.

That evening, after taking supper at the City Tavern with his friends, Jefferson returned to his rooms early to speak to his landlord, Benjamin Randolph. Mr. Randolph, he knew, was a fine cabinetmaker, and Jefferson had a project for him. He explained that what he wanted was a travel lap desk convenient for writing that had, as well, an adjustable book rest for reading. The desk should be equipped with a drawer that could be locked and within which he could store paper stock and written papers. It was to be fitted to hold supplies of ink, nibs for his pens, and sand for blotting. Randolph was happy to oblige.

When it was finished, the multipurpose desk met all Jefferson's specifications and was a fine piece of furniture. Crafted of beautiful ma-

The desk on which Thomas Jefferson wrote the Declaration of Independence. "On that little desk was done a work greater than any battle, loftier than any poem, more enduring than any monument." (Courtesy of the National Museum of American History, Smithsonian Institution)

hogany, it was as small as possible and lightweight, with a maximum use of space. Neither its designer nor its builder could have anticipated that this little desk would come to be revered by future generations.

Soon after he was settled at Mr. Randolph's, and with his mind still on the Virginia Convention, Jefferson hastily drew up a plan for the kind of constitution he felt his "country" (Virginia) should have. As he wrote this document, he was able to clarify and articulate his own views on society and government. He sent it off to Edmund Pendleton, then Virginia's Speaker of the House, with George Wythe, who was returning to Williamsburg for a brief stay. After stating that the "Legislative, Executive, and Judiciary Offices shall be kept forever separate," the document granted voting privileges to a far broader spectrum of the people than had been provided for in the past. The people would be the source of authority. Many years later, Jefferson would write that "a government is republican in proportion as every member composing it has an equal voice in directing its concerns."[5]

His plan also guaranteed religious freedom and freedom of the press, and abolished the ancient inheritance laws that Virginians had brought from England. This last proposal would change the existing system from inherited privilege to one of merit. All heirs should have equal rights—male and female alike, he stated, granting a new dignity to womanhood. As the devoted father of a daughter, and with a deep respect for the intelligence of women, Jefferson saw these ancient inheritance laws as an instrument for the "accumulation and perpetuation of wealth, in select families," which had formed an artificial aristocracy in Virginia. Abolishing these laws, he believed, would lay the foundation "for a government truly republican."[6] He proposed, instead, an aristocracy of virtue and talent. His courage and his farsighted vision of an ideal America are all the more remarkable when one considers that Thomas Jefferson belonged to the small, closely knit Virginia aristocracy of land and slave owners.

But his plan arrived too late. A draft, called the Virginia Declaration of Rights and prepared chiefly by George Mason, a Fairfax County planter who was a close friend of Washington and the Lees, had already been accepted. The Virginia assembly did adopt Jefferson's preamble to his "plan of government," a recital of all the wrongs King George III had committed against Virginia.

George Mason was, like Jefferson, a champion of individual liberties. In his "Declaration" he stated that "all men are by nature equally free and independent and have certain inherent rights . . . among which are the enjoyment of life and liberty, with the means of acquiring and possessing property, and pursuing and obtaining happiness and safety." In simple, straightforward language, Mason went on to state the rights of man, including freedom of the press and free exercise of religion. Yet George Mason, George Washington, Richard Henry Lee and his brother Francis Lightfoot Lee, as well as Thomas Jefferson, all owned a substantial number of slaves. Indeed, in the floor debate in the Virginia assembly on Mason's Declaration of Rights, "the point was made that Mason's assertion could not be applied to slaves because they owned no property; that they were, in fact, *themselves* property."[7]

About a week later, Jefferson moved to a cooler and quieter section of Philadelphia. He had found lodgings in a new brick house owned by Jacob Graff Jr. (Jefferson spelled it Graaf), a newly married young bricklayer. The house, situated on the southwest corner of Market and Seventh Streets, was three stories high, "five windows wide and

The house on Market Street in which Thomas Jefferson wrote the Declaration of Independence. By Benjamin Ridgeway Evans. (Courtesy of the Historical Society of Pennsylvania)

four windows deep." He rented the second floor, which consisted of a furnished parlor and bedroom. There were only a few other houses nearby. He took with him the little desk that Benjamin Randolph had made, along with a revolving Windsor chair that he had also ordered.

Before the end of the month, the Virginia delegation received instructions from the convention at Williamsburg to propose a declaration of independence and to call for foreign alliances and the confederation of the colonies. Richard Henry Lee hastened to comply.

On June 7 he rose in the State House in Philadelphia and, in a three-part resolution, moved "that these United Colonies are, and of right ought to be, Free and Independent States; that they are absolved from all allegiance to the British Crown, and that all political connection between them and the State of Great Britain is and ought to be, totally dissolved." The fiery Lee, who had lost the fingers on one hand in a hunting accident, gestured for emphasis with the hand wrapped in a black silk handkerchief. He went on to propose that the colonies immediately "take the most effectual measures for forming foreign Alliances." Finally, he urged that "a plan of confederation be prepared and transmitted to the respective Colonies for their consideration and approbation."[8] This would be known as the Articles of Confederation and Perpetual Union.

John Adams jumped to his feet and seconded the motion. Congress was in an uproar. It sat until 7 p.m., then adjourned until "punctually at ten o'clock" the next day, Saturday, June 8. Heated debates continued all that day.

Many of the states were still under instructions to vote against a declaration of independence. Their delegates argued that the time was not right. John Dickinson of Pennsylvania, in particular, made a desperate plea for time, but all the delegates from New England, Virginia, and Georgia argued that the debate had ended when American blood was shed at Lexington. The radicals, led by John Adams, Richard Henry Lee, and George Wythe, pointed out that the declaration would simply "declare a fact which already exists." Through all the debate, Thomas Jefferson said not a word but sat quietly taking notes.

Finally, a compromise was effected. The resolution would be postponed for three weeks, until July 1. But a committee would be appointed at once to prepare the declaration. In this way, should Congress agree, no time would be lost in drafting it. It was clear, Jefferson would say later, that the moderates were "not yet matured for falling from the parent stem."[9]

Drafting a resolution was a necessary task because the mere assertion of independence by Congress was considered inadequate. It was essential, Congress felt, to clearly state the reasons for the resolution in such a manner that the colonists would understand the need for the action and would be inspired to fight for independence.

The facts must also be explained to the rest of the world. Congress understood that it must promote the American cause and justify the severing of ties with Great Britain and the establishment of America's own government. The support of other nations might be critical to the new nation's success.

At this point, the tide was running strongly toward independence. Canvassing, intriguing, caucusing, and persuading were needed behind the scenes. Never one to allow himself to be drawn into the battles be-

The fiery Richard Henry Lee, who proposed "that these United Colonies are, and of right ought to be, free and independent States." (Courtesy of the National Archives)

ing waged among the delegates, Jefferson was always on good terms with the older, more conservative leaders and retained their confidence. Now he and Sam Adams, a delegate from Massachusetts and a man with great skill in political organization and management, met regularly to devise plans and assign individual tasks to other members.

On Wednesday, June 13, Richard Henry Lee did what Thomas Jefferson wanted so desperately to do himself: he left Philadelphia to return home to Virginia to take part in the formation of the new government. But Congress had other plans for Thomas Jefferson. He, along with Benjamin Franklin, John Adams, Roger Sherman, and Robert R. Livingston—representing the northern, middle, and southern colonies—were appointed to a Committee of Five to draft the declaration.

All the men elected were distinguished. Each represented a different colony. Franklin, from Pennsylvania, was, at seventy, one of the most commanding figures of his time. His name was known throughout the colonies and in Europe. Adams represented Massachusetts. At forty-one, he was one of the most famous patriots in New England, and he had a fine reputation as a political thinker and speaker. His name, too, was known in London. Sherman, fifty-five, was the most distinguished patriot in Connecticut, and Livingston, from New York and the only one younger than Jefferson, was destined for a brilliant career.

But Thomas Jefferson, who had just turned thirty-three, was the one chosen to write the declaration. All the members recognized that he could disagree politically yet remain on friendly terms socially. He was unyielding in his principles, they knew, but he "bore the olive branch." He was the one man who knew the history, the law, and the principles of government thoroughly, who had an unshakable faith in the ability of men to govern themselves, and who wrote graceful, elegant prose.

Accordingly, when the committee first met at the stone farmhouse several miles outside the city where Dr. Franklin was recuperating from gout, they discussed the general content or "articles" of the document, then nominated Jefferson "to draw them up in form and cloath them in proper dress." Jefferson accepted the assignment, later saying of it simply, "The committee for drawing the Declaration of Independence desired me to do it. It was accordingly done."[10]

Forty-six years later John Adams would give a somewhat different version. He *and* Jefferson were asked to "make the draught [draft]," he said. Then

> Jefferson proposed to me to make the draught.
> I said, "I will not."
> "You should do it!"
> "I will not."
> "Why?"
> "Reasons enough."
> "What can be your reasons?"
> "Reason first—You are a Virginian, and a Virginian ought to appear at the head of this business. Reason second—I am obnoxious, suspected, and unpopular. You are very much otherwise. Reason third—You can write ten times better than I can."
> "Well, if you are decided, I will do as well as I can."
> "Very well. When you have drawn it up, we will have a meeting."[11]

Benjamin Franklin, when he was the chief spokesman for the American colonies in London. He worked diligently there to bring Great Britain and her American colonies together in friendly understanding. (Courtesy of Independence National Historical Park)

# A Revolutionary Document

FOR THE NEXT seventeen days Jefferson isolated himself in his lodgings in Mr. Graff's house. His decision to move there had been a wise one. The house, remote from the center of the bustling city, afforded him the quiet he needed to think and to write.

Although Jefferson later indicated that he had had no books before him as he wrote, certainly his encyclopedic mind recalled much that he had read over the past years. John Locke's *Second Treatise on Civil Government,* which set forth his doctrine of natural rights and the right of revolution, had continued to have a profound influence on Jefferson. And the writings of Lord Bolingbroke had convinced him that there should be no restraints on individual reason in any field, including religion.[1]

In all likelihood, he would probably have had with him his Commonplace Book and a copy of his own version of the Virginia constitution. Its preamble had been adopted by the Virginia assembly. He would have had, as well, George Mason's draft of the Virginia Declaration of Rights, which had just been published in Philadelphia.

He would also likely have had a copy of his *Summary View of the Rights of British America,* written two years before, in which he had articulated his theory that Saxon law was the origin of English common law and had cited the Saxons as a precedent to justify the American colonies' establishment of their own government and laws.[2]

As he pondered the task now facing him, Jefferson knew that the time had come to express the conclusions he had reached slowly, gradually, as he had read the historians, the philosophers, and the old lawyers, and had thought carefully about their ideas and copied them into his Commonplace Book. He would call now on all this earlier reading, on his writing, on his legal experience, and on his understanding of independence as he had personally experienced it, and he would distill the ideas in his mind from these many sources into one short document.

He would try to write with what John Adams called his "peculiar felicity of expression." He would write simply, clearly, logically.

Almost forty-nine years later, in May 1825, Jefferson would articulate this in a letter to Henry Lee:

> This was the object of the Declaration of Independence. Not to find out new principles, or new arguments, never before thought of, not merely to say things which had never been said before; but to place before mankind the common sense of the subject, in terms so plain and firm as to command their assent, and to justify ourselves in the independent stand we are compelled to take. Neither aiming at originality of principle or sentiment, nor yet copied from any particular writing, it was intended to be an expression of the American mind, and to give to that expression the proper tone and spirit called for by the occasion.[3]

This is precisely what it became. The absence of *new* ideas would eventually be considered one of its greatest strengths. The Preamble to his Declaration was, indeed, "an expression of the American mind." But it was more than that. It was a stirring expression of the ideas of the Enlightenment which eloquently summed up the philosophy behind the argument for the revolution: the creation of a new political system, and the vindication of the rights of man.[4]

He would articulate his own deep faith in the possibility of forging a new nation based on the principle that the people have the right to govern themselves: governments are instituted among men to *protect* their rights.[5] He would convince a "candid world" that the American colonies were justified in seeking to become an independent nation.

His routine followed a pattern that varied only slightly. He arose each day at dawn, when there was just enough light in the sky by which to read; soaked his feet in a basin of cold water, which he believed helped to ward off colds; played his violin softly for a while; and then sat in his chair in the sunny second-floor parlor, propped his new desk on the table, took his quill pen in hand, and began to write.

As he wrote, he was conscious of the fact that he might be expected to read this declaration aloud to the assembled Congress. This troubled him because he rarely spoke publicly; he preferred to write. One of his early biographers, who knew him, said that when Jefferson began to speak in public, his voice "sank in his throat" and became "guttural and inarticulate." John Adams would say of him, "During the whole Time I sat with him in Congress, I never heard him utter three sentences together."[6]

Now Jefferson thought carefully about how the Declaration should be read and heard. In fact, he marked his rough draft with what appear to be diacritical accents—marks that would help him if he were asked to read it.

Since his days at the Reverend Maury's school, Jefferson had been enthralled by Homer. He once compared Patrick Henry to Homer, whispering to a friend during one of Henry's impassioned speeches, "He speaks as Homer wrote." Jefferson so admired Homer's perfection as a poet that he wrote that even if a passage from Homer should be printed in the manner of prose, "it would still immortalize its author."[7] He was intrigued by the way in which Homer rhythmically measured his language "as a piece of music is divided into bars." Clearly interested in the link between music and oratory, Jefferson felt that prose should have the same rhythms as music. He owned several books on musical theory that addressed precisely this topic. Prose, as well as poetry, could profit from being written "in measured cadences."

Bending his head over his little writing box, sipping the tea that Bob had quietly placed in front of him, he put his thoughts on paper, adding, "interlining," and crossing out as he went along. He wrote quickly and easily, but he revised constantly, always searching for the better word, the happier phrase, the smoother transition. As a page became too difficult to read because of all the changes, he copied it "fair," then repeated the process. He worked on it in sections, rather than as one continuous text, until he was almost finished.

He chose his phrases carefully until the sound and the sense were perfectly matched, and he could hear the pitch and cadence and rhythm of what he wanted to say. He composed, as do many good writers, for the ear as well as for the eye.

Jefferson knew too that the power of words does not always lie in the political ideas they express, but rather in the emotional resonance of their images. Thus, he was able, as was no one else, to convert George

Rough draft of the Declaration of Independence. Jefferson aimed for the ease and simplicity of good conversation as he wrote and rewrote the document, always searching for the best word, the best phrase, the smoothest transition. (Courtesy of the Library of Congress)

Mason's statement of equality and rights expressed in his Virginia Dec-laration of Rights into eloquent and memorable language and to make it uniquely his own.[8]

He understood that should the colonies win their independence, the Declaration would become an extremely important document. The fate of the colonies might rest on it. He had been given the mandate of con-vincing the world that the colonists had a legal and a moral right to sep-arate from Great Britain. They were *not* rebelling against established political authority, but were a free people maintaining long-established *rights* against a usurping king. Revolution, he knew, was not legal ac-cording to British law as stated by William Blackstone.* War was con-sidered lawful only when it became "necessary." His task, then, was to plead his country's cause in terms of the rights of men. His appeal would be to a higher law, "the Law of Nature and of Nature's God."

In one long, simple sentence whose haunting cadence imparts to it a quality of deep solemnity, Jefferson immediately set the new nation among all the powers of the earth, and elevated their quarrel with Britain from a simple political dispute to a major event in history:

> When in the Course of human events, it becomes necessary for one people to dissolve the political bands which have connected them with an-other, and to assume among the powers of the earth, the separate and equal station to which the Laws of Nature and of Nature's God entitle them, a decent respect to the opinions of mankind requires that they should declare the causes which impel them to the separation.

He continued with a succinct expression of a common humanity—of all groups, all races, all faiths, and both sexes:

> We hold these truths to be self-evident, that all men are created equal, that they are endowed by their Creator with certain unalienable Rights,

---

*William Blacktone, a British jurist and educator, wrote *Commentaries on the Laws of England* (1765–69), the most comprehensive single treatment of the body of English law.

that among these are Life, Liberty and the pursuit of Happiness. That
to secure these rights, Governments are instituted among Men, deriving
their just powers from the consent of the governed. That whenever any
Form of Government becomes destructive of these ends it is the Right of
the People to alter or to abolish it, and to institute new Government, laying its foundation on such principles and organizing its powers in such
form, as to them shall seem most likely to effect their Safety and Happiness. . . . But when a long train of abuses and usurpations, pursuing invariably the same Object evinces a design to reduce them under absolute
Despotism, it is their right, it is their duty, to throw off such Government,
and to provide new Guards for their future security.

No longer was Jefferson a young lawyer writing a legal brief. He had
become a deeply committed man, pouring his own emotions—his faith,
his burning passion for his country and for the rights of mankind—into
electrifying phrases.

Jefferson was able to distill a complex combination of political and legal thought into a lyrical statement that made the "truths" uttered by the
Declaration so "self-evident."[9] They were, indeed, the "common sense"
of the matter. They were not new; rather, as John Adams described
them, "they *realized* the theories of the wisest writers" of the seventeenth and eighteenth centuries, philosophers whose writings had had
such a powerful influence on Jefferson.

Jefferson's Declaration would stamp on the American mind the doctrine of natural rights and would grant the people the right of revolution, which was to him the most important part of his document. Governments are instituted among men to protect their *rights,* he wrote.
The people had the *right* to govern themselves. Echoing Locke, Jefferson here put forth a philosophy that affirmed the right—and the duty—
of a people to overthrow a government that violated the principles on
which it had been established and to reclaim that power to establish a
new government. For the first time in history, the right of revolution
would be legal. The Declaration was, and remains, a revolutionary
document.[10]

When Jefferson used the phrase "created equal" in his Declaration, he
meant that no one held authority over any other by right of birth or as a

gift from God. He believed, with the Enlightenment philosophers, that in the eyes of nature every child is born equal. Nature did not decree the inequality of blacks to whites. Nature did not pronounce the female inferior to the male.[11]

Previously, in 1770, when Jefferson had tried, unsuccessfully, to win freedom for a slave, he had pleaded in court: "Under the law of nature all men are born free." This concept of equal rights given at creation to all human beings, regardless of race or gender, by "Nature's God" echoes his *Summary View of the Rights of British America*, written two years before. Men were born to freedom, not to slavery, he had written. The God of the Declaration did not own men, nor did he believe that other men should own men. As one historian has written, "Equality was . . . the most radical and the most powerful ideological force let loose in the Revolution."[12] It would become the defining characteristic of the American nation and would ultimately change the world.[13] It is this concept that is, perhaps, the foremost reason that Jefferson still lives. Yet there were those at the time who believed that this did not apply to slaves because slaves were property.[14] Thus, the tragic juxtaposition of American freedom and American slavery haunts us to this day.

When Jefferson spoke of pursuing happiness, he meant a public happiness that is measurable and that is, indeed, the test and justification of any government. Two years before, in *Summary View*, he had spoken of happiness as the object of government, and of the right of the people to live "under such laws and regulations" as would "promote public happiness." And John Adams, in his "Thoughts on Government," wrote that "the happiness of society is the end of government as . . . the happiness of the individual is the end of man."[15]

Jefferson had almost certainly encountered the phrase "the pursuit of happiness" in his voluminous reading and may have liked the sound of it. It had been widely used in England since 1690, and was also used extensively in the colonies. Locke had written "All men desire happiness" in *An Essay Concerning Human Understanding*.

Eighteenth-century philosophers believed in happiness. The English poet Alexander Pope called happiness "Our being's end and aim"; the French philosopher Jean-Jacques Rousseau pronounced, "Happiness is the end of every sentient being; it is the first desire impressed on us by nature, and the only one that never leaves us." Another French philosopher, François Voltaire, said simply, "Happiness is the object, the duty, and the goal of all sensible men."[16]

But European philosophers had never considered the pursuit of happiness a right. Happiness was too far removed from the circumstances of the Old World. In the New World, however, the idea that the "pursuit of happiness" was a right was not exceptional. Indeed, it had appeared in George Mason's Virginia Declaration of Rights adopted by the Virginia assembly just two months before, on May 12. That document included, among the inherent rights of men, "pursuing and obtaining happiness and safety." But it was Thomas Jefferson whose beautifully wrought prose brought human life to a new level by declaring the pursuit of happiness the natural right of every individual and made securing happiness the object of government. By so doing, Jefferson "gave currency to an expression which was to influence deeply and even to mold American life."[17] "It was Jefferson's responsiveness to the historical moment, not his originality that brought him to the fore."[18]

All the while that he was writing, Jefferson never for a moment forgot his own personal anguish. When he had left Virginia for Philadelphia early in May, his mother had just died, he had lost a young child, and he had left behind an adored wife who was dangerously depressed. He longed to be back at Monticello with her. Was he sacrificing her to this cause? he brooded. His control of his fiercely burning emotions came through in a letter he wrote to John Page: "Every letter brings me such an account of her health, that it is with great pain I can stay here."[19]

But he did stay, and he continued to write his Declaration until he was satisfied that he had done the best he could. Only then did he put the sections together in a simple form: an introduction that sets the American Revolution within the whole "course of human events" and describes it as absolutely "necessary"; a preamble, a clear, concise, and dignified statement of political philosophy that explains the Declaration's rationale to "mankind" and establishes the right of revolution against tyrannical authority; the application of that philosophy to the

American colonies; a sustained attack on King George III by a dramatic presentation of the ways in which the colonists' rights have been invaded; and a solemn renunciation of the political ties between the colonies and Great Britain. Its primary purpose was *not* to declare independence. Rather, it was intended as a formal justification of an act already accomplished.

He made a fair copy that he gave first to John Adams, asking for his corrections, then sent it by messenger to Dr. Franklin, who was still suffering from gout and was confined to his rooms. They changed only a few words, "interlined in their own handwritings." He prepared another fair copy incorporating their changes and sent it to the committee. On Friday, June 28, he presented it "unaltered to the Congress."* He had entitled it simply "A Declaration by the Representatives of the United States of America, in General Congress assembled."[20]

Now as the delegates sat in their high-backed cushioned chairs, shuffling papers on the tables in front of them, or whispering behind cupped hands, the Declaration was read aloud, then left on the table for their perusal. There was no discussion. Numerous other matters of ordinary business were dealt with, and then Congress adjourned until "nine o'clock Monday next."

Such was the reception of the Declaration of Independence.

Mr. Jefferson was left to wait until after the weekend for any word of approval. But his job was done, and he would try not to brood on it. On Saturday he bought a straw hat for ten shillings, a map, and spurs, and paid his wine merchant and his barber.

Monday morning, July 1, dawned bright and cloudless. By eight-thirty, when Jefferson walked from his lodgings toward the State House, the bricks and cobbles were already giving off heat. As he walked up the three steps and through the wide double doors of the building, he was grateful for the cool of the hallway inside.

The tension mounted as the members began to assemble. That day they would vote on Lee's resolutions that the colonies were free and independent states.

---

*The original copy, "with the corrections of Dr. Franklin and Mr. Adams interlined in their own handwriting," is commonly known as the Rough Draft.

John Dickinson, his face pale against his plum-colored coat, rose to defend for the last time the conservative point of view. He spoke for nearly an hour.

John Adams answered him in what Thomas Jefferson would describe years later as "a power of thought and expression that moved us from our seats."[21] As Adams spoke, pounding his hickory walking stick on the floor for emphasis, a storm broke outside and he had to raise his voice against the roll of thunder. It grew dark. Candles were brought in. Still the debate raged on. It continued for nine hours, with no break for dinner. Even Sam Adams, who rarely spoke in Congress, spoke that day, quietly and convincingly, rising on his toes in his characteristic manner as he ended a sentence.

Finally the delegates from South Carolina requested that the decision be postponed until the next morning so they might have time to reconsider. Everyone understood the significance of voting for independence. A unanimous vote was essential. Colonies that voted against independence would not be included in the confederation and so would become, in effect, enemy states. No one wanted this to happen.

The delegates understood, too, that voting for independence meant jeopardizing their lives as well as their fortunes. They knew that English law provided that traitors could be partly strangled, their bowels torn out and burned before their eyes, their heads then cut off, and their bodies quartered.

They recognized, also, that once Congress voted formally, its decision was final. A vote on independence taken too soon could destroy Congress. In order to prevent this, they had the day before turned themselves into a Committee of the Whole, in which both debate and vote were unofficial—a trial balloon, so to speak. No colony would be forced to leave Congress because of what was recommended in the committee. When Congress became a Committee of the Whole, President John Hancock had stepped down, and Benjamin Harrison had taken the chair as head of the committee. Everyone else remained where he was.

During the past weeks, more and more of the delegates had come over to the side of the patriots. Their faith was proving greater than their fear. When they met that Tuesday morning, South Carolina had made the decision to join their ranks. John Dickinson, who could never bring himself to vote for independence, and Robert Morris, both of Pennsylvania, had stayed away, allowing their state to vote "aye" without them. And Caesar Rodney, who had ridden eighty miles in darkness and heavy rain, arrived from Delaware drenched and covered with mud just in time to cast the deciding vote in favor of independence. Only the New York delegates, still waiting for instructions from home, did not vote. But their vote was promised, and within a few days they too sent approval. Independence was established.

The next day, John Adams, writing to his wife, Abigail, expressed the momentous significance of the decision:

> Yesterday, the greatest question was decided, which ever was debated in America, and a greater, perhaps, never was nor will be decided among men. . . . The second day of July, 1776, will be the most memorable epocha in the history of America. I am apt to believe that it will be celebrated, by succeeding Generations as the great anniversary Festival. It ought to be commemorated, as the Day of Deliverance, by solemn acts of Devotion to God Almighty. It ought to be solemnized with Pomp and Parade, with Shews, Games, Sports, Guns, Bells, Bonfires, and Illuminations, from one End of this Continent to the other, from this Time forward, forever more.
>
> You will think me transported with Enthusiasm but I am not.—I am well aware of the Toil and Blood and Treasure, that it will cost Us to maintain the Declaration, and support and defend these States.—Yet through all the Gloom I can see the Rays of ravishing Light and Glory. I can see that the End is more than worth all the Means. And that Posterity will tryumph in that Days Transaction, even altho We should rue it, which I trust in God We shall not.[22]

But the momentous "Epocha" that so excited John Adams would be reduced to a historical footnote by the event that was to follow two days hence.

On Wednesday, July 3, the delegates turned their attention to the paper that Jefferson had placed before them the preceding Friday. Once again, the white-paneled chamber in the State House resounded with long and heated debate. It lasted for the greater part of the third and fourth days of July. It was not a happy time for Thomas Jefferson. Word by word, sentence by sentence, page by page, his document was criticized, ripped apart, changed—by men whose talents for writing certainly did not equal his.

As he listened to the often rude criticism, he sat silently squirming in his seat. He did not speak on behalf of his "instrument." But feisty John Adams, angered at the evident distress of his friend and at the mutilation of what he considered a brilliant document, kept jumping to his feet to defend it, fighting for every line as Jefferson had written it as though he were fighting for his life. Jefferson would remember him for this always with gratitude and affection.

The pragmatic Benjamin Franklin, too, tried in his own way to comfort his young colleague and to soften the blows. Sitting beside Jefferson, he leaned over and whispered a story:

When I was a journeyman printer, one of my companions, an apprentice Hatter, having served out his time, was about to open a shop for himself. His first concern was to have a handsome signboard with a proper inscription. He composed it in these words: "John Thompson, Hatter, makes and sells hats for ready money," with a figure of a hat subjoined. But he thought he would submit it to his friends for their amendments. The first he shewed it to thought the word "hatter" tautologous, because followed by the words "makes hats" which shew he was a hatter. It was struck out. The next observed that the word "makes" might well be omitted, because his customers would not care who made the hats. If good and to their mind, they would buy, by whomsoever made. He struck it out. A third said he thought the words "for ready money" were useless as it was not the custom of the place to sell on credit. Everyone who purchased expected to pay. They were parted with, and the inscription now stood "John Thompson sells hats." "Sells hats," says his next friend? "Why nobody will expect you to give them away. What then is the use of that word?" It was stricken out, and "hats" followed it, the rather, as there was one painted on the board. So his inscription was reduced ultimately to "John Thompson" with the figure of a hat subjoined.[23]

It was not until years later that Jefferson could appreciate the humor of Franklin's story.

Now Jefferson was saddened as he heard deleted the greater part of a passage that revealed his own feelings: "We must endeavor to forget our former love for them [our "unfeeling brethren"], and hold them as we hold the rest of mankind, enemies in war, in peace, friends. We might have been a free and a great people together."[24]

But what Jefferson regarded as the most grievous change was the elimination by Congress of what John Adams called Jefferson's "vehement philippic against negro slavery,"[25] denouncing the king's determination "to keep open a market where men should be bought and sold." Here Jefferson was using the word "men" in the broad sense of "mankind": that is, the entire human species, for those who were bought and sold were most assuredly female as well as male, children as well as adults.

Jefferson had written: "He [the king] has waged cruel war against human nature itself, violating its most sacred rights of life and liberty in the persons of a distant people who never offended him, captivating and carrying them into slavery in another hemisphere, or to incur miserable death in their transportation thither."

This passage says clearly that Jefferson considered Africans captured into slavery not a separate category of beings, but human beings—with the same sacred rights of life and liberty that are the natural endowments of all human beings. But he was talking about natural rights, not social or political equality.

In deference to South Carolina and Georgia, "who had never attempted to restrain the importation of slaves, and who on the contrary still wished to continue it," this paragraph was struck out. "Our northern brethren also I believe felt a little tender over those censures; for tho' their people had very few slaves themselves yet they had been pretty considerable carriers of them to others," Jefferson wrote of it later.[26]

But Jefferson's acknowledgment that the colonists had been willing participants in the slave trade undermined his assertion that "the *Christian* king of Great Britain" was alone responsible for "the cruel war against human nature."[27]

Congress continued to question, edit, and harden the phrases, but much of Jefferson's direct, precise prose was left intact. The delegates speedily approved the preamble, making only two minor changes. To the concluding paragraph they added two references to God, an appeal "to the supreme judge of the world," and "a firm reliance on the protection of divine providence." Jefferson's final words, "we mutually pledge to each other our Lives, our Fortunes and our sacred Honor," they agreed could not be improved. In spite of what Jefferson may have thought, his colleagues were not ruthless, and the Declaration emerged a stronger, yet thoroughly Jeffersonian, document.

An unusually severe thunderstorm on the night of July 3 brought a cold and dreary morning with a bracing north wind on July 4. When Jefferson arose at dawn, as was his custom, he noted in his little Account Book that the temperature was sixty-eight degrees Fahrenheit at six o'clock. While his mind must assuredly have been on the coming debate, a part of it was also on his Patty, for at some point during the day he paid for a thermometer and seven pairs of women's gloves. As the day progressed, the sun came out and the temperature rose to seventy-six degrees. Later, it became oppressively hot and humid in the crowded State House chamber, even with the windows open.

The delegates continued their debate, but they were becoming increasingly uncomfortable and irritable. Next door to the State House was a livery stable from which swarms of flies emerged. They entered the delegates' room through the barely open windows, alighting on the legs of the delegates and biting hard through their silk stockings. The men in turn lashed furiously at the flies with their handkerchiefs, but to no avail. Years later Jefferson would say that the debate that day came to an end and a vote was taken merely to get away from the flies. Treason was preferable to discomfort.

Late in the afternoon, Benjamin Harrison announced that the delegates had agreed to the document. The situation that afternoon was essentially the same as that on July 2. Twelve colonies voted in the affirmative, while New York remained silent.*

Now Benjamin Harrison read aloud the title: "A Declaration by the Representatives of the United States of America in General Congress

---

*New York adopted a resolution approving and supporting the Declaration on July 9. It was laid before Congress on July 15. It then became The Unanimous Declaration of the Thirteen United States of America.

Assembled." Overcome by the magnitude of the occasion, he paused, then continued. The delegates sat in complete silence as the haunting cadence of the words of the preamble echoed in the hall.

As Mr. Harrison read the body of the document, Jefferson's stinging indictment of the king, relentlessly repeating "He has . . ." nineteen times, listed all the specific grievances against George III. This steady piling up of offenses became a mournful bell tolling the death of American allegiance to the king.

The final section asserts that for men accustomed to freedom, there is only one choice:

> We, therefore, the Representatives of the United States of America, in General Congress Assembled, appealing to the Supreme Judge of the world for the rectitude of our intentions, do, in the Name, and by the Authority of the good People of these Colonies, solemnly publish and declare, That these United Colonies are, and of Right ought to be Free and Independent States; that they are Absolved from all Allegiance to the British Crown, and that all political connection between them and the State of Great Britain is and ought to be totally dissolved; and that as Free and Independent States they have full Power to levy War, conclude Peace, contract Alliances, establish Commerce, and to do all other Acts and Things, which Independent States may of right do.—And for the support of this Declaration, with a firm reliance on the protection of divine Providence, we mutually pledge to each other our Lives, our Fortunes and our sacred Honor.

Nowhere is Jefferson's "peculiar felicity of expression" more evident than in the closing sentence. The members of Congress had chosen well.

Suddenly, time was of the essence. It was urgent that the Declaration be printed for immediate distribution to the states for proclamation. There was no time even for Charles Thomson, Secretary of the Congress, to make a copy of the draft with its amendments or to transcribe it into the Secret Journal he had been keeping of the proceedings. He simply left space in the volume for the attachment of a printed copy.

Jefferson, as the author and head of the Committee of Five, personally delivered the document to the Market Street shop of John Dunlop, printer to Congress. Later in the evening, Thomson joined him at the shop to help in the task of proofreading. In an effort to get the job done as quickly as possible, Dunlop cut the manuscript into sections and assigned each to a different compositor. The manuscript got so cut up and dirtied in the process of printing that it was discarded, and thus the historic copy actually approved by Congress did not survive.

Mr. Dunlop was able to publish the entire text of the Declaration in his *Pennsylvania Packet,* and before sunset that night the *Pennsylvania Evening Post* came streaming off the press with the terse announcement:

This day the

CONTINENTAL CONGRESS

Declared the

UNITED COLONIES FREE

And

INDEPENDENT STATES

But it had been inserted just at press time on a back page.

Jefferson kept for his own files the original "Rough Draft" from which he had made the copy that he presented to Congress on June 28. From this he made additional copies to send to his friends who were anxious to know what was happening. He wanted them to see the way the document read before it was "mangled" by Congress. His pride wounded by the changes, Jefferson wrote in the margin, "a different phraseology inserted."[28] His friend Richard Henry Lee assured him by return post that "the thing is in its nature so good that no cookery can spoil the dish for the palates of free men."[29]

His old friend John Page, addressing him as "My dear Jefferson," wrote simply, "I am highly pleased with your declaration. . . . God preserve the United States. We know the Race is not to the swift nor the Battle to the Strong. Do you not think an Angel rides in the Whirlwind and directs this Storm?"[30]

Precisely at twelve noon on July 8, 1776, the Declaration of Independence was proclaimed by the sheriff of Philadelphia and read aloud by his deputy to the crowds that had gathered in the Pennsylvania State House yard. Then the crowd, led by the mayor of Philadelphia and other city officials, marched down the street to hear it read once again at the Court House.

That evening, under a star-filled sky, bonfires were lit throughout the city, battalions paraded on the commons, and church bells tolled. The coat of arms of George III was removed from the State House and brought to the commons, where, as the crowd of spectators cheered, it was placed on a pile of casks and burned. The lead would be used to mold bullets for Washington's army.

Quietly watching from the sidelines was Thomas Jefferson. No one except the members of Congress knew that he was the author. Cheers and celebrations continued all night, although they were not for him.

Within a few days the Declaration reached General George Washington, who had chased the British from Massachusetts and was now facing them in New York City. It was read at the head of each brigade of the Continental army amid "demonstrations of joy." Similar scenes were enacted throughout the colonies as the news arrived.

It was not until August 2 that the Declaration was finally hand lettered on parchment and laid on the table to be signed by the members. Jefferson signed his name simply *TH Jefferson*. He was one of many. He knew, as did all the members gathered round the table, that if the war with England were to be lost, all those who signed could be hanged for treason. The story is told that as they were signing, John Hancock urged all the members to hang together, to which the wise and witty Benjamin Franklin retorted, "Yes, we must indeed all hang together, or else, most assuredly, we shall all hang separately."[31] The signed parchment copy was kept in a secret place until January 18, 1777.

John Dickinson was not among the signers. He still fervently hoped for an eventual reconciliation with Great Britain. Although Dickinson had led the opposition and refused to change his mind, he never lost the respect of the radicals. And he was patriot enough to ride off to join his regiment and fight to defend the Declaration.

# 16

# Legal Reform in Virginia

HIS TASK COMPLETED, Thomas Jefferson's thoughts turned now to his Martha. It seems likely that she had suffered a miscarriage and was having great difficulty recuperating from it both physically and emotionally. In the eighteenth century, childbearing exacted a harsh toll on both mother and baby. In Martha's case the circumstances were always particularly complicated. Recent medical opinion speculates that she may have been suffering from diabetes, a condition not readily diagnosed, or treated, in eighteenth-century Virginia, and one that is often aggravated by pregnancy. But there is little doubt that she was seriously ill.

When a letter arrived from her, begging her husband to come home, Jefferson immediately set about trying to arrange a leave from Congress. But he realized suddenly that, one by one, the older members had all gone, leaving him the sole guardian of Virginia's vote in Congress.

Desperately, he wrote to Richard Henry Lee, imploring him to return to Philadelphia to relieve him: "For God's sake, for your country's sake, and for my sake, come. I receive by every post such accounts of the state of Mrs. Jefferson's health that it will be impossible for me to disappoint her expectation of seeing me. . . . I pray you to come. I am under a sacred obligation to go home."[1]

But Lee would not be hurried.

Jefferson remained in Philadelphia through a sweltering August, attending to the business of Congress. He served on committees and wrote reports. And he collaborated once more with John Adams and Benjamin Franklin, this time on the design for a seal of the United States. The motto "E Pluribus Unum" was the result. Franklin's suggestion, "Rebellion to tyrants is obedience to God," was adopted for the reverse side. Jefferson was so pleased with Franklin's motto that he used it himself, stamping it on the wax with which he sealed his own letters.

Finally, Jefferson could wait no longer. He bought some hats and guitar strings, settled his accounts for his lodgings and his horses, and packed his belongings. On Tuesday, September 3, the red-haired aristocrat and the slender, dark-haired slave, each riding one horse and leading another with their packs, set out for Monticello. On the way they stopped at The Forest, where Martha and little Patsy had been staying while Jefferson was in Philadelphia. Now they all returned to Monticello. Jefferson and his family would have eighteen days together on their mountaintop.

By October Martha seemed to have recovered some of her strength, and she agreed to accompany her husband to Williamsburg for the meeting of the Virginia Convention. George Wythe graciously made his house available to them. As they were preparing for the trip, Jefferson felt a sense of well-being, a jubilance at the thought of returning to his familiar haunts in Williamsburg, of once again taking his seat in the legislature there and having a hand in preparing the laws of Virginia—so dear to his heart. And he would have his wife at his side. Never again, he vowed, would he be far from her. He would concentrate his efforts on the local scene.

Autumn in Williamsburg with her husband seemed to make Martha blossom again. But they had been in Williamsburg just a few weeks when Jefferson was faced with a wrenching decision. A letter arrived by messenger from John Hancock, offering Jefferson the post of commissioner to France. He would serve with Benjamin Franklin and Silas Deane, who were already in France. The war was not going well, and French aid was sorely needed. Jefferson's ability with words, his knowledge of French, his intelligence, and his diplomatic skill were well known in Congress.

"If it is your pleasure, one of our armed vessels will meet you in any river in Virginia that you choose," Richard Henry Lee had written by way of inducement.[2]

Jefferson kept the messenger waiting for three days as he agonized over his response. But he knew he couldn't go. Martha was in the early stages of another pregnancy and certainly could not be expected to endure the rigors of a trip across the sea—a voyage that might take up to two months in cramped quarters and in possibly rough weather. And he couldn't leave her home without him.

The letter he finally sent to John Hancock declining the post serves as an example of his unusual reserve and shyness. "No cares for my own person, nor yet for my private affairs would have induced one moment's hesitation to accept the charge. But circumstances very peculiar to the situation of my family, such as neither permit me to leave nor to carry it, compel me to ask leave to decline a service so honorable and at the same time so important to the American cause."[3]

He could not expose his personal life to public view. He could not tell the president of Congress, in simple and direct words, that his wife was ill and expecting another baby.

17

## Religious Liberty

"WELL AWARE THAT the opinions and belief of men depend on their own will, but follow involuntarily the evidence proposed to their minds; that Almighty God hath created the mind free, and manifested his supreme will that free it shall remain by making it altogether insusceptible of restraint. . . ." With these stirring words Thomas Jefferson began what he considered to be his proudest success, his Bill for Establishing Religious Freedom. In fact, nothing else that he ever accomplished would bring him greater satisfaction—or more unjust charges of impiety or atheism.

When Thomas Jefferson took his seat in the newly formed Virginia House of Delegates in Williamsburg in October 1776, most of the faces there were familiar ones. Only Peyton Randolph was missing. He had died suddenly while dining with Jefferson at the home of a friend. He was fifty-four years old. Over the years Jefferson's respect and affection for his older cousin had deepened, and Randolph's sudden death was a sharp blow.

Edmund Pendleton was the new Speaker, and Robert Carter Nicholas, Thomas Nelson, and Benjamin Harrison were among some of Jefferson's old friends. Patrick Henry had been elected the first governor of the Commonwealth of Virginia, and Jefferson's dearest friend, John Page, was president of the Council of State, which acted as the legislature's upper house and as an advisory committee to the governor.

It was here that Jefferson first met James Madison, a shy, twenty-five-year-old delegate from Orange County, Virginia. It marked the beginning of a friendship that would last for the rest of their lives.

Patrick Henry's elevation to the governorship had left a vacuum of leadership in the assembly, and Jefferson was quick to fill it. While he became a leader in day-to-day legislative procedure, his effectiveness was primarily the result of his tact, his enduring friendships, his genuine feeling for Virginia, and the force of his ideas. Just five days into the session, on October 12, when the House called for a general revision of the laws of Virginia, Jefferson was appointed chairman of a committee of five men who were instructed to "reform the entire structure of law so as to strip it of all vestiges of its earlier monarchical aspects and to bring it into conformity with republican principles." Their mandate was to repeal, amend, or revise the entire code of English law then in force in Virginia.[1]

Exempted from this would be "the ancient statutes, particularly those commented on by Lord Coke," whose language was simple, and meaning clear. Jefferson had acquired great respect for "old Coke" since his student days, when he had called him "an old dull scoundrel." The mandate to the committee also provided that they introduce new laws where necessary; and finally, that they report the whole for action by the legislature. The choice of Thomas Jefferson to head this committee was evidence of his stature. At just thirty-three years of age, he had become the principal agent of legal reform in Virginia.

The assignment captivated Jefferson. Here was his chance to bring to fruition, through the law, his vision of a happy and virtuous society. Here was an opportunity for him to accomplish, through the law, what he had not been able to achieve at the Virginia Convention of 1776. He seemed to understand that there were only certain times in the history of nations when fundamental reforms were possible. This was such a time. All his earlier reading had prepared him well for the task.

The other members of the committee were Edmund Pendleton, George Wythe (who resigned his seat in the Continental Congress in order to accept what he considered a more important assignment), George Mason, and Thomas Ludwell Lee, another liberal assemblyman. But both Mason and Lee soon excused themselves, offering the reason that since they were not lawyers, they considered themselves unqualified. Jefferson, Wythe, and Pendleton, therefore, apportioned the work among themselves, although the bulk of it fell to George Wythe and Thomas Jefferson, leaving them free to express their own ideas. This would be an opportunity for Jefferson to work closely with the man who had been his mentor, and whom he esteemed above all others.

To Jefferson fell the revision of the criminal code as well as proposals for bills on education and religion, among others. The first of these would result in humane criminal laws, which eliminated the death penalty for all crimes except murder and treason. His bill on education would become a detailed plan for implementing a system of public education in Virginia, something that had never been attempted in any country in the world. And his bill calling for complete religious freedom, protecting all people against religious intolerance and persecution, would become his proudest success.

The revision of the laws would occupy the men for the next three years. They worked separately, with periodic meetings, so much of the time Jefferson worked at home. In fact, his own library was so vast that he could not have accomplished the job as well anywhere else. He added to his library constantly. When Peyton Randolph died, Jefferson purchased the books he had left, including some rare Virginia manuscripts.

It was Jefferson who was responsible for the introduction of more bills than any other single member of the Virginia General Assembly* during the years 1776–79. His accomplishment was remarkable. "He was himself a veritable legislative drafting bureau."[2]

In the meantime, the war was going badly, and in mid-December of 1776, Jefferson received a letter at Monticello from Gov-

---

*With the ratification of the Virginia Constitution in 1776, the Virginia House of Burgesses had officially changed its name to the Virginia General Assembly.

ernor Patrick Henry appointing him county collector of blankets and rugs for the freezing soldiers in New Jersey. The winter of 1776–77 was the coldest in anyone's memory. The wells at Monticello went dry, and water had to be dragged up the winding road to the mountaintop. And there was continuing worry about Martha, who was expecting a baby in the spring.

In the middle of May, Jefferson was granted a leave of absence from the spring session of the legislature to be with his wife when their child was born, and he went home to Monticello with high hopes. These were realized when, on May 28, his friend Dr. George Gilmer delivered Martha of a son. There was much rejoicing among family, friends, and servants, for a son was very special to Virginians with their deep sense of family pride.

But their joy turned quickly to sorrow: "Our son died 10 H, 20 M. p.m.," Jefferson wrote seventeen days later.

It was shortly after this that Jupiter and Suck lost their first known child, Aggy, who was just two months old.

Unaware of the Jeffersons' tragedy, John Adams had written, "We want your Industry and Abilities here extreamely. . . . Your Country is not yet, quite Secure enough, to excuse your Retreat to the delights of domestic Life. Yet, for the Soul of me, when I attend to my own Feelings, I cannot blame you."[3] But Jefferson stayed close to Martha and couldn't answer Adams's letter until August.

Work on the mansion continued very slowly, and Monticello's wells remained dry for the rest of the year. Jefferson, as always, buried his grief in work and continued his revision of the laws of Virginia. In October, he forced himself to leave Martha to take his seat at the fall meeting of the House of Delegates, but he was ten days late.

The year 1778 found Jefferson busy once again on his mountaintop, interspersing work on the laws with the supervision of the plantation that he loved. He was also staying close to Martha, who was once again expecting a baby. Ninety thousand bricks were made that year, and in one month during the summer, more than fourteen thousand were laid. He was constantly experimenting in his garden. In the spring, he added many trees to his orchard—cherry, apple, pear, quince, plum, apricot, and bitter almond—and in the fall he received the shoot of an Italian olive tree from his Italian friend Philip Mazzei's neighboring plantation. As Jefferson planted the tiny olive tree, he reflected that it would take ten years to bear fruit.

"Our third daughter born," Jefferson recorded in his precise manner on August 1, 1778, at 1:30 a.m. They named her Mary. She would come to be known as Maria, and by the family as Polly. Her sister Patsy was now almost six.

There had been much anxiety over this birth, particularly in light of the babies they had lost and of Martha's fragility. Jefferson did not take his seat in the assembly until he was certain that both Martha and the baby were out of danger. The session was almost over when he arrived in Williamsburg.

As the year 1779 dawned, work on the laws was nearing completion, and Jefferson was pleased with what he saw emerging from the three years of effort. What he had been striving to create was a more favorable climate for the freedom and happiness of his countrymen. Having written the charter of the new nation in his Declaration of Independence, he was now determined to establish that document's passionate principles of freedom, equality, and self-government in the laws and institutions of Virginia. He was laying a foundation for what he would later describe as "a government truly republican."[4]

In his Bill for Establishing Religious Freedom, the reform closest to his heart, Jefferson was drafting what he considered the "fulfillment of the philosophy of the Declaration of Independence." But here he would find himself ahead of his generation, and he would have to fight hard to accomplish his goal. Indeed, he would refer to prerevolutionary Virginia as a land of "religious slavery."[5] He would later describe the decade-long struggle to effect the enactment of the bill as "the severest contest" in which he had ever engaged.[6] Passions were never as high as when questions of religion were involved.

One of Jefferson's friends, the brilliant and pious Edmund Pendleton, would lead the opposition to Jefferson in his battle for the separation of church and state. In spite of this, Jefferson, looking back on the struggle many years later, described Pendleton as

the ablest man in debate I have ever met with. He had not indeed the po-
etical fancy of Mr. Henry . . . but he was cool, smooth & persuasive . . .
his conceptions quick, acute, and full of resource; never vanquished. . . .
You never knew when you were clear of him, but were harassed by his perseverance until the patience was worn down of all who had less of it than
himself. Add to this that he was the most virtuous and benevolent of men,
the kindest friend, the most amiable and pleasant of companions, which
ensured a favorable reception to whatever came from him.[7]

Religious dissent had been a powerful force in the founding of some
of the American colonies. Roger Williams and William Penn, the
founders of Rhode Island and Pennsylvania, respectively, had been
early crusaders in the cause of religious liberty. Virginians, on the other
hand, living in the oldest and most populous of the British colonies, had
brought with them the Established (Anglican) Church of England. Its
settlers had not migrated to escape religious intolerance but instead
sought to re-create the England they had left.

Thomas Jefferson had grown up in the secure shelter of the Church
of England, which had been Virginia's officially established religious institution since 1619. He attended its church, learned from its clergy, received communion, and shared in its political and social prestige. He
would later attend its college and serve as a vestryman for his church in
Albemarle County, as leading planters were expected to do. He contributed generously to local churches and throughout his life maintained
warm personal friends among the more enlightened clergy.

But early on, Jefferson had developed his own strong belief in complete intellectual and religious freedom. Sometime after 1764, when he
obtained a copy of Henry Saint-John Bolingbroke's *Works*, he had absorbed that philosopher's methods of historical criticism and scientific
doubt. As he weighed the evidence with a legal mind, he began to question the authenticity of the Bible as a historical document.

While Jefferson was not a religious dissenter, he always regarded religion as a strictly private affair, and he believed strongly that his personal views had no bearing on any public conflict. He had great respect
for the honest opinions of all men, found the teachings of Jesus "the
purest system of morals ever before preached to man,"[8] and looked

with complete tolerance on forms of religion other than Christianity. But it was this tolerance that caused many people to think of him as an atheist.[9]

In Virginia, both believers and dissenters were forced to pay taxes for the support of the Anglican Church. Now, the colony's large population of Methodists, Presbyterians, and Baptists, many of whom were fighting in the war, were demanding greater religious freedom. In response, Virginia had adopted a Declaration of Rights, drawn by George Mason and adopted in 1776, that granted "the free exercise of religion" to all citizens.[10]

Nonetheless, in 1777 the Anglican Church of England remained the established church in Virginia, with George Washington and Patrick Henry as its most notable defenders. But by then Thomas Jefferson and his young friend James Madison had already begun fighting to ensure freedom of religion.

While most Virginians were tolerant of dissenting sects, Jefferson demanded much more than tolerance. The state, he insisted, had no business restricting or supporting *any* religious belief or practice. Nor did the church have the right to dictate truth. There must be absolute freedom of religious conscience and opinion, and there must be a separation of church and state. He strongly objected to the special privileges that had made it possible for the Anglican clergy to become an artificial aristocracy, allowing them to exercise an unwarranted degree of authority. No reform was more important to him than the disestablishment of the Anglican Church. The mind must be free from authority of any kind, he insisted.[11]

"Our rulers can have authority over such natural rights only as we have submitted to them. The rights of conscience we never submitted, we could not submit. We are answerable for them to our God. The legitimate powers of government extend to such acts only as are injurious to others. But it does me no injury for my neighbor to say there are twenty gods, or no god. It neither picks my pocket nor breaks my leg," Jefferson would write in 1782.

"Reason and experiment have been indulged, and error has fled before them," he continued. "It is error alone which needs the support of government. Truth can stand by itself. . . . Reason and free enquiry are the only effectual agents against error."[12] Religious matters must not be subject to common law and to acts passed by the assembly. They must be taken out of the jurisdiction of the common law.

As an Enlightenment thinker, Jefferson was here laying the principles of freedom of religion and separation of church and state on the grounds of *reason* and *right,* making them not only accessible to but the right of all mankind.[13]

The Statute of Virginia for Religious Freedom, as Jefferson's Bill for Establishing Religious Freedom ultimately came to be known, is divided into three parts: the preamble, which makes up three-quarters of it; the enacting clause; and the final statement. The preamble is an eloquent manifesto of the sanctity of the human mind, arguing not only for religious liberty but for intellectual liberty as well. It illustrates how the larger cause of freedom of the mind was by now a part of Jefferson's philosophy of religious liberty.[14]

In the enacting clause, Jefferson prohibited the use of force in religion, thereby protecting all individuals from persecution for their religious beliefs and granting equal protection to all persons and all religions. All religions would be equal in the eyes of the law:

> No man shall be compelled to frequent or support any religious worship, place, or ministry whatsoever, nor shall be enforced, restrained, molested, or burthened [burdened] in his body or goods, nor shall otherwise suffer, on account of his religious opinions or belief; but that all men shall be free to profess, and by argument to maintain their opinions in matters of religion, and that the same shall in no wise diminish, enlarge, or affect their civil capacities.

These were strong words in eighteenth-century Virginia.

Jefferson ended his bill with the doctrine that churches had no right to dictate truth: ". . . and finally, that truth is great and will prevail if left to herself . . . errors ceasing to be dangerous when it is permitted freely to contradict them." Then, well aware that he was departing from parliamentary practice, yet mindful of the possibility that one religious group might someday gain a majority in the Virginia legislature and thereby have the power to repeal this ordinance, Jefferson wrote into the bill itself a final clause affirming his belief that religious freedom was a natural right:

> Though we well know that . . . to declare this act irrevocable would be of no effect in law, yet we are free to declare that if any act shall be hereafter passed to repeal the present, or to narrow rights hereby asserted . . . such act will be an infringement of natural right.[15]

Jefferson was not an atheist. He did not deny the existence of God, he simply had a different concept of God. During the seventeenth and eighteenth centuries, Deism was a predominant theology among English-speaking intellectuals.[16] Jefferson probably considered himself a Deist. Deists believed in one God, a just and benevolent creator who was the source of the "laws of nature" and the moral sense, and who, after creating the world and the laws governing it, stepped back and refrained from interfering with the operation of those laws and rejected every kind of supernatural intervention in human affairs. No mystical revelation would provide the answers to the questions of human beings. Reason was their only dependable guide.[17] Jefferson never rejected Christianity or the moral teachings of Jesus. But the Christianity he accepted was based on reason.[18]

The Enlightenment's questioning attitude toward all institutions—as well as concern for individual rights, the rule of reason, and the human capacity for self-improvement and self-government—found its way into many of America's most cherished state documents, including the Declaration of Independence. But "no less eloquent, and far more original than the Declaration, was Jefferson's [Bill for Establishing Religious Freedom]."[19] "Our civil rights have no dependence on our religious opinions," Jefferson declared. Religion and government are separate spheres. A man's religion is personal, not political, and each denomination should maintain itself through voluntary contributions. There must be no state interference in any form.

Jefferson's bill was savagely attacked and not enacted into law by the General Assembly of Virginia until January 16, 1786, while Jefferson was in Paris as U.S. minister to France. Its passage was accomplished, after much struggling and maneuvering, with the skillful aid of his young friend James Madison. Indeed, as Jefferson had anticipated, many members of the Virginia legislature proclaimed the bill an attack on the Christian religion, but despite this, it passed with such a decisive majority that it came to be seen as a "hinge between ages."

For the more than fourteen hundred years before its passing, it had been a universal assumption that religious solidarity of all the people in one recognized state church was essential to social and political stability.[20] Jefferson's bill changed that.

Jefferson's passionate concern for religious freedom cannot be doubted. It radiates through his extraordinary document. "There is nothing to compare with the elegant, emotive lyricism that lies within [its] formal cadences. One must read it aloud to appreciate the perfection of the rhythms and the immaculate choice of words."[21] Once again, as in his eloquent Declaration, Thomas Jefferson's "masterly pen" has shown us the power of the word—that ideas matter, and that words, beautifully shaped, can reshape lives.

In the 1850s a German theologian traveling in the United States came to the conclusion that "the United States are by far the most religious and Christian country in the world; and that, just because religion is there most free."[22]

The Statute of Virginia for Religious Freedom revealed its author as the foremost advocate of the entire separation of church and state in Virginia. A major symbol of religious liberty, and one of the noblest documents in American history, it remains Thomas Jefferson's most passionate state paper and one of his greatest contributions to humanity.

❧ 18 ❧

# "Public Service and Private Misery"

DURING THE YEARS 1776 to 1779 Jefferson had been active on every important committee in the Virginia House of Delegates, drawing innumerable reports and bills. Over the course of these years he easily assumed leadership of this group and soon attained the power and popularity that had belonged to Patrick Henry. He became the symbol of the rising tide of democracy. It was not surprising, then, that as Henry's term as governor neared expiration, Jefferson's friends nominated him for that office. Jefferson's instincts told him to decline. He had talked recently about retirement from politics altogether. Martha's health was steadily declining, and he knew that he would not be able to take her to Williamsburg with him. The governorship would mean another separation from her and his children.

But his friends were adamant, and he understood that it was his duty to accept. He wrote to Richard Henry Lee: "In a virtuous government, and more especially in times like these, public offices are, what they should be, burdens to those appointed to them, which it would be wrong to decline, though foreseen to bring with them intense labour, and a great private loss."[1]

That he eventually accepted the nomination and was elected governor of Virginia has been called the great misfortune of his life. No period of his career laid him open to more abuse.

At the beginning of 1779, most Americans had been certain that the Revolutionary War was coming to an end. France had entered on the American side, and people thought that England, unable to gain victory, would give up the struggle. But suddenly, just when Jefferson was elected governor, the war entered a new and ominous phase. The British, unable to destroy Washington's army in the north, determined to "unravel the thread of rebellion from the southward."[2]

Virginia was virtually defenseless. She was open to attack on her long exposed coastline as well as from hostile Native Americans spurred on by the British in the Blue Ridge Mountains and on the frontiers beyond. She had no regular army for her defense, since all the regular soldiers were in the Continental army in the north. Even those were often ragged and hungry, for Congress had no money to pay them. Inflation was making paper money worthless.

All able-bodied freemen still at home were enrolled in the militia, but they were untrained, undisciplined, and often unarmed. They were called to action only at the sound of an alarm. And they had to fight against English soldiers, the best-trained troops in the world, who were being supplied by the world's greatest navy.

Smallpox, also, was causing a great loss of lives. Extremely contagious, often fatal, and with no known cure, it had felled thousands of soldiers. "The smallpox is ten times more terrible than Britons, Canadians and Indians together," John Adams wrote.[3]

Such was the state of affairs when Thomas Jefferson became governor of Virginia on June 1, 1779. He had just turned thirty-six. The next day he stood, in powdered wig and fashionable dress, in the great hall of the House of Delegates, where he had served as a burgess for so many years, to express his thanks to the General Assembly. Martha was not there to hear him, or to share with him the warm wishes and letters of congratulation that poured in from all over the colonies. "I will not congratulate you, but my country," an old friend wrote.[4]

Jefferson now found that the British advance on the South was controlling all his thinking and his actions. But there was little he could do except watch the lengthening shadow of war move steadily closer. As governor, he found himself playing an entirely different role from that of reformer and political leader in the legislature. Remembering all too well the power of the royal governors, the framers of the Virginia Constitution had stripped the governor of the state of virtually all power. The state was, in effect, ruled by the Council of State, which consisted of eight members chosen by joint ballot by both houses of the assembly. Among the members were several of Jefferson's friends: John Page, James Madison, John Walker, and Jacquelin Ambler (who had won Rebecca Burwell from him so long ago). The governor simply carried out its decisions. He was essentially a figurehead.

Nothing in Jefferson's background had prepared him for executive leadership. His strength lay in legislation. This student of the law, this classical scholar, had not been trained to be a war chief. He was not the military leader that the moment called for.

Throughout, Jefferson complied with General Washington's wishes that the needs of Virginia be subordinated to the needs of the main armies, the "grand army," as he called it, and that the best trained troops be sent to support them. So Jefferson sent men, money, and arms both north and south, although they were desperately needed at home. He continued to rely on the poorly armed and increasingly unwilling militia.

Jefferson remained in the governor's palace in Williamsburg until April 1780, when the capital was moved inland to Richmond for security. Richmond was then a sleepy, commercial town, and Jefferson quickly set about drawing elaborate plans for the new capitol. Once again, he had an opportunity to indulge his delight in architecture.

He rented a beautiful house from a relative, and on a cold day in April, he brought Martha, the girls, and his slaves to live in Richmond, along with assorted household goods.

One month later, just after he had begun his second term as governor, Charleston, South Carolina, fell to the British. This was considered the worst disaster of the war.

As Jefferson continued to grapple with the seemingly insoluble problems of war—the devastating loss of lives, and the knowledge that the British were moving steadily closer—his mind was also on his family. Martha was expecting another baby. As always, the family lived in a state of terrible apprehension, until the night of November 30, when, at 10:45 p.m., amid the all-too-familiar atmosphere of crisis, Lucy Elizabeth was born. The little girl seemed to thrive very quickly, and within a month after the delivery, Martha too had regained her strength.

During these troubling months Jefferson managed once again to demonstrate his capacity for friendship. He found the time to befriend a young colonel in the Continental army whom George Washington had sent to him.

James Monroe was a twenty-two-year-old Virginian who had served with distinction in the north but had become bewildered and discouraged after he was wounded at the Battle of Trenton in December 1776. He was at a loss now as to what to do. Jefferson kindly took him under his wing, recommended a legal career, and offered to guide him in his studies. He helped him solve his military problems as well. He sent the young soldier to the South to establish a line of communication between the capital of Virginia and the Carolinas. Monroe's letter to Jefferson a short time later is a tribute to the compassion and understanding that Jefferson exhibited and to the friendship that was formed: "A variety of disappointments . . . nearly destroyed me. . . . Had I not formed a connection with you I should most certainly have retir'd from society. . . . I feel that whatever I am at present in the opinion of others or whatever I may be in future has greatly arose from your friendship."[5]

The year 1781 began ominously. Brigadier General Benedict Arnold had demonstrated daring and skill in a gallant fight for the American cause from Ticonderoga to Saratoga (1775–77). In the spring of 1779, however, he suddenly turned traitor and transmitted military intelligence about the American army to the British. Now he was in command of a British army that would invade Virginia from the coast and wreak untold havoc.

Favored by good winds and a strong tide, Arnold's fleet swept rapidly up the James River to Richmond, where his troops set fire to strategic parts of the city. The raid destroyed stores and crippled morale. It damaged arms and ammunition, clothing, food, and many important government papers before Arnold escaped by another timely shift in the wind. The governor was mortified. He had been caught off guard.

Overnight, the man who had written the Declaration of Independence, reformed ancient laws, served on important committees, championed the rights of the people, and steadily supplied General Washington with troops, arms, and horses was condemned because he couldn't keep the British out of Virginia.

Jefferson promptly wrote a frank letter to General Washington acknowledging his failure. Washington replied with gentle words of comfort and, finally recognizing the seriousness of the situation, sent 1,200 regulars, under the Marquis de Lafayette, to Virginia. Lafayette was a wealthy young French nobleman who had come to America at the age of nineteen and volunteered to fight in the Continental army. Now, at twenty-three, he was a major general, highly regarded by Washington. Although he arrived too late to capture Benedict Arnold, his arrival marked the beginning of a long friendship between him and Jefferson. Although the two men had little in common except their high ideals and mutual respect, over the years they forged a warm friendship that lasted throughout their lives.

The war continued to rage on Virginia's soil and in her waters. Jefferson did what he could. All that Virginia had of men and resources were enlisted in the cause. In fact, so many men were in service during the planting season that Jefferson feared there wouldn't be enough food raised to feed the people.

And there seemed to be no end to Jefferson's personal misery. On a raw, rainy day in April, at ten o'clock in the morning, little Lucy Elizabeth, only five months old, died. Public service was taking a terrible toll. "I think public service and private misery inseparably linked together," Jefferson would later write to James Monroe.[6] He was more certain now that he would retire from office at the conclusion of his second term—June 2, 1781.

By May the legislature, fearful of another attack on Richmond, made plans to meet instead in Charlottesville, on May 24. Jefferson's second term of office would expire on the second of June, but the assembly had not yet found time to arrange for a new election. When May ended, Virginia had no governor.

During this time, Lord Cornwallis was pushing up the coast from the Carolinas into Virginia, and Colonel Banastre Tarleton and his cavalry were galloping toward Charlottesville under instructions to capture Thomas Jefferson and the members of the legislature.

John Jouett, a captain in the militia and a citizen of Charlottesville, was in the Cuckoo Tavern in Louisa County late on the evening of June 3 when Tarleton's legion swept by on the main road. Suspecting their destination, "Jouett quickly mounted his fine horse and rode furiously toward Monticello by a less used and shorter route. Galloping over rocks and fallen trees, his face lashed by branches, he covered the forty miles to the top of the mountain several hours ahead of the enemy, arriving shortly before dawn."[7]

As he came pounding up Monticello's winding road, the clatter of the horse's hoofs awakened Jefferson and several members of the legislature who were his guests at the time. They were startled to hear this outlandish-looking figure in scarlet coat, military hat, and plume, his face streaked with blood, tell them that Tarleton was on his way with 180 green-coated dragoons and 70 red-coated cavalry.

Only Jefferson took the news calmly. He quietly ordered that a carriage be brought round and that Caractacus, his favorite—and fastest—horse, be taken to Monticello's blacksmith to be shod. Then he awakened Martha and the children and insisted that they and their guests have a leisurely breakfast. He insisted also that Jack Jouett stop long enough to refresh himself with a glass of Madeira wine. Years later, in his old age, Jouett, who had come to be called Virginia's Paul Revere, would laugh and say that he would "do it again for another glass of Mr. Jefferson's Madeira."[8]

Soon Jouett turned his horse back down the hill to warn the other members of the assembly in Charlottesville, all of whom fled immediately.

Jefferson was confident that Tarleton's heavily armed men could not possibly equal Jouett's pace and that there was time to spare. Besides, he reasoned, he was no longer governor, and the British would not be interested in capturing him. But he was wrong. As the author of the Declaration of Independence, he was one of the most wanted men in America.

After breakfast, Jefferson's guests left also, but Martha and the children remained in the house. Suddenly, a young officer came rushing up to the door to tell Mr. Jefferson that the British were almost to the foot of the mountain. Only then did Jefferson hurriedly bundle his family and a few servants into the waiting carriage and send them off to his friend Colonel Edward Carter's nearby Blenheim Plantation, across the James River. Jupiter, as always when the family traveled, was their coachman. But Jupiter's wife, Suck, remained behind and was one of the slaves carried off by the British. It would be six months before she was returned to Monticello.[9]

As soon as the carriage pulled out, Jefferson told two trusted servants—his butler, Martin Hemings, and Caesar—to hide the silver plate and other valuables, and he ordered his horse brought to a point in the road between Monticello and nearby Carter's Mountain. Then he walked through the woods, cutting across his land to the valley between the two mountains. When he reached his horse, he began walking it over a path toward Carter's, pausing to look back at Charlottesville through a telescope he had brought along. The city was quiet.

Deciding that there was still time to remove some of his papers from the house, he started back toward Monticello. He was fearful that when the British reached Monticello they would set fire to it. Suddenly he noticed that the little dress sword he had been wearing at his waist was gone. It had slipped out of its scabbard, he guessed, as he knelt down to sight his telescope. He went back to retrieve it. Before leaving again, he decided to have another look at the city below. This time he saw that

Charlottesville was swarming with Tarleton's dragoons. Jefferson mounted his horse and galloped into the woods on Carter's Mountain. The sword had saved his life.

As Tarleton's troops, under a Captain McLeod, arrived at Monticello, Martin was handing down the last of the silver to Caesar, who was under the wooden floor of the front portico. A glimpse of white through the trees warned Martin, and he quickly slammed down the plank, leaving his comrade imprisoned below. There Caesar would remain, cramped and silent, without food or light, for the next eighteen hours.

Martin, standing on the plank, received McLeod with dignified politeness. The captain returned the courtesy. He was under orders from Tarleton to capture Governor Jefferson, but he was not to disturb anything in the house. McLeod even locked the door to Jefferson's study and gave the key to Martin. But the soldiers plundered the wine cellar. They broke the necks off the bottles with their swords, drank some of the wine, and poured out the rest.

One of the dragoons, anxious to locate Jefferson, put a pistol to Martin's chest, cocked it, and threatened to fire unless the slave revealed his master's whereabouts. "Fire away, then!" Martin retorted. Jefferson's faith in his servants was well founded. The family never forgot their devotion.

Meanwhile, Jefferson had joined his family at Blenheim. Later, he took them to Poplar Forest, his property in Bedford County, where he felt certain they would be safe.

At the same time that Tarleton's men were pursuing the governor and the members of the legislature in Charlottesville, Cornwallis had advanced up the James River to Jefferson's plantation at Elk Hill, probably the most valuable of all his farmlands. Here Jefferson was not so lucky. Describing the devastation a few years later, he said that the ruthless Cornwallis had

destroyed all my growing crops of corn and tobacco; he burned all my barns, containing the same articles of the last year; having first taken what corn he wanted; he used, as was to be expected, all my stock of cattle, sheep and hogs for the sustenance of his army, and carried off all the horses capable of service; of those too young for service he cut the throat;

and he burned all the fences on the plantation, so as to leave it an absolute waste. He carried off also about 30 slaves. Had this been to give them freedom he would have done right, but it was to consign them to inevitable death from the small pox and putrid fever raging in his camp.[10]

Jefferson's friends in the legislature finally realized that he had been serious when he said he would not seek a third term. Now they heeded his advice and elected Thomas Nelson as governor. It was then that the military tide turned. In the south the British were pushed back to Charleston and Savannah. In the north George Washington and a French admiral named de Grasse began a fortunate union that forced the British commander Cornwallis on the defensive. Cornwallis surrendered his entire force of seven thousand men at Yorktown on October 19, 1781.

Although Jefferson had hated the job of governor, he had worked tirelessly to solve what were essentially insoluble problems. His fear of overstepping the strict legal rights of the office even in an emergency, his allocation of Virginia's resources to the common cause rather than to its own defense, and his fleeing to safety from Tarleton's dragoons—just as Samuel Adams and John Hancock had fled from Lexington at Paul Revere's warning—all served to brand him a coward. Jefferson was industrious, he was attentive to details, and he was careful to abide by all the measures taken by the legislature. Yet a legend grew up about his inefficiency. His faithful dedication to public duty served, in the end, to brand his administration a failure.

# 19

# "One Fatal Stain"

THOMAS JEFFERSON'S HABIT of keeping records of everything continued throughout the years. His extraordinary attention to detail went even beyond his Garden Book and his many memorandum books.

He also kept notes—jotted on loose sheets of paper—teeming with facts and opinions on every branch of learning.

"I had always made it a practice whenever an opportunity occurred of obtaining any information of our country, which might be of use to me in any station public or private, to commit it to writing. These memoranda were on loose papers, bundled up without order, and difficult of recurrence when I had occasion for a particular one," he would write years later.[1] Indeed, over the years he kept notes on everything—the weather, the crops, household expenses, his travels, the letters he wrote and received, the books he bought and read, and the buildings he admired, all revealing the utilitarian cast of his ingenious mind. He was an inveterate collector, but his collections—and his records—were for use, as were his reading and writing.[2]

Thus, in the fall of 1780, when Jefferson received a letter from Philadelphia from Marquis François de Barbé-Marbois, secretary of the French legation to the United States, requesting answers to a list of twenty-three queries (questions) about Virginia for the French government, he was ready.

In his characteristic manner, he seized this opportunity to organize his notes, think about them, and, through further study, pursue some of their scientific and philosophical implications. He sent his answers off to Marbois one year later, on December 20, 1781. But he continued to gather information in order to expand their scope and enrich the text. Later, he compiled the whole into what would evolve into his only book, *Notes on the State of Virginia*. It was a project that gave free rein to his imagination and to his passion for learning. Jefferson did not originally intend the work for publication. It was meant to be his answer to the Frenchman's questions, a friendly sharing of scientific knowledge with a group of French philosophers—in three hundred pages. It would come to be considered one of the most important expressions of the cultural life of the early American republic, a masterpiece of American literature.

Demonstrating his extraordinary range of knowledge, Jefferson's *Notes* became a rich combination of hundreds of useful scientific facts with a proud description of the beauty of his "country." It was at once factual and lyrical, a celebration of the land's capacity to support life.

Jefferson described Virginia's climate and crops, its resources for commerce and communication, its wilderness landscapes, its history, its archaeology, its native societies. He seemed to grasp the vastness of the possibility of America.

In glowing passages he gave Europeans their first glimpse of Virginia's natural beauty, he cataloged facts, he proved that American animals were larger than their European counterparts, and he defended the American Indian against the disparaging claims made by the famous French naturalist Georges-Louis Leclerc, comte de Buffon.

Director of the Jardin du Roi (the Royal Garden) in Paris, and author of the multivolume natural history *Histoire naturelle, générale et particulière,* Buffon was perhaps the most influential and widely known natural historian of the late eighteenth century. His assertions that New World animals were smaller than their Old World counterparts, and that domestic animals introduced into America were diminished in size and quality from their European ancestors, were all the French knew. Furthermore, Buffon contended, the unsuitability of the North American climate for animal life also affected human beings. It was colder and more humid, he said, and thus "everything languishes, decays, stifles."

Jefferson declared Buffon's dismal descriptions to be "just as true as the fable of Aesop." Describing American minerals, trees, plants, fruits, and animals, he went on to disprove Buffon's statements, taking special pains to refute his theory of the degeneracy of people of the New World.[3]

To counter Buffon's remarks about the American Indian, Jefferson asserted that American Indians were brave and manly, affectionate to their children, and strong in their attachments to family and friends. They were eloquent speakers, their reasoning abilities were strong, and their imagination "glowing." He hoped for "cultural and physical amalgamation of Indians with white Americans."[4]

As he had done in the Declaration of Independence, Jefferson submitted "facts . . . to a candid world." Are American animals smaller? he asked. He would find out. The European bear, he learned, weighed 153 pounds, the American 410. In Europe the beaver grew to 18 pounds, in America to over 40. And he found specimens to ship to the comte to prove his points.[5]

To counter the French concept that the environment of the New World was physically debilitating, and fearful that America's new government might fail if Europeans believed that the new country was inferior to the countries of Europe, Jefferson was here attempting to prove that America was indeed a chosen land, and that its experiment in self-government would prevail. He defended his country's honor and created a confidence in it that would encourage military and financial support from European countries, particularly France.[6]

His pride in America shone throughout. America's French allies had simply wished to understand the physical features, population, and laws of Virginia. They would get much more than they had bargained for.

In Query II, "Rivers and Navigation," Jefferson predicted the importance of the Mississippi River to western settlers: "The Mississippi will be one of the principal channels of future commerce for the country westward of the Allegheny."[7] Some twenty years later, the Louisiana Purchase and the Lewis and Clark expedition would prove him correct.

He dedicated his answers to Query VII to his own favorite subject of research, Virginia's climate.[8] From his days as a student in Williamsburg, Jefferson had been noting rainfall and temperatures in his memorandum books. Now he could use those statistics to refute Buffon's assertions about America's climate and, at the same time, provide information to American farmers who wanted to know what crops to plant and when.[9]

As Jefferson continued ostensibly answering Marbois's questions, he was actually setting down his views on politics, religion, science, education, and philosophy—an index, as it were, to his own mind. In language he thought the Europeans would understand and based on his limited observations, Jefferson was describing his world in his time as he saw it. *Notes on the State of Virginia* also became his view of how life in America *should* be, his vision of the possible, his dream for the future. As he was explaining America, he was becoming part of the larger world. His book would take its place among the best of Enlightenment literature. But it brought to the fore, in tragic counterpoint, the problem of slavery in his country, and his own inner conflicts about it.[10]

In his response to Query XIV, which deals with the administration of justice and the laws of Virginia, Jefferson referred to the revision of the laws which he and George Wythe had recently completed. These would probably not be voted upon, he said, until "a restoration of the peace* shall leave to the legislature leisure to go through such a work."

It was here, embedded within his response to this query, that Jefferson called for the abolition of slavery. But in so doing, he included perhaps the most troubling passage in all his writings, advocating colonization of freed blacks to a distant place:

> To emancipate all slaves born after passing the act . . . and further directing, that they should continue with their parents to a certain age, then be brought up, at the public expence, to tillage, arts or sciences, according to their geniuses, till the females should be eighteen, and the males twenty-one years of age, when they should be colonized to such place as the circumstances of the time should render most proper, sending them out with arms, implements of household and of the handicraft arts, feeds, pairs of the useful domestic animals, &c. to declare them a free and independent people, and extend to them our alliance and protection, till they should have acquired strength.

He went on to justify this colonization with what one historian has called Jefferson's "moral honesty":[11]

> Deep rooted prejudices entertained by the whites; ten thousand recollections, by the blacks, of the injuries they have sustained; new provocations; the real distinctions which nature has made; and many other circumstances, will divide us into parties, and produce convulsions which will probably never end but in the extermination of the one or the other race.

Jefferson was firmly convinced that black people could never be incorporated into white society on equal terms, at least in his lifetime. He believed that the mutual fear and resentment that already existed between the two races were so strong that a cohesive biracial society could never exist. His only solution was a plan of gradual emancipation and ultimate colonization to a new country they could claim as their own,

---

*The Revolutionary War was still going on.

and where they could be recognized as "a free and independent people." But, he stipulated, they must have "the essential powers of self government and self improvement" after they had been "sufficiently trained by education and habits of freedom to walk safely by themselves."[12] Throughout his life, Jefferson never wavered in his conviction that American blacks must be "removed" when freed.

When he was nearing the age of eighty, he wrote in his autobiography: "Nothing is more certainly written in the book of fate than that these people are to be free. Nor is it less certain that the two races, equally free, cannot live in the same government."[13]

Invoking the "limited sphere of my observation," he specified "the real distinctions which nature has made," both "physical and moral," and included color, "that immoveable veil of black which covers all the emotions." "I advance it, therefore, as a suspicion only, that the blacks, whether originally a distinct race, or made distinct by time and circumstances, are inferior to the whites in the endowments both of body and mind."[14]

In this, Jefferson may well have been influenced by David Hume, one of the Enlightenment's major intellectual heroes. In his essay "Of National Characters," Hume had written: "I am apt to suspect the Negroes and in general all the other species of men . . . to be naturally inferior to the whites. There never was a civilized nation of any other complexion than white, nor even any individual eminent either in action or speculation. No ingenious manufactures amongst them, no arts, no sciences."[15] Even John Locke "appears to have had no objection to slavery as it was practiced as a matter of property in the English colonies."[16]

Hume, along with many prominent intellectuals of the Enlightenment, defined man in terms of mental and psychological characteristics. Thus he put forth the view that "the mental life of non-whites, especially Indians and Africans, [was] significantly different from that of whites."[17] Many eighteenth-century philosophers argued that Indians and Africans could have no abstract ideas, could not engage in prudent reasoning, nor could they understand or appreciate true religion. This evaluation of nonwhites became "one of the problems of eighteenth century thought: the justification of European superiority over the rest of mankind."[18] The first American edition of the *Encyclopaedia Britannica* (Philadelphia, 1798) contained articles substantiating this view and repeated the same theories in subsequent editions even into the twentieth century.[19]

Some historians have mused that while Jefferson hated slavery, perhaps by expressing "suspicions" that blacks were inferior to whites, he was able to "preserve his inner equilibrium, and make it possible for him to live temporarily with an institution that, he constantly assured himself, was in the course of eventual extinguishment." Indeed, most of Jefferson's friends and neighbors contended that "slavery was the most humane condition for an inferior order of men."[20]

But Jefferson was not *defending* slavery. Rather, he was speaking out for emancipation, while at the same time explaining the problems that emancipation would pose. He recognized that blacks "were equally entitled, as a people, to reclaim the rights of self-government their enslavement had denied them." "The institution of slavery," he said, "was not set above the principles proclaimed in 1776" in the Declaration of Independence.[21]

His indictment of slavery is nowhere better stated than in his reply to Query XVIII, which asked about the "particular customs and manners" of Virginia. Here, Jefferson chose to respond by discussing one topic only—the evil effects of slavery:

> There must doubtless be an unhappy influence on the manners of our people produced by the existence of slavery among us. The whole commerce between master and slave is a perpetual exercise of the most boisterous passions, the most unremitting despotism on the one part, and degrading submissions on the other. Our children see this, and learn to imitate it; . . . the parent storms, the child looks on, catches the lineaments of wrath, puts on the same airs in the circle of smaller slaves, gives a loose to the worst of passions, and thus nursed, educated, and daily exercised in tyranny, cannot but be stamped by it with odious peculiarities. The man must be a prodigy who can retain his manners and morals undepraved by such circumstances. . . . And can the liberties of a nation be thought secure when we have removed their only firm basis, a conviction in the

minds of the people that these liberties are the gift of God? That they are not to be violated but with his wrath? Indeed I tremble for my country when I reflect that God is just: that his justice cannot sleep forever.[22]

The existence of slavery, Jefferson believed, was as degrading to the master as to the slave. Not only was slavery a moral wrong, it was a violation of the natural order of things, a crime against humanity. The very freedom that had just been won by a revolution with such sacrifice could not, he was certain, survive as long as the institution of slavery remained.[23]

Many years later, in 1825, Jefferson's granddaughter Ellen, completing a five-week-long wedding trip to Boston with her new husband, wrote to her grandfather of the beauty of New England: "It has given me an idea of prosperity and improvement, such as I fear our Southern States cannot hope for, whilst the canker of slavery eats into their hearts, and diseases the whole body by this ulcer at the core."[24]

Her grandfather responded that "the rustic scenes" Ellen had left in Virginia "do not want their points of endearment. Nay, one single circumstance changed, and their scale would hardly be the lightest. *One fatal stain* deforms what nature has bestowed on us of her fairest gifts."[25] That circumstance would change, he prophesied. Slavery would be abolished.

Indeed, Jefferson had concluded his response to Query XVIII: "I think a change already perceptible, since the origin of the present revolution. The spirit of the master is abating, that of the slave rising from the dust, his condition mollifying, the way I hope preparing, under the auspices of heaven, for a total emancipation, and that this is disposed, in the order of events, to be with the consent of the masters, rather than by their extirpation."

John Adams, upon reading the *Notes*, pronounced that the "passages upon slavery, are worth Diamonds, they will have more effect than Volumes written by mere Philosophers."[26]

# 20

# "That Eternal Separation"

W HEN JEFFERSON WAS NEARING completion of his *Notes*, the Marquis de Chastellux, a handsome young Frenchman who had been one of the commanders of the French army at Yorktown and who was a scholarly member of the French Academy, came to visit Jefferson at Monticello. This meeting with Chastellux, and the friendship that developed, was the beginning of a fondness for the French people that would last for the rest of Jefferson's life.

"Let me describe to you," the marquis wrote, "a man, not yet forty, tall, with a mild and pleasing countenance, but whose mind and understanding are ample substitutes for every exterior grace. An American, who, without ever having quitted his own country, is at once a musician, skilled in drawing, a geometrician, an astronomer, a natural philosopher, legislator, and statesman. . . . It seemed as if from his youth he had placed his mind, as he had done his house, on an elevated situation from which he might contemplate the universe."[1]

Monticello was not completed at the time Chastellux visited. The house that Chastellux saw, in fact, was not the elegant mansion of Jefferson's imagination, but rather a depressing conglomeration of "scaffolding, dust, mud, noise, and debris"—a skeleton house that was rising around its inhabitants. But enough had been done to impress the marquis with its elegance and classic symmetry: "Mr. Jefferson is the first American who has consulted the fine arts to know how he should shelter himself from the weather," he would write.[2]

Chastellux saw very little of Jefferson's wife, Martha, during his visit, and his description of her tells us only that she was "mild and amiable." Martha was expecting another baby any day, and she was keeping to her room. Jefferson and Chastellux, though, stayed up far into the night, drinking punch and enthusiastically reading poetry aloud to one another by candlelight.[3]

Just a few days after Chastellux departed, on May 8, 1782, Martha gave birth to an unusually large baby girl, whom they named Lucy Elizabeth, after their infant of the same name who had died just a year before. This was their sixth child, three of whom had died as infants. Their two surviving daughters, Martha (Patsy) and Mary (Maria, or Polly), were ten and four years old respectively. This time, baby Lucy seemed to thrive, but her mother was unable to regain her strength.

Day by day she grew steadily weaker and seemed to be wasting away in front of Jefferson. Half nurse, half companion, Jefferson sat with her for hours on end, holding her hand, reading to her, willing her to live. When she slept he wrote his *Notes* in a little room just off the bedroom, near enough to hear her stir. All other ordinary activities—even correspondence—were suspended. While Martha lingered for four months, her husband was rarely out of calling distance.

Occasionally, he would take time out to stroll around the grounds hand in hand with Patsy and little Polly. By now he had begun to stock his grounds with white-tailed deer, and father and daughters often stopped to feed them.

Martha continued to decline.

Her husband revealed his feelings in the final lines of a letter to his understanding young friend James Monroe: "Mrs. Jefferson has added another daughter to our family. She has been ever since and still continues very dangerously ill."[4]

One day, as Jefferson and Martha were reading together, Martha asked for a pen and, recognizing that she was slowly slipping away, wrote from memory a stanza from *Tristram Shandy,* a favorite book of theirs:

> Time wastes too fast: every letter
> I trace tells me with what rapidity
> Life follows my pen. The days and hours
> Of it are flying over our heads
> Like clouds of windy day, never to return—
> More everything presses on—

Her strength ran out. She couldn't go on. But Jefferson, who knew the passage as well as Martha, and knew too that its author, Laurence Sterne, had written it to a loved one as he was dying, completed it:

—and every
Time I kiss thy hand to bid adieu,
Every absence which follows it, are preludes to
that eternal separation
Which we are shortly to make!

Just before she died, Martha made one last anguished plea to her husband. Some of the favorite house servants had been allowed to come in to see her, and they listened as she struggled to hold back the tears and to tell her husband some of the things she hoped he would do. Her greatest concern, she whispered, was for her three little girls, and her fervent wish was that the children not be brought up by a stepmother, as she had been after her mother died. It was passed down in the Jefferson family tradition that quietly, solemnly her husband promised that he would never marry again. But he continued to reassure her—and himself—that she was not dying.

When she sank into a final coma, "he was led from the room almost in a state of insensibility by his sister, Mrs. Carr, who with great difficulty, got him into the library, where he fainted, and remained so long insensible that they feared he never would revive," Patsy described it years later.[5]

Alarmed by her brother's reaction, fearful that he too was dying, Martha Carr frantically called out to Elizabeth Eppes, still bending over her lifeless sister, "Leave the dead and come and take care of the living!"[6]

But it was ten-year-old Patsy, patient, sensitive, understanding, who finally drew her father out of the stupor into which he had fallen:

He kept his room three weeks, and I was never a moment from his side. He walked almost incessantly night and day, only lying down occasionally when nature was completely exhausted, on a pallet that had been brought in during his long fainting fit. My aunts remained constantly with him for some weeks—I do not remember how many. When at last he left his room, he rode out, and from that time he was incessantly on horseback, rambling about the mountain, in the least frequented roads, and just as often through the woods. In those melancholy rambles I was his constant companion—a solitary witness to many a burst of grief, the remembrance of which has consecrated particular scenes of that lost home beyond the power of time to obliterate.[7]

A bond was forming between father and daughter that would never be broken.

Martha was buried beneath the great oak tree on the side of their mountain, beside the bodies of their three tiny children and not far from where Dabney Carr lay buried.

The simple note in Jefferson's Account Book for September 6, 1782, reads, "My dear wife died this day at 11:45 A.M." Martha was only thirty-three years old. Her husband had just turned thirty-nine. The inscription he wrote for the slab of white marble that would mark her grave probably tells more about his love and devotion than other words could convey:

To the memory of
Martha Jefferson
Daughter of John Wayles;
Born October 19th, 1748, O.S.*
INTERMARRIED WITH
THOMAS JEFFERSON
JANUARY 1ST, 1772
Torn from him by death
September 6, 1782:
This monument of his love is inscribed
* * *

Then, in Greek, so most could not read it, two lines from Homer's *Iliad:*

If in the house of Hades men forget their dead,
Yet will I even there remember my dear companion.

And he went beyond this epitaph. He destroyed every letter that he and Martha had exchanged over the years. He would never be able to

*Old Style.

reread them, never reopen old wounds. He would ensure, also, that their letters to each other would not become public property, that they would never be open to prying eyes.

Forty-four years later, after Jefferson himself had died, a secret drawer was discovered in a private cabinet that contained locks of hair and other little mementos of his wife and each of the children, including those who had died, all labeled in his own handwriting. Although carefully arranged, everything gave evidence of having been frequently—and lovingly—handled.

Suddenly, life seemed meaningless for Jefferson. She who had been "the cherished companion of my life," and with whom he had lived for ten years "in unchequered happiness," had been snatched away from him. As he rode his horse through the Albemarle hills, or paced the floors of Monticello, there seemed little reason to go on living. What remained for him? Even filled as Monticello was with his children, his sister and her children, and the servants, the house became for him an empty shell, devoid of the spirit that had given it its beauty.

Redheaded, freckle-faced Patsy, at ten already large boned and growing tall like her father, became his shadow, riding with him five or six miles a day and trying to lessen his grief simply by being there.

In anguish Jefferson wrote to his sister-in-law Elizabeth Eppes, "This miserable hand of existence is really too burthensome to be borne and were it not for the infidelity of deserting the sacred charge left me, I could not wish its continuance a moment. . . . The care and instruction of our children indeed affords some temporary abstractions from wretchedness."[8]

He did honor the sacred charges left to him, and in November took his own and all the Carr children to be inoculated against smallpox at Ampthill, the home of his friend Archibald Cary, who had lent it to him for that purpose. He remained with them as their "chief nurse," caring for them all until they recovered.

From Ampthill he wrote to the Marquis de Chastellux that he was just "a little emerging from the stupor of mind which had rendered me as dead to the world as was she whose loss occasioned it." Before her death, he continued, "my scheme of life had been determined. . . . A single event wiped away all my plans and left me with a blank which I had not the spirits to fill up."[9]

Edmund Randolph thought his friend's inconsolable grief, in contrast to the stoic silence with which the Virginia gentry normally dealt with loss and death, was somehow abnormal. A shocked Madison dismissed the stories of his friend's behavior as "altogether incredible."[10]

But Martha's death was, indeed, a turning point in Jefferson's life, completely changing its inner rhythm and direction. Her loss, he told an acquaintance three years later, "was the only circumstance which could have brought me to Europe."[11]

# PART III

## *Facing the Enlightenment*

# 21

# A New Door Opens

B Y THE TIME Jefferson returned to Monticello from Ampthill, Congress had thrown him a lifeline: they offered him a commission to negotiate peace in Paris. His friends in Congress, Madison foremost among them, guessed correctly that now he would welcome this opportunity.

Jefferson took Polly, now four years old, and Little Lu, as he called her, to Eppington, where Martha's half sister, Elizabeth Eppes, had offered to care for them. The ten-year-old slave Sally Hemings went with them as their "nurse-maid," or babysitter. Patsy, Jefferson decided, much to her delight, was old enough to accompany him. But the ship that was to carry them to France was caught in the ice at the entrance to the Chesapeake Bay, and a provisional peace treaty was signed before they could sail. By the middle of May he and the children were all back at Monticello. For Jefferson it was a quiet summer, filled with haunting memories of Martha.

His unmarried sister, Anna, came to stay with him. His brother, Randolph, Anna's twin, lived simply on his own lands nearby. A well-liked and kindly man, Randolph had not inherited his older brother's keen intelligence, but the two maintained an affectionate relationship.

In June word came that Jefferson had been elected to Congress. His term would begin in November. He was pleased that he could once again lend a hand to "the laboring oar."[1]

He tried hard to keep busy in the interim. He wrote to Madison that "unremitting occupations" were the only palliative for loss and grief. He began to classify and catalog his entire library, which by now had grown to 2,640 volumes. Working alone, he arranged the books, not in the traditional alphabetical order, but according to Sir Francis Bacon's divisions of knowledge: Memory, Reason, and Imagination. Jefferson's classification scheme renamed these History, Philosophy, and Fine Arts, what he considered the three principal categories of human knowledge.[2]

His list opens a window into the brilliance of his mind. The Library of Congress would later adopt this method.

He then began an orderly index of all the letters he had written and received, which he called a "Summary Journal of Letters." From then on, for the rest of his life, he kept a careful record of all his letters. It is from these tens of thousands of letters that his thoughts and activities can be pieced together like a mosaic. He seemed always to be writing. The act of writing was for him the act of thinking. He clarified his own thoughts as he wrote.

He used the summer, also, to instruct Patsy, now nearing eleven, and the six Carr children. He was concerned about their education because there were relatively few good schools in Virginia at that time, and none near Monticello for the girls. He worried particularly about Patsy and wrote to Marbois in Paris, "The chance that in marriage she will draw a blockhead I calculate at about 14 to 1." This meant that the future education of her children would "rest on her own ideas and direction without assistance."[3] Mr. Jefferson was taking no chances.

In October, after he had once again settled Polly and Little Lucy with their Aunt Eppes, Jefferson set out for Philadelphia. He was accompanied by Patsy in the phaeton and his servant James Hemings on horseback. When they arrived there, they discovered that Congress had unexpectedly moved to Annapolis, Maryland. With a heavy heart, Jefferson decided that it was not wise to take his daughter with him to Annapolis, and so prevailed on Mrs. Hopkinson, widowed mother of Francis Hopkinson, a friend and fellow signer of the Declaration of Independence, to care for her in Philadelphia. That city was more of a metropolis than Annapolis, and Patsy could acquire more "taste and proficiency in the arts" there. He then made arrangements for her to study under the guidance of several tutors.[4]

When he felt comfortable that Patsy would be happy with the kindly Mrs. Hopkinson, he tended to his own affairs, then hurried to catch up with Congress. As soon as he arrived in Annapolis, he wrote to his daughter the first of many letters to his children that he would continue to write for the rest of his life. Written during long periods of separation, these letters allow a glimpse into the soul of Thomas Jefferson and reveal a side of him not visible in the other memorials he left behind. Letters of advice, of love and tenderness, and often of wit, they show how deeply interested he was in every detail of their young lives, and how difficult it was for him to be apart from them. He had become both father and mother.

Annapolis, Nov. 28th, 1783

My dear Patsy—After four days' journey, I arrived here without any accident, and in as good health as when I left Philadelphia. The conviction that you would be more improved in the situation I have placed you than if still with me, has solaced me on parting with you, which my love for you has rendered a difficult thing. The acquirements which I hope you will make under the tutors I have provided for you will render you more worthy of my love; and if they cannot increase it, they will prevent its diminution. . . . With respect to the distribution of your time, the following is what I should approve:

From 8 to 10, practice music.

From 10 to 1, dance one day and draw another.

From 1 to 2, draw on the day you dance, and write a letter next day.

From 3 to 4 read French.

From 4 to 5, exercise yourself in music.

From 5 till bed-time, read English, write, etc.

Communicate this plan to Mrs. Hopkinson, and if she approves of it, pursue it. . . . I expect you will write me by every post. Inform me what books you read, what tunes you learn, and inclose me your best copy of every lesson in drawing. Write also one letter a week either to your Aunt Eppes, your Aunt Skipwith, your Aunt Carr, or the little lady [her sister Polly] from whom I now inclose a letter, and always put the letter you so write under cover to me. Take care that you never spell a word wrong. Always before you write a word, consider how it is spelt, and, if you do not remember it, turn to a dictionary. It produces great praise to a lady to spell well. I have placed my happiness on seeing you good and accomplished; and no distress which this world can now bring on me would equal that of your disappointing my hopes. If you love me, then strive to be good under every situation and to all living creatures, and to acquire those accomplish-

ments which I have put in your power, and which will go far towards ensuring you the warmest love of your affectionate father,
Th. Jefferson

P.S.—Keep my letters and read them at times, that you may always
have present in your mind those things which will endear you to me.[5]

One can't help wondering whether Patsy's father realized that he had
neglected to allow any time for amusement—or even for meals.

Yet Patsy strove to comply. Cheerful, loving, and enthusiastic, she
took to heart her father's advice and tried hard to pattern herself after
him. That he was consistently loving and kind softened for her the effect
of his moralizing. Secure in the knowledge that she would always be
dear to him, she was not burdened by fear that his love was conditioned
on her good behavior. She didn't always follow his instructions. She occasionally let as much as two months slide by without writing or sending the copies of her lessons that he requested.

When Congress finally did assemble in Annapolis, Jefferson discovered that many of his old friends were no longer there. They were occupied elsewhere, and Congress was filled with new, younger members.
In this group, Jefferson stood out and quickly assumed leadership. His
work during the next five months would leave a permanent imprint on
American life.

One of the first orders of business for Congress was the acceptance of
George Washington's farewell. At that time Washington could have become a king or a dictator, but he chose instead to relinquish his command of the army and retire to Mt. Vernon, his plantation in Virginia.
Jefferson was chosen chairman of the committee to arrange the ceremonies, and he drew up a simple but dignified and impressive order of
proceedings scheduled to take place two days before Christmas. Then,
characteristically, he quietly stepped aside.

At the ceremony in the emotion-packed room, as Washington spoke
of his departure from "the great theatre of action" and bid Congress "an
affectionate farewell," spectators and congressmen alike wept. Jefferson
called it "an affecting scene."[6] When Thomas Mifflin, the president of
Congress, rose to reply, there were few in the audience who did not realize that Thomas Jefferson had written his speech.

Yet that very evening, Jefferson could once again shift easily into a different role. From a leader in Congress and a writer whose words stirred the hearts and minds of his countrymen, he could become a concerned father, anxious to instruct his daughter. He admonished Patsy: "I omitted . . . to advise you on the subject of dress, which I know you are a little apt to neglect. . . . be you, from the moment you rise till you go to bed, as cleanly and as properly dressed as at the hour of dinner or tea. . . . Nothing is so disgusting to our sex as a want of cleanliness and delicacy in yours."[7]

Jefferson took no part in the gay social life swirling around him in Annapolis. As members of Congress attended lively balls and parties given by wealthy socialites of the city, Jefferson remained at home, reading and writing. Still deeply depressed by Martha's death, he admitted his "gloom" to a new young friend, a Dutchman named G. K. von Hogendorp. In a rare show of his emotions, Jefferson told him, "I have been happy and cheerful. I have had many causes of gratitude to Heaven; but I have also experienced its rigors. I have known what it is to lose every species of connection which is dear to the human heart—friends, brethren, parents, children."[8] Yet he couldn't bring himself to include the word "wife."

Jefferson worked tirelessly in Congress and continued to put his unique stamp on the future of his country. Indeed, he immersed himself in public affairs in an attempt to steel himself against the pain of Martha's death. During the next five months he was a member of nearly every important committee. He drafted thirty-one state papers. One of these, his "Notes on the Establishment of a Money Unit and of a Coinage for the United States," imposed the decimal system and established the dollar as the basic American currency. He had already simplified the laws of Virginia. Now he was attempting to simplify the arithmetic of money. Once again, he was introducing logic and order into his world. Congress accepted his plan, but not his equally simple system of weights and measures.

One of Jefferson's most important contributions during that period was his "Report" of March 22, 1784. A few months earlier he had been appointed chairman of a committee to deal with the question of the future government of the vast new territory called the Northwest. Virginia had ceded her claims to the land north and west of the Ohio River to the country. She had, in effect, given away an empire. Now Jefferson's "Report" simply and concisely outlined a plan of government for all the western lands. It allowed for new territories to be admitted to the Union on an equal footing with the thirteen original states and provided in detail for ten new states, stipulating that their governments be republican and include no hereditary titles. It further stated that "neither slavery nor involuntary servitude" would be permitted in any new states taken into the Union after the year 1800.

Nearly all the southern delegates voted against the antislavery proposal. All the northern states voted in favor, which would have just carried it. But one of the two delegates from New Jersey (John Beatty) was ill and therefore absent. Thus, that state's vote was not counted, and the measure was defeated.

Jefferson, writing to a French historian several years later, said, "The voice of a single individual would have prevented this abominable crime from spreading itself over the new country. Thus we see the fate of millions unborn hanging on the tongue of one man, and Heaven was silent in that awful moment."[9]

Although the section on slavery was voted down, slavery never did flourish in the Northwest Territory. Here Jefferson showed himself to be a prophet once again—a major architect of American expansion. His "Report," although never put into effect, became the basis of the Northwest Ordinance of 1787. This law, which came to grips with how a nation should deal with its colonial peoples, reaffirmed Jefferson's fundamental principle that new states be admitted "on an equal footing with the original States." Further, the ordinance stated, "There shall be neither slavery nor involuntary servitude in the said territory."

Jefferson had one more important duty to fulfill for Congress, and in this he was to anticipate the next five years of his own life. Congress recognized that friendly trade relations had to be established with foreign countries as quickly as possible if the United States were to survive as a nation. Now Jefferson was asked to prepare a new list of instructions for diplomatic agents to follow in negotiating treaties with other countries. Nothing like this had been done before. But once again, Jefferson had thought carefully about the subject, and he was prepared.

Among his suggestions was one that endorsed sending a mission to Europe to negotiate with those countries with which the United States had no formal connection. Two representatives were already there: Benjamin Franklin had been minister to France since 1776; and John Adams, who had been in Europe since December 1779, was minister to The Hague in Holland. John Jay of New York had resigned as minister to Spain and was returning home. Now Jefferson was nominated to be the third, replacing Jay. On May 7, 1784, Congress appointed Thomas Jefferson minister plenipotentiary to negotiate treaties of commerce with the maritime powers of Europe and those of Africa that bordered on the Mediterranean Sea.

Suddenly, Jefferson's mind was filled with plans—for his family, for Monticello, for his forthcoming trip. He immediately sat down to write letters. His first was to William Short, a bright and enthusiastic young man of twenty-five whose studies Jefferson had been guiding. Connected to Jefferson by marriage (he was the nephew of Henry and Robert Skipwith, each of whom had married half sisters of Martha Jefferson), Short had attended the College of William and Mary, where he studied law under George Wythe (who had been named the college's first professor of law) and was one of the founders of Phi Beta Kappa. He had served as its president from 1778 to 1781. After graduating from college, Short practiced law and, at the age of twenty-four, was elected to the Virginia Executive Council of State.[10]

Jefferson asked Short to accompany him to France as his private secretary. He offered him bed and board, assurance that he would give him "little trouble," and a salary of one thousand dollars a year.[11] Jefferson would later refer to Short as his "adoptive son."

"Friends grounded Jefferson."[12] Friendship was essential to him and he drew much satisfaction from the friendships of young men whose potential was clear, who sought knowledge as he did, and whose views he could help shape just as his own views had been influenced by George Wythe, Francis Fauquier, and William Small in Williamsburg so many years before.

In what is perhaps the clearest expression of what friendship meant to Jefferson, he wrote to his good friend James Madison, asking Madison to accept as a "tender legacy" Peter Carr, son of his sister Martha and Dabney Carr, and to oversee the boy's education while he was gone: "I will not say it is the son of my sister, tho her worth would justify my resting it on that ground; but it is the son of my friend, the dearest friend I knew, who, had fate reversed our lots, would have been the father to my children."[13]

To Madison he also extended a warm invitation:

> I hope you have found access to my library. I beg you to make free use of it. . . . Monroe is buying land almost adjoining me. Short will do the same. What would I not give [if] you could fall into the circle. With such a society I could once more venture home and lay myself up for the residue of life, quitting all its contentions which grow daily more and more insupportable. Think of it. To render it practicable only requires you to think it so. Life is of no value but as it brings us gratifications. Among the most valuable of these is rational society. It informs the mind, sweetens the temper, cheers our spirits, and promotes health.[14]

William Short, a young protégé of Jefferson's, acted as his chargé d'affaires and private secretary in France. Jefferson thought of him as his "adoptive son." By Rembrandt Peale, 1806. (Courtesy of the Muscarelle Museum of Art, College of William and Mary)

James Madison, Jefferson's
cherished friend and political
ally in the Virginia legislature.
Madison guided the Constitution
through the convention and, while
Jefferson was in Paris, kept him
informed of developments in
America. By Charles Willson
Peale. (Courtesy of the Gilcrease
Museum, Tulsa, Oklahoma)

He invited Martha Carr and her entire family to remain at Monticello, and he extended an invitation to pass the hot season there to his wife's half sister Ann Wayles and her husband, Robert Skipwith, and to his own sister Anna Scott Jefferson. His plantation was left in the care of his overseer.

In the last letter he wrote before leaving for Europe, he asked his sister-in-law Elizabeth Eppes to continue to care for his two little girls. They were too young to risk the perils of an ocean voyage. He would take the almost-twelve-year-old Patsy with him to share the big adventure. And he made arrangements to take James Hemings, his nineteen-year-old slave, with him. At long last the door to Europe was open to him. Perhaps it would be the door to a new life as well.

# 22

# "Behold Me on the Vaunted Scene of Europe"

Thomas Jefferson hurried to Philadelphia from Annapolis—the trip took four days—then celebrated his arrival by attending "the playhouse." He spent the next two weeks dealing with the endless details of preparing for the trip. He shopped in Philadelphia for many of the things that he and Patsy would need for their journey, including furnishings and bedding for their cabin aboard ship. There was much to be done, and therefore not enough time to make the long trip back to Virginia to see his two little children.

There were no papers for him to study, no precedents to guide him in his new role. He would simply have to learn as he went along. To begin his education, he decided to tour the northern states before he departed for France and to see and absorb all that he could.

He collected Patsy, and together they set out for a trip through New England in the little time remaining. Patsy, sitting straight beside her father in the phaeton and dressed in the best clothes he could purchase for her in the city of Philadelphia, was delighted with the pocket money her father had given her for souvenirs along the way.

Since he would be dealing with questions of commerce in Europe, Jefferson met with the governors of each of the states that he and Patsy visited, and discussed with them their commercial needs. Father and daughter went as far north as New Hampshire, then returned to Boston. There, on July 4, 1784, the eighth anniversary of the Declaration of Independence, they boarded the newly built and beautiful ship *Ceres*. The next morning, just as dawn was breaking over Boston Harbor, they set sail for Paris, France.

There were only five other passengers, "all of whom Papa knew," Patsy wrote to their friend Mrs. Elizabeth Trist in Philadelphia. There was "fine sunshine all the way, with a sea as calm as a river."[1] The trip was remarkably short—only nineteen days from land to land—with favorable winds most of the way. When they were becalmed for three days off the coast of Newfoundland, they spent the time fishing.

In contrast to his usual activity, Jefferson used the voyage to relax and enjoy his fellow passengers, sharing with them the fresh apples and oranges and the fine wines he had brought on board. He did take some time, though, to learn Spanish with the help of a grammar and two copies of *Don Quixote*—one in English, the other in Spanish—that he had brought with him.

Jefferson looked forward to seeing friends, such as Chastellux and Lafayette, both of whom were waiting for him in France. He looked forward, also, to adding to his store of knowledge: he would gather facts and make comparisons, and he would send home to America the useful information he gathered.

This tall, spare man in black, now forty-one years old, knew American life and the American people, and he understood the workings of his government. No one else in America was better qualified to represent it than he. He may not have realized it at the time, but he had become, after George Washington and Benjamin Franklin, the most famous national figure in America.

As he paced the deck, thinking, he resolved to correct the impression in Europe that the United States was a loose confederation of states. He would convince the Europeans that his country was a nation worthy of their respect.

They landed in Portsmouth, England, near the end of July, then crossed the English Channel to Le Havre, France, in a tiny boat in a violent rainstorm. The cabin on the vessel was so small that they had to crawl into it, and Patsy teased her distinguished father about his long legs. From Le Havre they followed the Seine River to Paris, where they arrived on August 6, 1784. The harvest season was just beginning, and Jefferson's farmer's eye appreciated the fertile fields along the way. But Patsy and her father looked in vain for the sun.

Once settled in Paris, they saw very quickly that before Jefferson could begin to conduct official business, they would have to be dressed properly. Their simple American clothes looked strange there, and they were warned that to be out of fashion was more criminal than to be seen in a state of nature. So Jefferson summoned the milliner, shoemaker, staymaker,* and dressmaker for Patsy, then ordered a suit, hat, shirts, knee buckles, and shoe buckles, as well as a sword, belt, and lace ruffles for himself.

About a week after the Jeffersons arrived in Paris, John and Abigail Adams, their eighteen-year-old daughter, Nabby, and seventeen-year-old son, John Quincy, came to France. Abigail and Nabby had arrived in London from Massachusetts just three weeks before. John and John Quincy had been in the United Netherlands (Holland), where John Adams had been negotiating a financial loan for Congress. The Adams family was overjoyed to be reunited after a four-year separation and went to live in a lovely house in Auteuil, adjoining the Bois de Boulogne, the former royal hunting park, and just beyond Passy, the little village west of Paris where the aged Dr. Franklin was living. Jefferson and Patsy were frequent guests at Auteuil and quickly came to love the house and its inhabitants.

Before Jefferson embarked on his official business, he located a school for Patsy and arranged to enroll her there. The school, called the Abbaye Royale de Panthemont, was considered the finest convent school in Paris. Mother Louise-Thérèse, the director of the school, was kind to Patsy, but the young girl couldn't bring herself to call her "Mother." She was lonely at first, but her father visited her for a while every day until her French improved. She knew very little French when she started, and the girls at school knew no English, so communication was almost impossible. In spite of this, she made friends quickly, and soon learned to chatter away in French. Her schoolmates began to call her "Jeffy," and she began to feel at home.

Immediately upon his arrival in Paris, Jefferson had gone to pay his respects to Benjamin Franklin. Now that Patsy was comfortably settled in school, he felt free to begin the work for which he had come to France. He, Franklin, and Adams, the triumvirate who had worked together in Philadelphia, reassembled and set to work to prepare the framework of new commercial relations between America and the Old World. Their

---

*Stays were a corset, stiffened with flexible bones, worn by women to shape and support the body.

objective was to negotiate as many treaties of friendship and commerce with European countries as they could.

The first meeting of the American ministers took place on August 30, 1784, amid a feeling of optimism. The three men were happy to be collaborators once again and confident that they would be successful in their negotiations. David Humphreys, the new commission's secretary, joined them.

🖎 Jefferson was a diligent and skillful diplomat, and he met many people through Franklin, but negotiating was a very slow process, and soon he was writing, "We do not find it easy to make commercial arrangements in Europe. There is a want of confidence in us."[2] He still found himself depressed much of the time. Paris winters are much more severe than Virginia winters, and he was disappointed by the gray Paris sky. It was many months before he could report a completely cloudless day—and Jefferson loved the sun. He longed for the red clay hills of Albemarle County and the view of the Blue Ridge Mountains from Monticello. And he was still mourning his Martha.

December found him ill and confined to his house for six weeks, and for some time afterward he remained "very weak and feeble," according to Abigail Adams.[3]

He looked forward eagerly to his friend Lafayette's anticipated return to France from America in January, but when Lafayette did come he brought devastating news: Little Lu had died in October. Jefferson's anguish can only be guessed at. His adored wife was gone, as well as four of their six children. Even his wife's little son, John Skelton, had died. All he had left were Patsy and Polly. "The sun of happiness [has] clouded over," he wrote, "never again to brighten." His gloom seemed to echo the wind and rain of Paris. He was ill for the rest of the winter.[4]

He wrote to Francis Eppes as soon as he was able, ending the letter: "Present me affectionately to Mrs. Eppes, who will kiss my dear, dear Polly for me. Oh! Could I do it myself!"[5] How he missed her! He knew, too, how Polly would suffer at the loss of her little sister, whom she called "my baby."

He didn't learn until May 1785 that the Eppeses had lost their own little Lucy at the same time. Both children had had whooping cough. Elizabeth Eppes had written to her brother-in-law immediately, but somehow it took almost seven months for her letter to arrive in Paris. "Life is scarcely supportable under such severe afflictions," she had written.[6]

When the sun finally began to shine again in March, and Jefferson could walk six to eight miles each day in the Bois de Boulogne, he began to feel a little better. He loved the sights and sounds of the country. The sun was always medicine for him. Now he resolved to have Polly come to him in France. He must keep what was left of his family together. He began planning her voyage immediately, but it would take two years to accomplish.

On May 2, 1785, Thomas Jefferson was notified of his election by Congress to succeed Benjamin Franklin as minister to the French court. Franklin had finally received the permission he had been requesting to retire and return home to America. At about the same time, John Adams was named minister to the court of St. James and began preparations to move to London.

Franklin's wit and learning, his wisdom and diplomacy, had won the hearts of the French people, and Jefferson had preferred to remain in the background during his first year in France. He deferred to the seniority and greater experience of his two colleagues, always asking their opinions first. Now he was on his own. He would be the only senior American statesman on the Continent to channel information between France and America and to influence the exchange of ideas.

Benjamin Franklin's network of well-placed friends was one of his most useful diplomatic and propaganda tools, and this became an important legacy for Thomas Jefferson. The Duke de La Rochefoucauld d'Enville, the Marquis de Condorcet, Georges-Louis comte de Buffon, and Antoine Lavoisier, France's most celebrated chemist, all became friends.

Jefferson had always had the utmost respect for Franklin and considered him the greatest American. Thus, Jefferson could say later, "On being presented to anyone as the minister of America, the common-place question used in such cases was, 'C'est vous, monsieur, qui remplace le Docteur Franklin?' ('It is you, sir, who replace Dr. Franklin?') I generally answered, 'No one can replace him, sir: I am only his successor.'"[7]

Immediately upon becoming minister to France, Jefferson, according to protocol, informed the French foreign minister, Charles Gravier, comte de Vergennes, of his appointment. It was Vergennes who had been the architect of the Franco-American alliance that had helped the colonies win the war with England.

Mr. Jefferson delivered a "letter of credence" to the king and, outfitted in full court dress, had his first official audience with Louis XVI, his beautiful queen, Marie Antoinette, and the royal family. But Thomas Jefferson was not impressed. He did not like the queen; he considered her unpredictable and devoted to pleasure and expense. And he knew that she was rumored to be unfaithful to the king. Of Louis XVI he said, he "loves business, economy, order and justice. He wishes sincerely the good of his people. He is irascible, rude and very limited in his understanding, religious bordering only on bigotry. He has no mistress, loves his queen and is too much governed by her."[8]

As was proper, Jefferson gave a dinner for about twenty people to celebrate his appointment. Among the guests were the Marquis de Lafayette and his lovely young wife, Adrienne. Her family, the Noailles, was one of the most powerful in France. Several other notable members of the French court, Commodore John Paul Jones, the courageous and daring naval hero of the American Revolution, and the Adams family were there as well. The outspoken Abigail Adams didn't like the etiquette of a French dinner party. The men, she complained, "rarely sit down before dinner, and often block the fireplace in the winter," shutting out all the fire from the ladies and leaving them very cold.[9]

Abigail Adams was the personification of New England pride and reserve, but she was captivated by Mr. Jefferson. This tall and engaging Virginian always had a funny story to tell or a witty observation to make. His fund of information on a multitude of topics was vast and stimulating. He was naturally courteous, his instinctive southern gallantry always evident. In a letter to her sister, Abigail described him as "one of the choice ones of the earth."[10]

The Marquis de Lafayette was a wealthy Frenchman who volunteered to serve in the Continental army. His friendship with Jefferson blossomed when Jefferson was in France. During the early stages of the French Revolution, Lafayette's moderate views enabled him to promote compromise between conflicting political factions. (Courtesy of Monticello/ Thomas Jefferson Foundation, Inc.)

While in France, Jefferson had been correcting and enlarging his *Notes on the State of Virginia.* Although he had submitted his answers to Marbois's queries in December 1781, he had continued to labor over a revision for three successive winters and had probably completed a fair-copy draft before leaving Monticello for France on October 16, 1783.[11]

Now he had two hundred copies printed privately, a few of which he shared with friends in Europe. The rest he sent to friends back in America: James Madison, James Monroe, and fellow members of the American Philosophical Society. Jefferson had been elected a member of the society in 1780. The oldest learned society in America, it was founded in Philadelphia in 1743 (the year of Jefferson's birth) by Benjamin Franklin to promote useful knowledge.

Jefferson was not interested in a large printing of the *Notes* for the public. He did hope that his book would be read by students at the College of William and Mary, in order to set them "into a useful train of thought."[12] But he was worried about having it circulated in America because of the sentiments he had expressed about slavery: "I have taken measures to prevent its publication. My reason is that I fear the terms in which I speak of slavery and of our constitution may produce an irritation which will revolt the minds of our countrymen against reformation in these two articles, and thus do more harm than good."[13]

Indeed, once Jefferson became a representative of the entire nation, not just his state of Virginia, he became virtually silent on the issue of slavery. In 1785 he told his friends in France not to expect him to participate actively in abolishing slavery in Virginia. Abolition was vital, he said, but he might impair his "usefulness"—"his ability to do good for his fellow men—by engaging in a futile and unpopular effort to hasten emancipation by governmental action."[14]

He wrote to a French friend Brissot de Warville: "You know that nobody wishes more ardently to see an abolition not only of the trade but of the condition of slavery. But . . . I am here as a public servant; and those whom I serve having not yet been able to give their voice against this practice, it is decent for me to avoid too public a demonstration of my wishes to see it abolished. Without serving the cause here, it might render me less able to serve it beyond the water."[15]

Yet, when a French bookseller got hold of a copy of his *Notes* and took it upon himself to print a bad French translation, and a well-known London printer asked Jefferson for permission to print the English original, he agreed. By so doing, Jefferson ensured that an authentic English edition, written in his own distinctive style, would be available. This would be published in London in 1787.

Suddenly, after the French publication, Jefferson's standing in the circle of men whose approval he valued most was enhanced. He was recognized as a man of science and letters, a representative of a free and reasonable society. To his own amazement, he was becoming a much-sought-after guest at the Paris salons.

Fashionable gatherings, known as salons, had been at the center of Parisian social and intellectual life since the latter part of the seventeenth century, and by the eighteenth century they had become centers of the Enlightenment. Here, the "salonnières," the cultivated women who founded the salons, brought together—on an equal footing—men of letters and men of power, and thereby transformed a social gathering for nobles into a serious working space where people of similar tastes and interests could exchange information and opinions on all manner of subjects.

The salonnières of the Enlightenment were intelligent, self-educated women who were reshaping the social forms of their day to meet their own social, intellectual, and educational needs. In an age when women did not have careers, the primary purpose of the salon was to give educated women a place to share ideas.[16]

Here in France, Jefferson, in addition to his role as a negotiator, could finally be the kind of person he wanted to be—a "detached philosopher," living a life of intellectual pursuits. He was entering the world of the French writers and philosophers whose works he had studied and drawn on when he wrote the Declaration of Independence. He had come face to face with the Enlightenment. The philosopher of the New World was confronting the Old World. He fell under its spell completely.

He was settling into his new routine and was expanding his circle of friends. But he remained homesick for America. Mail was exasperatingly slow—the packet of mail from New York came only once a month—and letters were often opened. He begged his friends for details, bits of information to help him stay in touch.

To Elizabeth Eppes he wrote, "Pray write to me, and write me long letters. . . . You always know facts enough which would be interesting to me to fill sheets of paper. I pray you, then, to give yourself up to that kind of inspiration, and to scribble on as long as you recollect any thing unmentioned, without regarding whether your lines are straight or your letters even."[17]

Most of all, he missed his little daughter. Now he stepped up plans to bring her to him.

Soon after his appointment as minister to France, Jefferson moved from the small house in which he had been living to a much grander one on the corner of the Champs-Elysées and the rue de Berri, called the Hôtel de Langeac. It was one of the most beautiful houses in Paris. Built in the latest fashion of former king Louis XV, it boasted a flush toilet. Jefferson remained there for the duration of his stay in France. William Short moved with him. Patsy came to spend every Sunday.

Jefferson immediately purchased "table furniture"—china, glass, table

Paris can be seen in the background of this view down the Champs-Elysées through the Grille de Chaillot. Thomas Jefferson's house, the Hôtel de Langeac, was on the left at the near corner. (Courtesy of the Bibliothèque nationale de France)

linen, silver, plated ware, lamps, and household utensils—and, captivated as he had become by French cuisine, found a good French cook named Adrien Petit, who, as *maître d'hôtel*, ran the house under Jefferson's meticulous supervision. Petit oversaw the kitchens, the wine cellar, and the stables, handled all household accounts, and directed the other servants.[18]

As a foreign diplomat, Jefferson was obliged to entertain graciously, and he felt justified in these expenses. But he soon found himself employing many more servants than he had anticipated. "It is the policy of this country to oblige you to a certain number of servants, and one will not touch what belongs to the business of another," Abigail Adams explained it.[19]

The allowance paid to the minister by the American government was totally inadequate for this kind of living, and Jefferson found himself in an awkward position. He couldn't afford the expense himself, and Congress was not prepared to deal with the issue. Abigail sympathized with him: "It would take two years of an American minister's salary to furnish the equipage of plate which you will find upon the tables of all the foreign ministers here," she wrote from England.[20]

Troubled by the situation, Jefferson wrote to his friend James Monroe in America and asked him to intercede for him with Congress. All the ministers who had come to Europe before Jefferson had come at a time when all expenses were paid and a sum allowed in addition for their time. Congress was no longer doing this, and Jefferson had spent almost a thousand guineas* of his own money, for which he was in debt. He asked nothing for his time, he told his friend, but thought his expenses should be paid. He did caution Monroe: "I pray you to touch this string, which I know to be a tender one with Congress, with the utmost delicacy. I had rather be ruined in my fortune, than in their esteem."[21]

Jefferson's role was developing into something quite different from what Congress had originally envisioned. The triumvirate who had set to work in the summer of 1784 was no longer together, and Jefferson's job was far more encompassing than had been anticipated. The outspoken defender of republican simplicity had become a member of a highly sophisticated society.

In 1782 his friend the Marquis de Chastellux had said of him that he was a man who "loves the world only insofar as he can feel that he is useful." Now, in Paris in 1786, Jefferson saw an opportunity to become more useful to the world. He would promote cultural relations between America and France by sending home examples of everything that was new, practical, and beautiful, examples that many of his countrymen had heard about but never seen.

The Paris of Louis XVI was bursting with creative energy in every branch of art, and in the midst of his many diplomatic duties, Thomas Jefferson managed to find time to indulge his appetite for all of it. He visited the many art galleries, exhibitions, and shops, purchasing works of art as he went. He rummaged in the bookstalls; he walked beside the river Seine or strolled under the fragrant foliage of the Bois de Boulogne with newfound friends. He shopped for his family and friends in America.

To his little Polly he sent "sashes" and Parisian dolls. To Peter Carr, the most brilliant of Dabney's children, he sent books and offered advice

---

*British coin worth one pound and one shilling (about $1.84 today).

and guidance in letters. He still felt, as he had in 1769, that "the only help a youth wants is to be directed what books to read, and in what order to read them."[22]

Jefferson "panted after the arts," his cousin Edmund Randolph would write of him many years later. The "vaunted scene of Europe," as Jefferson had described it, with its rich texture of art, architecture, and antiquity, absorbed his critical eye and finely tuned curiosity.[23] For the first time, he was meeting major artists with international reputations, visiting them in their studios and watching them work. He began to collect art and books to send home to Monticello. Monticello would reflect his Enlightenment ideals.

Before he left Monticello for France, he had been commissioned by Congress to have a marble statue made of George Washington. He was to choose "the most masterly hand" to undertake the assignment.[24] Now he arranged to have Jean-Antoine Houdon, a warm, generous, and affable man, whose reputation as a sculptor, Jefferson assured his fellow Americans, was unrivaled in Europe, undertake the task. In order to ensure that he could execute an exact likeness, Houdon made the long voyage to America to see Washington for himself, rather than relying on a portrait by Charles Willson Peale that Jefferson had brought with him. Jefferson was involved in all the planning, until the sculpture was finally completed in France and then sent home to be erected in Richmond, Virginia.

Jefferson sent books and wine to George Washington, James Monroe, and James Madison. For Madison he also purchased Diderot's new *Encyclopédie méthodique.* Denis Diderot, a French philosopher and man of letters, was editor in chief of the *Encyclopédie,* one of the principal literary monuments of the French Enlightenment. As the first encyclopedia to bring together the great minds of the time, it would have an enormous influence on the whole of Europe.

Their shared love of books was one of the powerful bonds between Jefferson and Madison. Madison reciprocated his friend's generosity by sending long, informative letters that kept him in touch with political developments in America.

Soon word came that Virginia had approved his Bill for Religious

Freedom on January 22, 1786. Madison, he felt certain, had worked hard to win the necessary votes to accomplish this. He wrote to his friend: "The Virginia Act for Religious Freedom has been received with infinite approbation in Europe and propagated with enthusiasm. . . . It has been translated into French and Italian, has been sent to most of the courts of Europe. . . . It is inserted in the new *Encyclopédie*."[25] His pride was evident.

⟋❧ 23 ❧⟍

# Dialogue between the Head and the Heart

Early in March of 1786, Jefferson received a letter from John Adams indicating that he thought that England might be ready to negotiate a commercial treaty with America. The wealth of the new nation depended on the growth of foreign trade, and it was essential to widen American markets.

Jefferson immediately rushed to England, only to realize that his friend had been far too optimistic. The two men were kept waiting endlessly and were treated rudely. When they were finally introduced to George III at Buckingham Palace, the king, in full view of surrounding courtiers, abruptly turned his back on the author of the Declaration of Independence without saying a word. Jefferson would never forget this insolence, and he had negative feelings toward England from then on.

He determined, though, not to waste this opportunity to see some of the country, so he and Adams toured together. Jefferson was particularly smitten with English gardening, and he took careful notes to aid him later in planning and maintaining an English garden at Monticello.

While in England, he had a model made of a polygraph, a portable copying machine that he had found in France. From that time on, he made copies of all his private letters and carefully and methodically preserved them as well as all his personal papers. Many years later, when he was an old man, a gentleman called on him to inquire about a lawsuit in which the man's father had been involved—nearly half a century before. Jefferson walked to a case, removed a batch of ancient papers from a cubbyhole, and in less that one minute produced the desired document.

⁓ This visit to London gave Jefferson an opportunity to strengthen his ties to the Adams family. And it was through the Adamses that he met a group of American artists who had moved to England. The group included the painters Mather Brown, Benjamin West, and John Singleton Copley. Now Jefferson sat for his portrait for the first time. It was painted by Mather Brown, whom Jefferson also commissioned to paint a portrait of John Adams. Jefferson would add these portraits to his collection of what he termed his "American worthies," hanging in his gallery at the Hôtel de Langeac. Brown, a native of Boston, was then a twenty-four-year-old student of the highly regarded artist Benjamin West.

While Mather Brown's painting is the first portrait of Thomas Jefferson, it is also, arguably, the most artificial, for it depicts him as a man of fashion. This was deliberate. Jefferson was demonstrating his awareness of the relationship between fashion and French politics. Jefferson liked the new freedom of dress he saw in the crowded Parisian art galleries and recognized its significance: "In society the *habit habillé* [dress coat] is almost banished, and they begin to go even to great suppers in frock [casual coat]: the court and diplomatic corps however must always be excepted. They are too high to be reached by improvement. They are the last refuge from which etiquette, formality and folly will be driven," he wrote to David Humphreys, the secretary of the American commission.[1]

Now he collaborated with Brown to create an image of an American who understood how important it was that, "as a minister to the French court, [he] achieve an ambassadorial appearance . . . yet at the same time not belie the ideals of an emerging nation that embraced the concept of republican simplicity." His carefully dressed and powdered hair, as well as his clothing, gives the painting an air of refinement. He would dignify the new American nation and ensure its credibility.[2]

Among the American artists to whom John Adams introduced Thomas Jefferson was the slender, black-eyed, and black-haired John

Trumbull, a dreamy young painter who had known Adams in Massachusetts. Thirteen years younger than Jefferson, Trumbull was the son of Governor Jonathan Trumbull of Connecticut, the only royal governor to embrace the patriot cause. The young Trumbull had come to London to study painting under Benjamin West. It was John Trumbull who introduced Jefferson to a lovely young woman who would, quite literally, sweep him off his feet.

When Jefferson returned to Paris from London in May, he had just turned forty-three, and he was a very lonely man. Martha had been gone for almost four years, Patsy was happily ensconced in school, and Polly was resisting her father's attempts to lure her to France. Until now there had been no hint of romance in his life. But at this time he was more vulnerable to an emotional attachment than he had been since Martha's death.

He always made friends slowly, and the pattern did not change in France. Gradually, though, he drew around himself a small circle of close friends, artistic men and women with whom he shared an enjoyment of all the arts that Paris had to offer—painting, architecture, plays, and concerts.

Jefferson particularly liked being part of the circle of friends and family of Lafayette and his delightful wife, Adrienne, as well as her aunt, Madame de Tessé, another member of the great Noailles family. Just two years older than Jefferson, she was young enough for Lafayette to call her his cousin. Madame de Tessé shared Jefferson's passion for freedom, as well as his love of the arts, particularly architecture and landscape gardening. Jefferson enjoyed talking with her and dined with the Tessés at least once a week. In fact, he formed a number of friendships in Paris with women who were attractive, intelligent, emancipated, and sophisticated. These became long-lasting attachments based on mutual interests and respect. Three of these women were among the most beautiful of their time. All were married.

He spent much time with the very lovely Angelica Schuyler Church, sister-in-law of Alexander Hamilton. She had grown up in New England, and at the age of eighteen had eloped with an Englishman, now a member of Parliament. Her friend Madame de Corny was young, witty, extremely pretty—and married to a man much older than she. Madame de Corny appreciated the company of the chivalrous Jefferson when her husband was away. She and Jefferson often took tea together or walked in the Bois de Boulogne, but she complained that he was too polite and too respectful. When she left Paris for a visit to England with her husband, she said she wanted to smuggle her devoted admirer in her pocket.

This was a time when women were still regarded as ornaments of society, and gallantry was in order. This Jefferson could practice to the ultimate. He liked women who were accomplished yet gentle, and objected to the idleness and dissipation of many of the ladies of the French upper class. He was particularly disturbed because he saw France as a land where marital fidelity was "an ungentlemanly practice." And as much as he admired intelligent women, he wrote to Angelica Church that the "tender breasts of ladies were not formed for political convulsion, and the French ladies miscalculate much their own happiness when they wander from the true field of their influence into that of politicks."[3]

In America, he said in another letter, this one to Mrs. Anne Bingham, a vivacious beauty half Jefferson's age, women knew their place, and were "too wise to wrinkle their foreheads with politics. They are contented to soothe and calm the minds of their husbands returning ruffled from political debate. They have the good sense to value domestic happiness above all other." They did not, as some Parisian women did, search for happiness outside their homes, "forgetting that they have left it behind in their nurseries."[4]

Mrs. Bingham, however, was quick to reply that French women "are more accomplished, and understand the Intercourse of society better than [women in] any other country." Describing the growing spirit of equality that these women were asserting, she wrote to Jefferson, "In what other Country can be found a [young and beautiful woman] who takes a lead in all fashionable Dissipation of Life, and at more serious moments collects at her House an assembly of the Literati, whom she charms with her Knowledge and her bel Esprit. The women of France interfere in the politics of the Country, and often give a decided Turn to the Fate of empires. . . . they have obtained that Rank and Consideration in society, which the Sex is intitled to, and which they in vain contend for in other Countries."[5]

Thomas Jefferson, for all his strictures about women and politics, enjoyed the company of these accomplished women. Their sympathetic manners, intellectual independence, and their passion for music, art, and architecture gave the lonely widower the emotional and intellectual support he craved, and they, in turn, found him irresistible.

To Madame de Tessé he would write from America in 1803, "[T]he friendship with which you honored me in Paris was among the circumstances which most contributed to my happiness there."[6]

Before he left London in May, Jefferson had invited John Trumbull to "come to Paris, to see and study the fine works there, and," as Trumbull put it years later, "to make his house my home, during my stay."[7] Jefferson was impressed by Trumbull's patriotic plan to paint some of the great scenes of the American Revolution. By giving the artist room and board, Jefferson was making a gesture that was without precedent: he was undertaking an act of patronage on behalf of his government.[8]

Trumbull accepted both in 1786 and in 1787. Soon after Trumbull arrived the second time, in August 1787, Jefferson sat for his portrait as part of Trumbull's painting *Signing of the Declaration*. It was Jefferson who suggested the subject, describing the scene in minute detail to the artist, even drawing a diagram from memory. Trumbull enthusiastically agreed. The scene actually portrayed was the meeting of June 28, when the committee named to draw up the document presented Jefferson's unedited draft to John Hancock, president of the Continental Congress.

This portrait of Jefferson is considered the most sensitive of all the Jefferson portraits. "In the eyes and in the aspect of the face, the artist has caught the visionary that was Jefferson at this period of his life."[9] It is considered a far better likeness than Mather Brown's painting.

Among the artists in Paris when Trumbull arrived were Mr. and Mrs. Richard Cosway, who had recently arrived from London. Richard Cosway was about Jefferson's age and the most popular miniature painter of his day—at a time when the miniature was a prized form of art. He was an extremely short man who was said to have a face like a monkey. He

A detail of the painting *Declaration of Independence,* by John Trumbull, showing, from the left, John Adams, Roger Sherman, Robert Livingston, Thomas Jefferson, and Benjamin Franklin presenting the document to John Hancock. (Courtesy of the National Archives)

was pompous and vain, and his elaborate dress—he wore a mulberry silk coat ornamented with strawberries—made him an easy target for caricature and satire. But the public liked his work, and he had amassed a fortune.

Cosway was married to the beautiful and talented Maria Hadfield, a twenty-seven-year-old artist in her own right. Maria was slim and graceful, with a mass of curly blonde hair, deep blue eyes, fair skin, and "modesty, beauty, and that softness of disposition which is the ornament of her sex and the charm of ours," as Jefferson described her.[10] Maria spoke many languages, but liked Italian best. She had been born in Italy of English parents and spoke English with a beguiling accent. She was the essence of femininity.

Maria's marriage to Richard Cosway had been orchestrated by her mother as a "marriage of convenience." Maria was a devout Catholic and had wanted to become a nun, but her mother had prevented it and arranged a match with Cosway. Now, after only five years of married life, Cosway was beginning to treat his wife callously. He flirted outrageously with the ladies who came to his salon, and he had had several flagrant

The beautiful Maria Cosway, whom Jefferson met in Paris, in a miniature painted by her husband, Richard Cosway. Jefferson's days with Maria, he told her, were "filled to the brim with happiness." (Courtesy of the Print Collection, Miriam and Ira D. Wallach Division of Art, Prints and Photographs, The New York Public Library, Astor, Lenox and Tilden Foundations)

affairs. Maria had tried hard in the first years of their marriage to please her husband, but she was aware that he was being unfaithful to her. She had come to fear and detest him. But she loved the world that Richard Cosway's success made possible for her and recognized her financial dependence on him.

The Cosways lived extravagantly and entertained lavishly. They numbered among their friends many of the English nobility. The Prince of Wales was rumored to have been intrigued by the lovely Maria.

Wishing to introduce the Cosways to Jefferson, Trumbull invited them and some friends to the Halle aux Bleds, the new, big, noisy Paris grain market where Jefferson had hoped to get some architectural ideas for a public market to be built in Richmond, Virginia. The most notable feature of the Halle aux Bleds was its giant dome. It resembled an inverted glass bowl, its sections held together with wood-ribbed framing, thus permitting light to flood the interior.

That day, when Jefferson first saw it, he was impressed by the "noble dome," but he was far more impressed by Mrs. Cosway. In fact, he was so distracted by her that, in order to get out of a dinner appointment that evening, he sent a note making up an excuse of pressing diplomatic business. Then this normally proper man went instead to the lovely park of St. Cloud, with its deep shaded lanes and its cascades tumbling from marble fountains toward the Seine, for dinner with his lively companions. When he learned that Maria was as accomplished in music as she was in painting (she sang, played the harp, and composed music), he arranged to end the memorable day with a visit to the renowned composer and teacher of the harp Johann Baptiste Krumpholz. Krumpholz's wife, Julie, a fine harpist herself, entertained them to a late hour. Reflecting on it later, Jefferson compared it to a long "Lapland summer day," filled to the brim with happiness.[11]

For the next month Thomas Jefferson and Maria Cosway were together every day. She had captivated him completely. It was one of the few instances in his life in which Jefferson broke through his natural reserve.

It seems likely that Trumbull accompanied them some of the time, but he left Paris for Germany at the beginning of September, and Richard Cosway, having work to complete, was content to leave his pretty wife on her own. Alone or in a "charming coterie,"[12] as Jefferson later described it, he and Maria saw something beautiful in Paris every day. And each day they had either breakfast or dinner together.

There were unforgettable days in their favorite haunts, and they were incredibly happy together. He was playing with fire, he knew, but he

The Halle aux Bleds, drawn by J.-B. Marechal, 1786, the noisy grain market in Paris whose dome so captured Jefferson's imagination. (Courtesy of the Bibliothèque nationale de France)

was happy and he didn't care. It was a golden September, and Thomas Jefferson had fallen in love.

For Jefferson, Maria was art and music and the embodiment of loveliness. She was bright and sensitive, although somewhat immature. Some of their friends called her a flirt, spoiled and self-centered, but to Jefferson she was charming and talented. For the first time since Martha had died, he felt carefree and alive. For a short while, he was young again.

Then, on September 18, while strolling together along the Seine on one of their daily outings, Jefferson, in a joyous mood, jumped over a low fence, caught his foot, and crashed to the ground. Attempting to break his fall with his right hand, he succeeded only in breaking his wrist.

He tried to keep the results of his mishap from Maria, holding the injured arm in his left hand until he had delivered her to her home. Returning to his own house, he summoned a surgeon, but the wrist was not set properly and was never to heal completely. Two years later the hand

Thomas Jefferson in Paris, by John Trumbull, 1788. (Courtesy of the White House Historical Association, White House Collection)

would still be withered, with swollen and crooked fingers. It stiffened seriously as he began to grow old and continued to cause him much pain,
making it difficult, if not impossible, to play his beloved violin. Now he
remained in excruciating pain, confined to his house for several weeks.

When word of the accident finally reached Maria, she sent a note,
with many little excuses: "I meant to have seen you twice. . . . Though
we were near your house, coming to see you, we were obliged to come
back, the time being much past that we were to be at St. Cloud, to dine
with the Duchess of Kingston." Then she added, "Oh I wish you was
well enough to come to us tomorrow to dinner and stay the evening. . . .
I would serve you, and help you at dinner, and divert your pain after with
good musik."[13] But Jefferson was unable to venture out of the house. He
was unable to be with Maria. And he was unable to write.

A few weeks later, on October 4, Jefferson learned that the Cosways
were planning to leave Paris the next day. Richard Cosway had completed his commissions in Paris and was eager to go to Antwerp to visit
the galleries there. Jefferson had to see Maria. So he attempted one last
excursion together. But as their carriage rattled over the pavement, his
shattered wrist, set badly in the first place, was shaken up even more.

"I have passed the night in so much pain that I have not closed my
eyes," he wrote laboriously to Maria with his left hand the next morning.[14] Plans to see her off that morning would have to be abandoned. He
had summoned another surgeon.

This time Maria replied promptly, blaming herself for having been
the cause of his pain. "Why would you go, and why was I not more
friendly to you, and less so to myself by preventing your giving me the
pleasure of your company? You repeatedly said it would do you no
harm. I felt interested and did not resist."[15] She went on to speak of him
as "unusually obliging." She would remember with "exquisite pleasure"
the charming days they had spent together and would long for the
spring, when she hoped to return to Paris. Meanwhile, would he send
her a line to Antwerp with news of his wrist?

The letter was more than he could bear. How could he wait for the
spring to see her again? He canceled the surgeon, got out of bed, hired
a carriage, and accompanied the Cosways to the post house at Saint-
Denis. There he provided dinner for them. Then, "having performed

the last sad office of handing you into your carriage . . . and seen the wheels get actually into motion, I turned on my heel and walked, more dead than alive," to his waiting carriage and was taken home.[16]

Three weeks later he wrote to a friend, "How the right hand became disabled would be a long story for the left to tell. It was by one of those follies from which good cannot come, but ill may."[17]

Soon reason began to triumph over passion. His head told him that it was folly for a man of forty-three, who had always before held himself in check, to give way now to amorous emotions. The way back could be hard to find.

So, "Seated by my fireside, solitary and sad," he wrote—painstakingly with his left hand—one of the most amazing love letters ever penned, "Dialogue Between the Head and the Heart." He called it a "history of the evening I parted from you." One of his biographers has called it "one of the most unusual tributes ever paid a pretty woman by a distinguished man."[18] It is, in fact, a rare insight into the emotions of this otherwise very private man, and reveals his need to convey to Maria some sense of his past, of his feelings, of himself. Perhaps, too, it was his way of sorting out his own turbulent emotions.

The letter, written in the form of a conversation between his head and his heart, the realist and the romantic, began with his heart telling his head, "I am, indeed, the most wretched of all earthly beings," and concluded by begging Maria to write to him: "If your letters are as long as the Bible, they will appear short to me. Only let them be brimful of affection." He goes on to tell her, "my health is good, except my wrist, which heals slowly, and my mind which mends not at all, but broods constantly over your departure."[19]

Jefferson sent the twelve-page letter, along with a love song by Sacchini, a prominent Italian composer of opera, that he had promised her. "Bring me in return its subject, Jours heureux [Happy days]!" he pleaded. He entrusted the packet to John Trumbull, who was to meet the Cosways in Antwerp and could be counted on to deliver it personally to Maria. He would carry most of their correspondence back and forth between them in order to avoid the prying eyes of the London and Paris post offices and of Mr. Cosway.

On Christmas Eve Jefferson sat by his fire and wrote another long letter to Maria: "If I cannot be with you in reality, I will be in imagination," he began. He wondered if she meant to disappoint him by not returning in the spring, as she had promised. But he could not live without hope. He ended, "Think of me much and warmly. Place me in your breast with those who love you most and comfort me with your letters."[20]

Maria wrote to him of her friends, of the gloomy London weather, of her own melancholy mood. She was painting all day, she told him, and playing music in the evenings. Her letters were *not* "brimful of affection," as he had requested. Certainly, they were not the letters of adoration he was writing to her. Gradually the correspondence lessened, and he began to plan a trip to the south of France to see firsthand the commercial seaport cities, inspect the agricultural regions of southern France and northern Italy, and try the healing effects of the mineral springs in Aix-en-Provence recommended for his wrist by his doctors. And, he hoped, he would forget the pain of his separation from Maria. His head would win over his heart.

But he would not leave until after he had attended the opening of the Assembly of Notables on February 22, 1787, which was delayed because of the death of Vergennes. Louis XVI had convened the group, made up of 144 nobles, both clergy and aristocrats handpicked by the king and his new finance minister, Charles-Alexandre de Calonne. The meeting was made necessary by the sad plight of the royal treasury. The French government was almost bankrupt. France was facing a financial crisis, and to resolve it, taxes had to be imposed on the church and the aristocracy. Until now taxes had been paid only by the poor, especially the peasants, and the middle class, the bourgeoisie: doctors, lawyers, merchants, manufacturers, and shopkeepers. Nobles and priests did not pay taxes. The king explained his purpose: "Gentlemen . . . my plans are far-reaching and important. I intend to relieve the people, increase tax revenue and diminish obstacles to trade."[21]

The Assembly of Notables opposed his plan, claiming that only the Estates General—an advisory body of representatives, similar to a parliament—could consent to new taxes. Representatives of the Estates General included members from all three estates: the clergy, the nobility, or great landowners, and the rest of the people. It was an ancient

institution, established before the development of the absolute monarchy, and had not met for 175 years. But the king understood that by calling the Estates General he would be relinquishing his own power. This
he refused to do.

Neither Thomas Jefferson nor anybody else recognized at the time
that they were witnessing the prelude to the French Revolution, a complicated series of happenings that would be spread over a period of ten
years, from 1789 to 1799, and would come to be considered one of the
most important events in European history. The Revolution would
strike at the traditional authority of kings, priests, and noblemen and
would spawn a worldwide movement toward the ideals of liberty and
equality.

Jefferson, for his part, advocated reformation in France rather than
revolution. He favored the rule of reason, not of force. Yet he hoped that
the spirit of resistance would never die.

It was at about this time that Jefferson learned of Shays's Rebellion in
his own country. In November 1786 a group of farmers and debtors in
western Massachusetts rose up against their creditors. Impoverished
back-country farmers, many of them Revolutionary War veterans, were
losing their farms through mortgage foreclosures and tax delinquencies.
Under the leadership of Daniel Shays they took up their muskets and
rebelled.

While Jefferson never condoned their use of force, the incident
helped crystallize his feelings about government. He came to see insur-
rection as an example of the need for expressions of discontent in a free
society. He articulated this in a letter to James Madison: "I hold it that
a little rebellion now and then is a good thing, and as necessary in the
political world as storms in the physical. . . . It is a medicine necessary
for the sound health of government."[22]

One week later, referring again to Shays's Rebellion in a private letter to Abigail Adams, he wrote, "The spirit of resistance to government
is so valuable on certain occasions, that I wish it to be always kept alive.
It will often be exercised when wrong, but better so than not to be exercised at all. I like a little rebellion now and then. It is like a storm in the
Atmosphere."[23] There was less need to punish the insurgents, he felt,
than to draw the proper lessons from the incident. Traditional American freedom, even though it occasionally manifested itself in violence,

was infinitely preferable to European tyranny. He had an unshakable faith in the right of men to govern themselves.[24]

⟨❧ 24 ❧⟩

# Changing the Shape of His Country

JEFFERSON SET OUT ALONE for the south of France on the last day of February 1787. After the wind and rain of Paris, he was looking forward to the warm blue skies of southern France and Italy. He had even left his servants at home in the hope that he would have no distractions and time to reflect quietly on all he saw.

He was enchanted with the French countryside. In Bordeaux, he made a thorough study of the wines and the vineyards. His experienced eye missed nothing. The rich fields reminded him of his own Virginia. But when he saw fields planted with clover, flax, and grain—in contrast to the tobacco planted in Virginia, which wears out the soil—he took careful notes. He was impressed by the French plan of crop rotation. He was always the questioning tourist, eager to learn what he could to bring back to his country. He talked to all the farmers he encountered, and in a letter to Lafayette, after telling him that he often wished his friend were with him, Jefferson recommended that Lafayette do the same. But, he wrote to him, "To do it most effectively you must be absolutely incognito. You must ferret the people out of their hovels, as I have done, look into their kettles, eat their bread, loll on their beds under pretense of resting yourself, but in fact to find out if they are soft." This knowledge could then be used to improve the lot of the common people by "the softening of their beds, or the throwing a morsel of meat into their kettle of vegetables."[1] On this trip he reaffirmed his belief that those who labor in the earth are God's chosen people, and that tillers of the soil have an instinct for order and justice.

Jefferson had long dreamed of visiting "the classic ground" of Europe and experiencing with his own eyes the remains of antiquity in their "purist form," rather than simply seeing them in books. Seven years before, when he had been governor of Virginia, his imagination had been fired by a picture of the Maison Carrée (Square House), a Roman temple in Nîmes, France, "the most beautiful and precious morsel of architecture left us by antiquity," he described it.[2] He had resolved, then, that Virginia's new state capitol in Richmond must be based on it. Since this would be the first building in the new nation designed exclusively to serve a republican form of government, he hoped that it might introduce a simple and pure style of architecture into American buildings.

Now he was in Nîmes, "immersed in antiquities from morning to night," and he could write to his friend Madame de Tessé, who shared his love of architecture, "Here I am, Madame, gazing whole hours at the Maison Carrée like a lover at his mistress." He described it as "simple and sublime . . . noble beyond expression."[3]

Soon he sent home to America plans for an adaptation of the building that he, with the help of the architect Charles-Louis Clérisseau, another Paris friend, had drawn. He described his feelings in a letter to his friend James Madison. It was essential, he told him, to establish "useful, noble" models: "But how is a taste in this beautiful art [architecture] to be formed in our countrymen, unless we avail ourselves of every occasion when public buildings are to be erected of presenting to them models for their study and imitation? . . . You see I am an enthusiast on the subject of the arts. But it is an enthusiasm of which I am not ashamed, as its object is to improve the taste of my countrymen, to increase their reputation, to reconcile to them the respect of the world, and procure them its praise."[4]

Once again, in architecture as he had in politics, Thomas Jefferson was changing the shape of his country.

From Nîmes Jefferson went on to Aix-en-Provence to try the waters there, noting carefully in his book that the temperature at the spout was ninety degrees Fahrenheit. The waters did not have the hoped-for healing results, and his wrist remained the same. But the sun was shining brightly, and his spirits were beginning to improve. After four days he left for Marseilles to see firsthand this seaport city and to attempt to further the commercial interests of his country. He found Marseilles "a charming" place, "all life and activity." In a playful letter to Madame de Tott, he described "the sounds of a Provencal city: the tinkling of the

The Maison Carrée in Nîmes, France, "the most perfect and precious remain of antiquity in existence." Jefferson said of it that he gazed at it for whole hours, "like a lover at his mistress." (From the collection of the author)

The Virginia State Capitol at Richmond, designed by Jefferson and modeled on the Maison Carrée. (Courtesy of the Library of Virginia)

bells on the mules, the braying of 300 asses, and the squabbling of 4,351 market women."[5]

When he crossed into Italy and saw the machines used there for cleaning rice, he determined that there was little difference between the Italian machines and those used in his own country. Thus the difference in taste must lie in the rice seed itself. So he hired a man named Poggio, a muleteer, to smuggle a sack of rough rice out of Italy for him—a practice punishable by death—and also filled his own coat pockets with as much rice as they could hold. When the muleteer and the diplomat met, safely, in Genoa, Jefferson sent the samples of the rice seed to South Carolina and Georgia so that planters there might experiment with it. Everywhere he was concerned with what might benefit American agriculture.[6]

Before leaving Paris, Jefferson had spent time with Patsy, then fifteen, and had promised to write her long letters every week. He used these to lecture her about the need for industry and activity. When Patsy wrote that she was having difficulty with her Latin, her father replied, "We are always equal to what we undertake with resolution." He went on to tell her, "Nobody in this world can make me so happy, or so miserable, as you. . . . Be industrious then, my dear child. Think nothing insurmountable by resolution and application, and you will be all that I wish you to be."[7]

Good-naturedly, Patsy responded by telling her father, "I am not so industrious as you or I would wish, but I hope that in taking pains I soon shall be. I have already begun to study more . . . for what I hold most precious is your satisfaction, indeed I should be miserable without it. You wrote me a long letter, as I asked you, it would have been much more so without so wide a margin."[8]

In another letter Jefferson couldn't refrain from offering Patsy more advice: "Determine never to be idle. No person will have occasion to complain of the want of time who never loses any. It is wonderful how much may be done if we are always doing."[9] Patsy well knew that her father practiced what he preached.

Jefferson had originally gone to the south of France in part to forget Maria Cosway. But when he returned to Paris in early June and discovered that she had not come as planned, he wrote to her of his trip: "Why were you not with me? So many enchanting scenes that wanted only your pencil to consecrate them to fame." If she was not coming back, he lamented, "What did you ever come for? Only to make people miserable at losing you?"[10]

Maria did return to Paris in August—without her husband—but she stayed in a remote section of the city and surrounded herself with an entourage that made it impossible for Jefferson to spend time with her alone. Childlike and spoiled, she was probably unable to comprehend the depth of his feeling for her.

Early in December, on the eve of her planned departure for England, Maria invited Jefferson to have breakfast with her the next morning to say good-bye. But when he arrived, Maria had already left. She had sent him a note the evening before, shortly after offering the invitation, which did not reach him in time.

"I cannot breakfast with you tomorrow," she had written. "To bid you adieu once is sufficiently painful, for I leave you with very melancholy ideas." Jefferson replied: "I went to breakfast with you according to promise, and you had gone off at 5 o'clock in the morning. This spared me, indeed, the pain of parting, but it deprives me of the comfort of recollecting that pain."[11]

Eight months later, when he was about to return home, he wrote to her, "I am going to America, and you to Italy. One of us is going the wrong way, for the way will ever be wrong which leads us farther apart."[12]

He never stopped hoping that she would someday come to America, where he could show her beautiful scenes of his country, "scenes worthy of your pencil."[13] She never came, and they never met again. The mood of gaiety and abandon that he had initially captured with her did not return, and his letters to her eventually became more restrained. His passion turned to tenderness. His head was now fully in control of his heart.

<br>

### ❧ 25 ☙

# "She Must Come"

BY THE SUMMER OF 1785 Jefferson had determined that Polly, now nine years old, must come to him, and in August he had set down in a letter to Francis Eppes the arrangements he felt it necessary to make.

First, he stipulated that Polly should travel in a good vessel sailing from Virginia in April, May, June, or July only. She must not sail at the time of the equinoxes, the time of violent storms.

The boat should have made at least one voyage, he told his brother-in-law, but must not be more than four or five years old. All vessels lost at sea, he explained, are either on their first voyage or are more than five years old. He suggested also that Polly be entrusted to the care of "some good lady passing from America to France, or even England, . . . who has had the smallpox." Fearing that the person who accompanied Polly might catch—and spread—a potentially fatal disease, Jefferson recommended that "a careful Negro woman, as Isabel, [be sent] if she has had the smallpox." He ended his letter with "kisses for dear Poll, who hangs on my mind night and day."[1]

Pirates were another ever present threat to American ships, and Jefferson worried about that also. His anxiety about her safety was that of a father *and* a mother:

> No event of your life has put it into your power to conceive how I feel when I reflect that such a child, and so dear to me, is to cross the ocean, and is to be exposed to all the sufferings and risks, great and small, to which a situation on board a ship exposes everyone. I drop my pen at the thought—but she must come. My affections have me balanced between the desire to have her with me, and the fear of exposing her; but my reason tells me the dangers are not great, and the advantages to her will be considerable.[2]

From the time just after his arrival in Paris, when he had first learned of the death of "Little Lu" and had resolved to have Polly come to France, Jefferson had been trying to convince her to make the journey. But he hadn't reckoned with the little girl's determination to remain with the aunt and uncle who had shown her unconditional love and affection. He wrote to her,

> I wish so much to see you, that I have desired your uncle and aunt to send you to me. I know, my dear Polly, how sorry you will be, and ought to be, to leave them and your cousins: but your sister and myself cannot live

without you, and after a while we will carry you back again to see your friends in Virginia. In the mean time, you shall be taught here to play on the harpsichord, to draw, to dance, to read and talk French, and such other things as will make you more worthy of the love of your friends; but above all things, by our care and love of you, we will teach you to love us more than you will do if you stay so far from us. . . . when you come here you shall have as many dolls and playthings as you want for yourself, or to send to your cousins whenever you shall have opportunities. . . . We shall hope to have you with us next summer, to find you a very good little girl, and to assure you the trust of our affection for you. Adieu my dear child.

Yours affectionately, Th. Jefferson[3]

Polly, living happily at Eppington with her loving aunt, uncle, and cousins, was reluctant to leave the only mother she had ever really known and the comfort of their sprawling white frame house to cross the ocean alone to be with the father and sister about whom she knew very little. She wrote back:

Dear papa—I want to see you and sister Patsy, but you must come to Uncle Eppes house.
Polly Jefferson[4]

And then she wrote:

Dear Papa—I long to see you, and hope that you and sister Patsy are well; give my love to her and tell her that I long to see her, and hope that you and she will come very soon to see us. I hope that you will send me a doll. I am very sorry that you have sent for me. I don't want to go to France, I had rather stay with Aunt Eppes. Aunt Carr, Aunt Nancy and cousin Polly Carr are here. Your most happy and dutiful daughter.
Polly Jefferson

It was going to be very difficult, Jefferson saw, to lure this child to France. And the Eppeses were no more eager to let her go than Polly was to leave them. They had grown to love her as their own and were still clinging to the hope that her father would change his mind.

Sensitively, tactfully, Jefferson appealed to them, stressing the "importance to the future happiness of the child that she should neither forget nor be forgotten by her sister and myself."[5]

Eventually, Francis Eppes devised a plan whereby Polly was tricked into going. A party was planned aboard a ship that was tied up at the dock at Eppington, to which Polly and her young cousins were invited. The children played together on the decks and in the cabins until Polly began to feel comfortable on the vessel. When she finally curled up in a corner and fell asleep after all the games and good food, the others crept away, leaving Polly in the charge of Andrew Ramsay, captain of the vessel. Aunty Eppes and her favorite cousin, Jack Eppes, were the last to tear themselves away.

Tucked in with her belongings was a note to her father from her anxious aunt: "This will, I hope, be handed you by my dear Polly, who I most ardently wish may reach you in the health she is in at present. I shall be truly wretched till I hear of her being safely landed with you. . . . For God's sake give us the earliest intelligence of her arrival."[6]

A beautiful young slave, Sally, Betty Hemings's fourteen-year-old daughter and the sister of James Hemings, who had accompanied Jefferson to Paris, remained on board with Polly. Although Jefferson had suggested that Isabel accompany Polly to France, Isabel was pregnant and about to give birth. It seems highly likely that the Eppeses chose Sally to go instead because, as part of the Hemings family, she had been at Monticello since she was two, and at Eppington with Polly all the while Jefferson was gone. Sally was loved by Polly, as well as by the Eppes family. Further, the Hemings were known to be intelligent and capable people. The Eppeses could feel comfortable in sending her.[7]

While Polly slept, the captain gave the order to weigh anchor, and by the time she awoke, the ship had already set sail. Polly Jefferson was on her way to France. She was first bewildered, then heartbroken when she began to comprehend what had happened. But Captain Ramsey's kindness and devotion to her soon helped her adjust, and in the five weeks they were at sea the two became very attached to one another. Polly ate at his table and often walked the deck with him, holding tightly to his hand. She was a sweet little girl with a sunny disposition, and she eventually came to enjoy her time on board the ship.

But the problem of separation repeated itself when she arrived in England. There, Captain Ramsay delivered her and Sally to Abigail Adams in London, who had offered to look after Polly until her father could come for her. Once again, Polly cried at having to leave the captain, whom she had grown to trust and love. Abigail Adams quickly won her heart, though, and Polly spent three happy weeks with her, awaiting her father's arrival.

But Jefferson, just back from his three-month trip and overwhelmed by the backlog of important paperwork that had accumulated during his absence, decided to send his trusted French steward, Petit, to collect Polly and Sally instead of making the trip to London himself. Once again, the little girl was devastated. Knowing no French, she was frightened of Petit—a strange man who spoke a strange language. She told Mrs. Adams that since she had left all her friends in Virginia to come over the ocean to see her father, she thought he would have taken the pains to come to England for her.

Polly finally arrived in Paris for a joyful reunion with her father and sister in the middle of July, two months after she had left Eppington. Patsy was given a week's holiday from school, and the two girls stayed home with their father. Patsy took her sister to the convent from time to time to familiarize her with it. When the little girl seemed comfortable there, Jefferson enrolled her, and she and Patsy returned together. Polly soon became a favorite of the girls and the mistresses, and within a year she was speaking and reading French easily, was learning to draw and to play the harpsichord, and was about to begin studying Spanish. The girls visited their father once or twice a week. It was at the convent that Polly was first called Maria, the name by which she chose to be known for the rest of her life.

Shortly after the girls' arrival in Paris, Jefferson saw to Sally's welfare as well: He paid to have her inoculated against smallpox by the highly acclaimed Dr. Robert Sutton, and he purchased appropriate clothing for her. He sent her to board with Madame Dupré, the Jefferson family laundress, for five weeks in order to learn to be a proper ladies' maid to his daughters; she was especially trained in needlework and the care of fine clothing. And when a French tutor was engaged for her brother James, Sally too may have participated.

Polly never ceased talking about Eppington, and her face lit up whenever she heard her Aunt Eppes mentioned. She missed all the Eppeses terribly, and while she eventually became happy in Paris, she longed for the day when they would be reunited.

Although she grew to love her father, Polly never became as close to him as Patsy was. Her ties were always to the family at Eppington.

Jefferson, though, became fully reconciled to life in France only after this child of his had crossed the ocean to him. He loved her deeply and was completely happy only when both his daughters were about. He considered them his jewels and enveloped them in a kind of motherly softness. He was firm with them, yet kind and always just. He never lost patience with them, and considered no need of theirs too small to attend to. He insisted on personally buying them all their clothes. In return, they, and ultimately all their children, revered and adored him.

## 26

## "Crusade against Ignorance"

DURING HIS YEARS in France, Jefferson was a diligent and skillful diplomat. He was dealing now with problems facing the United States, not simply those of Virginia. He was becoming more aware of the value of a strong central government, which could require individual states to honor America's treaty obligations, to protect the country's vulnerable northern and southern borders and secure the allegiance of the area west of the Allegheny Mountains, and to garner the respect of foreign countries.

He struggled to reduce America's debt to France for aid during the Revolutionary War by negotiating favorable treaties of navigation and commerce with Prussia and Morocco. He worked hard to obtain the commercial rights for his country that would make it possible for it to pay off all its debts to Europe. He worked out a plan whereby a league of nations would restrain pirates on the high seas, he gained a lowering of French duties on American products, and he tried to do away with an existing monopoly on the distribution and collection of taxes on tobacco by the farmers-general* in France.

During the summer of 1787, the fight in America to ratify a constitution that would unite the states under a more central government was rocking the Pennsylvania State House. The Constitutional Convention was in session there to work out the details. In frequent letters to Jefferson, Madison kept his friend up to date on developments. Many of the ideas in the Constitution had originally been Jefferson's, and Jefferson was happy for that, but, he told Madison, he was disturbed at the omission of a list of the rights protected by government: "freedom of religion, freedom of the press, protection against standing armies, restriction against monopolies, . . . habeas corpus laws, and trials by jury." He added that "a bill of rights is what the people are entitled to against every government on earth . . . & what no just government should refuse."[1]

As a direct result of Jefferson's objections, in 1791 a Bill of Rights, drafted by Madison, was made part of the Constitution. The first of its ten amendments stated: "Congress shall make no law respecting an establishment of religion, or prohibiting the free exercise thereof; or abridging the freedom of speech or of the press; or the right of the people peaceably to assemble and to petition the Government for a redress of grievances." Thus, several years after its passage, the Virginia statute's protection of the right of religious freedom became federal law via the U.S. Constitution.

Through the elegant dialogue and friendly banter of their letters, the friendship between Jefferson and Madison quickly grew into a working partnership. They "understood each other as allies."[2]

Jefferson looked upon the First Amendment with "sovereign reverence" because, as he explained in a letter to the Danbury, Connecticut, Baptist Association in 1802, it denied Congress the authority to make "law respecting an establishment of religion, or prohibiting the free exercise thereof," thus building a wall of separation between church and state.[3] This powerful metaphor has reverberated down through the cen-

---

*In prerevolutionary France, the farmers-general were a syndicate that had the right to collect certain taxes on behalf of the king. The system, which was open to abuse, was abolished by the Revolution.

turies and has been accepted by many as a concise description of the Constitution's church–state arrangement, despite differing interpretations. Since 1947, when Supreme Court Justice Hugo Black cited the First Amendment in a decision forbidding the State of New Jersey to spend state education funds for religious education, there has been ongoing passionate debate about Thomas Jefferson's original intentions for his wall.

Jefferson also feared the omission from the Constitution of the principle of rotation in office, particularly in the case of the president. Unless the Constitution expressly prohibited it, he reasoned, the president might be reelected for his lifetime. He wrote Madison long letters expressing his views. When the Constitution was completed, it outlined the general powers that were to be exercised by the new national government and became the highest law of the land, but it did not specify a term limit for the president or other officials.

While he was in France, many Frenchmen looked to Jefferson for advice on the rapidly approaching revolution. He watched carefully as the French people groped toward freedom, and to their leaders he preached moderation. The monarchy, he told Lafayette and his other French friends, must not be overthrown all of a sudden. There must be a gradual movement toward individual freedom and self-government. Reforms must be worked out patiently; sudden change could be dangerous. He cautioned his liberal-minded friends to make haste slowly. Once again, he showed himself to be an idealist who tempered his idealism with common sense, a dreamer who dreamed with his eyes open.

When asked by a French friend to explain what he meant by "government by the people," he replied that people should be introduced into every department of government to the extent that they are capable. He went on to explain that they are not qualified to *be* the executive, but they are qualified to *choose* the executive; they are not qualified to legislate, but they are qualified to *choose* the legislators; they are not qualified to judge questions of *law*, but they are capable of judging questions of *fact*.[4]

In Europe at this time, the Enlightenment was in full bloom, and Jefferson agreed with the prevailing thought that men could be free and happy if they came to know more about everything. The American experiment in self-government could only work if it was conducted by intelligent, well-informed, and reasonable people.[5] Education was the one true agent of change. To his old friend George Wythe he wrote from Paris, "I think by far the most important bill in our whole code is that for the diffusion of knowledge among the people. No other sure foundation can be devised, for the preservation of freedom and happiness." He went on to say, "Preach, my dear Sir, a crusade against ignorance; establish and improve the law for educating the common people."[6] Jefferson recognized that the time in which he was living was a time of possibilities.

A stream of young men—whose fathers had written to Jefferson from America requesting counsel for their sons—came to his house. To all of them he extended hospitality, advice, and inspiration, in part from his innate kindness, but motivated also by a strong sense of duty. He believed that he was training these young men to serve their country. They, in turn, appreciated his consideration of their opinions and his treatment of them as equals.

Some young men he counseled through letters. One of these was Thomas Mann Randolph Jr., the tall, dark son of Jefferson's cousin and lifelong friend since his days at Tuckahoe. Young Randolph had studied at the University of Edinburgh, in Scotland, for three years. During that period Jefferson wrote to him, advising him in his studies. After graduating with honors, Randolph wrote to Jefferson to tell him that he had decided on a career in politics. Jefferson responded happily that his country would have much for him to do. "It will remain . . . to those now coming on the stage of public affairs, to perfect what has been so well begun by those going off it," he wrote.[7]

In April, Jefferson received a disturbing letter from Patsy. In it she told her father that she had decided to remain in the convent and become a Catholic nun and would like his permission to do so. As a Protestant, Jefferson was dismayed.

Characteristically, he did nothing for a few days. Then he went to the convent, spoke quietly to Mother Louise-Thérèse, and withdrew both Patsy and Polly. He went to find his girls, greeted them warmly, and told them simply that he had come to take them out of school. They immediately drove home together. The subject of Patsy's letter was never mentioned by father or daughter.

Jefferson soon saw to it that Patsy was introduced into society at the brilliant court of Louis XVI. As usual, he shopped for the new wardrobe that was required (and for Sally as well, who would accompany her), selecting beautiful gowns with extremely good taste. Patsy, now a tall, attractive sixteen-year-old with deep blue eyes and reddish hair in tiny curls that framed her face, moved easily and happily from her role as student to her new role as Mademoiselle Martha, mistress of her father's household. Added to her duties was one she also seemed to love, tutoring her younger sister.

Polly was not as happy. She missed the attention of the adoring nuns and her classmates at the convent. She began to spend a part of most days in the home of the Lafayettes and became the special friend of their daughter Anastasie. She also developed a lasting friendship with Catherine (Kitty) Church, daughter of Angelica Church.

Both Patsy and Polly met many diplomats in their father's home. Patsy, in addition to being her father's hostess, occasionally filled in as secretary when William Short was away. As a result, she came to understand what was happening in France. The winter of 1789 was a severe one, and hundreds of people in Paris died of starvation. The girls witnessed mobs of hungry people roaming the streets, searching for food, and Patsy could see why the people might revolt. They had lost faith in their king and in the Assembly of Notables, which had been called into session for the emergency.

❧ 27 ❧

# A Summer of Violence

BACK IN AMERICA, on April 14, 1789, George Washington was notified by Charles Thomson, secretary of the Continental Congress, that he had been unanimously elected the first president of the United States. John Adams was named vice president, an office that Benjamin Franklin thought should have carried the title "His Superfluous Excellency."

George Washington, by James Peale, as the first president of the United States. (Courtesy of the Emmet Collection, Miriam and Ira D. Wallach Division of Art, Prints and Photographs, The New York Public Library, Astor, Lenox and Tilden Foundations)

When the news reached Jefferson, knowing that Washington much preferred the quiet of Mount Vernon to the turmoil of politics, he wrote to him, "Nobody who has tried both public and private life can doubt that you were much happier on the banks of the Potomac than you will be at New York."[1]

His respect for George Washington amounted almost to reverence. He knew Washington would accept the position out of the same sense of duty toward his country that he had. He wrote to Francis Hopkinson of "our great leader whose executive talents are superior to those, I believe, of any man in the world, and who alone, by the authority of his name and the confidence reposed in his perfect integrity, is fully qualified to put the new government so under way, as to insure it against opposition."[2]

Shortly before four o'clock on the afternoon of July 4, 1789, many of the Americans in Paris gathered for a gala dinner at the Jeffersons' house. A radiant Patsy was her father's hostess, and the Lafayettes were the honored guests. Coffee was poured for the first time from a silver coffee pot that Jefferson had designed. Ten days later the Bastille, the Paris prison that was the hated symbol of feudal tyranny in France, was stormed by French mobs and all the prisoners released. The French Revolution had begun.

Just three days before, Lafayette, who had been elected vice president of the Assembly of Notables, presented his "Declaration of the Rights of Man and of the Citizen," in which he had incorporated many of Thomas Jefferson's suggestions. After much debate, it was adopted by the National Assembly, the former Estates General, on August 26, 1789, but the king would not approve it. Ultimately, though, the declaration would become the basis for a French constitution as well as for similar statements of law in other European nations.

On the day of the fall of the Bastille, Polly, returning to their house on the Champs-Elysées from a visit to the Lafayettes', witnessed firsthand the violence of the mob. It was a frightened little girl who finally ran into her father's arms. She was so disturbed by what she had seen that she became ill and spent several days in a darkened upstairs room, the shutters closed against the noise outside.

All the Jeffersons became prisoners in their own home. Food and candles grew scarce. Some of the servants fled. And Jefferson began to fear for the safety of his daughters.

As the year 1789 progressed, events in Paris were fast spinning out of control. Yet even as Jefferson witnessed the disturbances, he believed that the revolutionary leaders were simply attempting to remodel the institutions of government to conform to Enlightenment principles.[3]

However, he had already written to John Jay, the American secretary for foreign affairs, requesting a leave of absence. He had been away from Monticello for five years and had not attended to any of his personal affairs in that time. Most important, he wished "to carry my children back to their own country."[4] He could return to France within six months, he told the secretary, but he would leave his daughters in America, in the care of their loving Aunt Eppes. "Their future welfare," he wrote to his sister-in-law, depended on it.

When his letter to John Jay went unanswered, Jefferson appealed to George Washington, adding that "there never has been a moment at which the presence of a minister here could be so well dispensed with."[5] Washington's permission for a six-month leave of absence finally arrived at the end of August 1789, and Jefferson immediately busied himself with preparations for the trip home.

On September 26, "a fine day," Jefferson and his daughters left Paris for Le Havre in his new London-made carriage. James Hemings and his sister Sally followed in Jefferson's old phaeton. Petit accompanied the group to Le Havre, but then returned to Paris. At Le Havre, the weather took a sudden turn, and they were met with a furious storm that kept them on shore for the next ten days. While they waited for the weather to improve, Patsy and Polly were frequently seen reading aloud to their father, who helped Polly pronounce some of the more difficult words.[6] One day, Jefferson walked ten miles in a blinding rain storm to find "a German Shepherd bitch big with pups, and bought her." Two puppies were born a few days later at Cowes, on the Isle of Wight, where the Jeffersons changed ships for the long ocean voyage, taking the puppies home to Monticello.[7]

On October 8, the sea now calm, the Jeffersons and their slaves started on their way to America. In France, Jefferson had commissioned paintings of Washington, Adams, Franklin, Madison, Thomas Paine, and Lafayette. Eighty-six packing cases filled with these and other paintings, drawings, books, wine, generous and thoughtful gifts for family and friends, a heavy marble pedestal for the bust of Lafayette, and all his papers had already been shipped to Virginia. William Short remained in France as acting chargé d'affaires and in charge of the Jeffersons' house as well.

James Hemings, who knew that on French soil he and his sister were considered free, had agreed, nevertheless, to accompany his master home. Both he and Sally had been paid regular wages by Jefferson since 1788. James had Mr. Jefferson's word that he would continue to receive a regular salary for his services and, if he taught a servant at Monticello the art of French cooking—which he had mastered and which Jefferson had come to love—he would be granted his freedom. James did indeed prepare his brother Peter to succeed him in the kitchen at Monticello. He was freed in 1796 and given money to go from Monticello to Philadelphia, where he wanted to live.

James's sister Sally, now not quite seventeen years old, had also agreed to return home with her master, after having extracted from him the promise of what her son Madison, many years later, would describe as "extraordinary privileges," including a "treaty" guaranteeing that any children born to her at Monticello would be granted their freedom at age twenty-one.[8]

Madison also claimed that, while in Paris, Sally had become Mr. Jefferson's concubine, and was returning home "enceinte [pregnant] by him."[9] Historians have long speculated on the possibility that a relationship did develop between Sally and Jefferson during the last year of their stay in Paris. While there is no documentation of any relationship, some things are known.

During the course of the twenty-six months that Sally had been in Paris she had matured into a very beautiful young woman, and one who probably recognized the importance of that beauty in a city where beauty was appreciated. Described by Abigail Adams as "good natured,"[10] Sally had learned to speak and understand the French language reasonably well and was comfortable moving about the city on her own. One can speculate that "seeing herself differently may have changed the way others, including Thomas Jefferson, saw her."[11]

Having lived at Monticello since she was a very young child, with a master who was always kind, Sally may at first have looked upon Thomas Jefferson as a father figure. Her own father, John Wayles, who died when she was two, had been the father of Jefferson's wife as well. In Paris, Sally observed Jefferson as a man who was by nature tender and gallant toward all women, was always dressed in the height of fashion, and seems to have recovered his spirits after his depression over his wife's death. By early in 1789, Jefferson's dalliance with Maria Cosway had come to a close.[12] It is not impossible, then, that there may have been a mutual attraction. A relationship between Thomas Jefferson and Sally Hemings could have developed.[13]

At Cowes, Jefferson and his family embarked on the *Clermont*, the British vessel that John Trumbull had arranged to have pick them up. They were her only passengers. For their accommodations on board ship Jefferson had requested "three master berths and berths for a man and woman servant, the latter convenient to that of my daughters."[14]

Jefferson was on deck at daybreak to hand a final letter to the pilot and to take a last long look at the receding shoreline as the ship, "in company with upwards of thirty vessels which had collected there and been detained, as we were, by contrary winds," weighed anchor and headed toward America. The American minister to France was on his way home.

Jefferson was never again as happy as he was during the last years he spent in France. It was one of the richest periods of his life in terms of personal friendships and freedom to indulge in cultural and intellectual pursuits. He had haunted the bookstores; he had attended the salons; he had indulged his love of art, theater, and music; and he was captivated by French cuisine. In his own words, he was returning home "charged, like a bee with the honey gathered on it," for the improvement of his own country.[15]

Yet the longer he had remained there, the more his pride in America had asserted itself. Paris, to him, was "empty bustle." The great mass of the people were oppressed, and even the nobility did not have the happiness enjoyed in America by every class of people, he told his friends. Paris, he thought, was a purposeless society, and life for Thomas Jefferson was empty when not purposeful. "My God! How little do my countrymen know what precious blessings they are in possession of, and which no other people on earth enjoy. I confess I had no idea of it myself," he wrote to James Monroe from France.[16]

Jefferson's affection for France would never waver, and his French friendships would be unaffected by the course of French politics, but he was returning to his own country with even stronger ties to it than when he had left, and with his faith in a democratic government renewed.

The *Clermont* arrived near the Virginia Capes after a pleasant voyage of just less than a month. But the fog was so thick that it was impossible to see. After standing off for three days, the captain, a bold and experienced seaman, determined to venture into Chesapeake Bay in spite of the weather. They beat against a strong head wind, lost their topsails, and were almost run down by a brig coming out of port and sailing before the wind. But they arrived safely at Norfolk about noon on November 23. Other ships whose captains were not as daring were kept at sea for another month by a storm that came up suddenly.

When the Jeffersons debarked, they were astonished to find a delegation from the legislature waiting to greet them. It was then that they learned that Thomas Jefferson had been nominated by President Washington and confirmed by the Senate to serve as secretary of state. His cousin and good friend Edmund Randolph had been named attorney general at the same time. Alexander Hamilton was secretary of the treasury, and John Jay was chief justice of the Supreme Court.

Jefferson's reply to the delegation was gracious but noncommittal. He did not accept the post, nor did he categorically refuse it: "That my country should be served is the first wish of my heart; I should be doubly happy indeed, were I to render it a service."[17]

The Jeffersons borrowed four horses from friends to draw their carriages and began a leisurely journey home, stopping along the way to visit relatives and friends. Polly, now called Maria, was overjoyed to be reunited with Aunty Eppes and all her young cousins, particularly Jack Eppes, who was now sixteen. Jack accompanied them on the remainder of the trip to Monticello.

It was at Eppington that an express rider caught up with them and handed Jefferson the official notification from George Washington of his appointment as secretary of state. He was not happy about it. He had hoped to return to France for a short period to complete his work there and then to retire from the political scene altogether. His family, his farm, his books called to him irresistibly.

But in the end, he wrote, "I found it better . . . to sacrifice my own inclinations to those of others." He couldn't refuse Washington: "But it is not for an individual to choose his post. You are to marshal us as may be best for the public good."[18]

When the slaves at Monticello learned that their master was on his way home, they requested a holiday on the day that he was expected. The overseer granted the request, and two days before Christmas they assembled at Monticello from all of Jefferson's farms. Young and old, men, women, and children, dressed in their finest, the women wearing their brightest turbans, all gathered to greet him. Some, growing impatient, started walking down the mountain and met the carriage just as it reached Shadwell, four miles away.

"Such a scene I never witnessed," Patsy wrote of it. They crowded around the carriage, then unhitched the horses and pulled and pushed the vehicle up the mountain to the front door of Monticello, shouting and singing all the way. "When the door of the carriage was opened, they received him in their arms and bore him to the house, crowding around and kissing his hands and feet—some blubbering and crying— others laughing. It seemed impossible to satisfy their anxiety to touch and kiss the very earth which bore him."[19]

When the girls alighted from the carriage, the people stood back respectfully, many holding their children up to see them, and quietly cleared a way for them. These two girls had left Monticello when they were only children. Now they were returning as young ladies, no longer Patsy and Polly but Martha and Maria, one a fully grown and stately young woman of seventeen, described as "a delicate likeness of her father"—fair-skinned, blue-eyed, redheaded, witty and graceful and skilled in the ways of court life, the other a "fairy-like" fragile eleven-year-old, even more beautiful and lovable than when she had left, whose haunting resemblance to her mother grew stronger with the passing of time. Thomas Jefferson and his daughters had come home to Monticello.

# PART IV

*"Splendid Misery"*

# 28

# Conflict in the Cabinet

JEFFERSON'S RESPECT for George Washington would not allow him to refuse the president anything, and he reluctantly accepted the post that was offered to him. But before he embarked on his career as secretary of state, he had one happy duty to perform at home.

Soon after the Jeffersons' return from France, Martha had become reacquainted with her second cousin Thomas Mann Randolph Jr. Now she announced to her father that she had fallen in love with him and wanted to marry him. She had just turned seventeen. Randolph, said to have descended on his mother's side from the Indian princess Pocahontas, was, at twenty-one, a handsome young man—no longer the childhood playmate who had climbed trees with her. Jefferson was delighted with her choice, and on February 23, 1790, he gave her away in marriage at Monticello. The wedding was a small affair with only the immediate families attending. The white gown she wore had been purchased for her by her father in Paris. The Reverend Mr. James Maury, Jefferson's old friend from his school days, performed the ceremony.

As part of their wedding gift, Jefferson gave the young couple Suck and her infant son Philip. Jupiter was not included in this gift, but he and his family were not separated. The newlyweds remained at Monticello for a short period of time. Philip, the only child of Jupiter and Suck to survive infancy, ultimately developed the same kind of relationship with Martha and Thomas Randolph's first-born son, Thomas Jefferson Randolph—known as Jefferson or Jeff—that existed between Jupiter and Jefferson. Many years later, Jeff Randolph would write of Philip that he was "small, active, intelligent, much of a humorist, [and] was my companion in childhood and friend through life."[1]

On a windy Sunday morning, March 21, 1790, wearing the red breeches and red waistcoat that were then the fashion in Paris, his reddish hair beginning to turn an untidy gray, the forty-seven-year-old

Miniature of Patsy (Martha) Jefferson at age seventeen, shortly before she married Thomas Mann Randolph Jr. By Joseph Boze, 1789. (Courtesy of the Diplomatic Reception Rooms, U.S. Department of State, Washington, D.C.)

Thomas Jefferson stepped off the Hudson River ferry and made his way through the narrow, crooked streets of lower Manhattan in New York, then the capital city, to the executive residence on "the Broadway," where he presented himself to President Washington, ready to assume his duties as secretary of state.

When Jefferson and Alexander Hamilton, secretary of the treasury, first met in New York, they had only respect for each other's reputation. But this was short-lived. Their disagreements began on foreign policy issues, Jefferson favoring close ties with France, Hamilton with England. Jefferson, fearing the same concentration of power in the hands of the national government that existed in England, was shocked by Hamilton's admiration for the British monarchy.

But their disagreements quickly revealed basic ideological and constitutional concerns as well. The best government was the one that governed the least, Jefferson believed. He had always had faith in the enlightened judgment of the people. Hamilton, to his way of thinking, was contemptuous of the common man. This became the basis for their feud. While Jefferson strove at the outset to cooperate, he was distressed to find himself in an atmosphere in which a republican system of government was not trusted. He viewed Hamilton as coveting personal as well as national power, betraying the Revolution and moving the country toward monarchy.

The two men also came into conflict over Hamilton's financial system. When Hamilton suggested that the federal government assume the states' war debts, Jefferson, along with Madison and others, foresaw that such a policy would strengthen the central government and thus weaken the role of the states. Jefferson argued that the Bank of the United States that Hamilton proposed would further jeopardize states' rights and was unconstitutional. There was, he said, no specific authorization in the Constitution for a national bank. The states, not Congress, had the power to charter banks. He believed that the Constitution should be interpreted "literally," or "strictly." In this way only, he felt, could the Constitution be preserved and liberty ensured.

Members of Congress began to take sides. Hamiltonians were called Federalists, while those who sympathized with Thomas Jefferson called themselves Republicans.* The framers of the Constitution had made no provision for political parties, and the idea of loyal opposition was unknown in America. People considered organized political opposition to be dangerous.

While Jefferson was the senior cabinet member, he had none of the glittering personal magnetism of the aggressive young Hamilton, and his persistent shyness made him appear cold. His simple clothes, his "laxity of manner," and his lack of "the firm collected deportment" expected of a cabinet minister were in sharp contrast to the erect military bearing of Hamilton and the brightly colored satins and expensive ruffles and laces he wore. Jefferson felt that finery was out of place in a republican government.

When, in the autumn of 1792, Hamilton published a series of ferocious attacks on his colleague in the *Gazette of the United States* in an attempt to drive him out of office, Jefferson made no reply. His friends did that for him.

---

*It is this party that would take the name, under President Andrew Jackson, of the Democratic Republican Party, which was soon abbreviated to the Democratic Party. The Federalist Party became known as the Republican Party.

Thomas Jefferson as secretary of state, 1791, after his return from France. (Courtesy of Independence National Historical Park)

Never a manipulator or an intriguer like Hamilton, Jefferson was scrupulous as an official. Although he opposed Hamilton's policies, his loyalty to President Washington was far more important to him. Even though he was unable to convince the president of the unconstitutionality of a national bank and Washington signed the bill establishing one, Jefferson reluctantly agreed to the president's strong urging that he remain in office. He would stay on, he told Washington, until the end of December 1793. But Hamilton and Jefferson, the chief officers in Washington's administration, remained, as Jefferson put it, "daily pitted in the cabinet like two cocks."[2]

Washington, unwilling to admit the existence of political parties, valued both Hamilton and Jefferson and recognized the important service rendered by each: "I regret, deeply regret, the difference in opinions which have arisen and divided you and another principal officer of the Government," he wrote to Jefferson. "I have a great, a sincere esteem for you both."[3]

Jefferson always had a strong distaste for personal controversy, and he understood that compromise was necessary for the preservation of the

Union. He was a skilled diplomat, and now he remembered Benjamin Franklin's rule: "Never contradict anybody." He tried hard to tolerate differences of opinion, believing it best to use the technique of asking questions and planting doubts and to look for ways to cooperate. In this way he continued to battle quietly for principles and policies but never for his own interests.

He labored diligently in his role as secretary of state and fully justified Washington's confidence in him. But his most notable accomplishment was calling attention to the dangers of Hamilton's policies and inspiring others to modify them in the years to come.

&#x32EC; While her father was in New York, Maria divided her time among the Eppes, her aunt Martha Carr and her Carr cousins living at Monticello, and her newly married sister and brother-in-law, who had recently moved to Varina, the estate given to the couple as a wedding gift by Thomas Mann Randolph Sr.

Once again, letters exchanged between father and daughters allow us a glimpse of their remarkable relationship. The lonely secretary of state wrote to Martha from New York: "Having had yourself & dear Poll to live with me so long, to exercise my affections and cheer me in the intervals of business, I feel heavily the separation from you." Then he went on, "[T]he happiness of your life now depends on the continuing to please a single person. to this all other objects must be secondary; even your love to me."[4]

Martha's reply was reassuring: "I assure you My Dear papa my happiness can never be compleat without your company. . . . I have made it my study to pleas [Mr. Randolph] in every *thing* and do consider all other objects as secondary to that *except* my love for you."[5] Martha's bond with her father was so strong that her husband never did displace him in her affections.

&#x32EC; On March 4, 1791, Vermont became the first state to be admitted to the Union after the original thirteen. Two and a half months later, taking advantage of an interval of relative quiet in the cabinet, Jefferson and James Madison decided to make a 920-mile trip from Philadelphia to Vermont and back.* In making a holiday trip up the Hudson River, Jefferson hoped to leave behind many of the bitter political controversies raging around him and rid himself of a recurring "violent" headache. Madison, too, was eager to escape the partisan politics in Philadelphia and to alleviate a troublesome stomach disorder. "Health, recreation and curiosity" were his objects, he told his friend.

In a letter to Maria, Jefferson described the route they would take: In about a week "I shall set out to join Mr. Madison at New York, from whence we shall go up to Albany and Lake George, then cross over to Bennington and so through Vermont to the Connecticut River, down Connecticut River by Hartford to New Haven, then to New York . . . and expect to be back in Philadelphia about the middle of June."[6]

Jefferson used the journey as an opportunity to make extensive scientific and botanical observations. He investigated the manufacture of maple sugar; he researched the "Hessian Fly," an insect that was destroying American wheat; he collected Indian dialects; he toured historic battlefields; and he completed some research for the American Philosophical Society.

While on their expedition, he delighted Maria by writing a letter to her on a piece of birch bark, "supposed to be the same used by the ancients to write on before the art of making paper was invented, and which being called the Papyrus, gave the name of paper to the new invented substitute."[7] The birch bark, Maria told her father, was "prettier than paper." She loved the piece he sent her, but she was not interested in the geography lesson he included. She was much more interested in her new niece: "My sweet Anne grows prettier every day," she reported.[8] Martha had made Thomas Jefferson a grandfather in January.

In the fall of 1791, just after Maria turned thirteen, her father spent a month at Monticello with her and then took her to Philadelphia with him. On the way, father and daughter stopped for a brief visit with President and Mrs. Washington at Mount Vernon. Here Maria and Nellie Custis, Mrs. Washington's granddaughter, became close friends,

---

*The capital had been temporarily transferred from New York to Philadelphia, and Jefferson traveled from Philadelphia to meet Madison in New York.

and Maria stayed on after her father left, continuing her trip to Philadelphia in the president's coach.

In Philadelphia Jefferson enrolled Maria in boarding school, but she spent several days each week with him in the small house he had rented on the banks of the Schuylkill River. There they spent many hours together under the trees that surrounded the house, where they had breakfast and dinner, wrote, read, and received company. "What would I not give that the trees planted nearest round the house at Monticello were full grown," he wrote to Martha.[9]

Maria's nineteen-year-old cousin Jack Eppes was now living with them and pursuing his studies under his uncle's supervision. Jack was reading law and attending classes periodically at the University of Pennsylvania. He somehow managed to arrange his schedule so that his time on the Schuylkill coincided with Maria's visits there.

Sometime late in August 1791, Thomas Jefferson received a letter from a sixty-year-old free black man living in Baltimore, Maryland, that must have startled him. It began, "Sir, I am fully sensible of the greatness of that freedom which I take with you on the present occasion; a liberty which Seemed to me Scarcely allowable, when I reflected on the distinguished, and dignified station in which you Stand; and the almost general prejudice and prepossession which is so prevalent in the world against those of my complexion."[10] The writer was Benjamin Banneker, a tobacco farmer whose father and grandfather had been slaves. His grandmother had taught him to read and write, and he loved mathematics. He had borrowed books on mathematics and astronomy, and by 1789 had become so proficient in astronomy that he could predict the weather and even a solar eclipse with considerable accuracy. Using his ability as an astronomer, he wrote and had published yearly almanacs. Now he sent his handwritten "copy of an Almanack which I have calculated for the Succeeding year" to Secretary of State Jefferson, citing this almanac as evidence of Negro ability.

Benjamin Banneker had already been recommended to George Washington as a surveyor, defining the boundary line and laying out the streets of the new capital city. The Georgetown *Weekly Ledger* soon described him as "an Ethiopian whose abilities as surveyor and astronomer already prove that Mr. Jefferson's concluding that that race of men were void of mental endowment was without foundation." Another government official stated that Banneker was "fresh proof that the powers of the mind are disconnected with the color of the skin, or, in other words, a striking contradiction to Mr. Hume's doctrine, that the Negroes are naturally inferior to the whites, and unsusceptible of attainments in arts and sciences."[11]

In his letter to Jefferson, Banneker had invoked the Declaration of Independence as proof that there "was a time in which you clearly saw into the injustice of a State of Slavery." "But how pitiable is it to reflect," he continued,

> that altho you were so fully convinced of the benevolence of the Father of mankind, and of his equal and impartial distribution of those rights and privileges which he had conferred upon them, that you should at the Same time counteract his mercies, in detaining by fraud and violence so numerous a part of my brethren under groaning captivity and cruel oppression, that you should at the Same time be found guilty of that most criminal act, which you professedly detested in others, with respect to yourselves.

Jefferson replied promptly:

> I thank you immensely for your letter of the 19th. instant and for the Almanac it contained. No body wishes more than I do to see such proofs as you exhibit, that nature has given to our black brethren, talents equal to those of the other colors of men, and that the appearance of a want of them is owing merely to the degraded condition of their existence, both in Africa and America. I can add with truth, that no body wishes more ardently to see a good system commenced for raising the condition both of their body and mind to what it ought to be, as fast as the imbecility of their present existence, and other circumstances which cannot be neglected, will admit.[12]

Jefferson went on to tell Banneker that he had taken the liberty of sending his almanac to his friend Monsieur de Condorcet, Secretary of the Academy of Sciences at Paris. By so doing, Jefferson was paying

Banneker a great honor. The academy was the foremost body of scientific learning in France, and Condorcet was one of that country's foremost scholars. He would provide Banneker's work with the exposure he believed it deserved.

It was at about this time that George Washington designated Thomas Jefferson as an unofficial assistant in laying out the as-yet-unnamed new capital city on the Potomac River. Once again Jefferson would utilize ideas accumulated during his years in France.

"Whenever it is proposed to prepare plans for the Capitol," Jefferson wrote to Major Pierre Charles L'Enfant, the first architect involved in planning the new city, "I should prefer the adoption of some one of the models of antiquity which have had the approbation of thousands of years." Somehow, the new nation's architecture must have in it a "ring of eternity." The best building examples that civilization had to offer must be the models.[13]

To Washington he suggested that the government circulate, free of charge, inexpensive copies of prints of outstanding architecture that Jefferson had brought home from Europe, in order to educate, and elevate, the taste of the citizens of nearby Georgetown. And he worked closely with the architect Benjamin H. Latrobe to design and build the Capitol building.

Latrobe would say of Jefferson, "You have planted the arts in your country . . . [through] your love and protection of the fine arts."[14] Years later Washington, D.C., would be considered by art historians to be the birthplace of the profession of architecture in America.

## 29

# "Our Own Dear Monticello"

"THERE HAS BEEN A TIME when . . . the esteem of the world was of higher value in my eye than everything in it. . . . But the motion of my blood no longer keeps time with the tumult of the world. It leads me to seek for happiness in the lap and love of my family, in the society of my neighbors & my books, in the wholesome occupations of my farm and my affairs, in an interest or affection in every bud that opens, in every breath that blows around me."[1] Thus did Thomas Jefferson reveal his true feelings to James Madison in June 1793. A few months later he reiterated those sentiments in a letter to Angelica Church: "I am going to Virginia. . . . I am then to be liberated from the hated occupation of politics, and to remain in the bosom of my family, my farm, and my books. I have my house to build, my fields to farm, and to watch for the happiness of those who labor for mine."[2] But the freedom to accomplish this—and the pleasure he derived from it—were made possible precisely by those slaves who labored for his happiness.

Thomas Jefferson resigned as secretary of state at the end of 1793, arriving home by mid-January 1794, certain that this was to be a permanent retirement. He was only fifty years old, but he was weary and sick of politics.

"The length of my tether is now fixed for life from Monticello to Richmond,"* he wrote to a friend. "My private business can never call me elsewhere, and certainly politics will not, which I have ever hated both in theory & in practice."[3] He gathered his family around him and pictured himself spending the rest of his days restoring his ravaged plantation, gardening, and enjoying his family.

He had found his house neglected and in sad need of repair. His restless mind was already planning the changes he would make. He would begin the radical alterations of Monticello that he had been considering since he had first been captivated by the ancient architecture he had seen in France. He would alter it to reflect French taste.

No doubt, also, Monticello as it stood in 1793 served as a bittersweet reminder of the happy days when his wife had been alive, and this played a large part in his decision to change it. And perhaps his statement to a visitor that "architecture is my delight, and putting up and pulling down, one of my favorite amusements" was a basis for his decision as well.

He determined that from the outside the house would appear to be

*A distance of about seventy miles.

one story only. But he would double its size in the manner of "all the new and good houses" in Paris. Thus, "the upper story was removed, the northeast front extended, and a new second level created for bedrooms within the height of the first floor. He referred to the new upper rooms as the 'Mezzaninos.'"[4]

And he would take advantage of the hillside site and put all the outbuildings beneath the terraces behind the house. In that way, the kitchen, laundry, smokehouse, meal room, pantry, and dairy would be hidden from view, connected to the main house by an underground passageway. But he was careful to provide for aboveground doors and windows for light and air.

He would use native American materials and traditions of craftsmanship to transform his home into something new. Roman and French classicism would be interpreted in red brick and white painted wood. It was a project he would pursue for the next sixteen years. He would build an extraordinary new house at the same time that he was fashioning a new government for his country.

His house would be modeled on the Hôtel de Langeac, the elegant town house he had rented in Paris: it would have "rooms of entertainment" as well as private spaces to form what could be called apartments; and he would value convenience over ceremony and architectural display.

He decided that he would erect a dome in the center of the structure, over the front parlor. It would be constructed of wooden ribs and radiating panes of glass, reminiscent of the Halle aux Bleds in Paris—and of that delightful afternoon in the summer of 1786 when he had met Maria Cosway. Construction of the dome, however, would not begin until 1800. In 1805, when the single sheet of glass that became its large circular window was finally put in place, and Mr. Jefferson's "sky-room" was completed, it became the first dome to be erected over a colonial American house.

Hemispherical forms had long fascinated Thomas Jefferson, and he had experimented with the combination of dome and octagon as early as 1770, when he had first seen it illustrated in Palladio's book. The contrast appealed to him.

The rooms in his house would be oval or octagonal, as he had seen in the exquisite châteaux of some of his friends in France. He seemed to recognize the importance of the play of light on architectural space. Perhaps also, in an age when artificial light was derived only from candles, his determination to have large windows that reached down to the floor, and even glass doors and skylights, grew out of his desire to have as much light as possible for his insatiable need to read. At the same time, nature itself in all its wonder became a constant presence in the rooms. Monticello looks out, not in. At every moment it reaches out to the landscape Thomas Jefferson loved: "And our own dear Monticello, where has nature spread so rich a mantel under the eye? mountains, forests, rocks, rivers. With what majesty do we there ride above the storms! How sublime to look down into the workhouse of nature, to see her clouds, hail, snow, rain, thunder, all fabricated at our feet! And the glorious Sun, when rising as if out of a distant water, just gilding the tops of the mountains, and giving life to all nature!" he had written to Maria Cosway in France years before.[5]

The entrance hall of Monticello, just inside the front portico, faces

Monticello's west front as it looks today. Jefferson situated Monticello's portico facing west toward the wilderness, but the east front looks toward Rome. He kept one foot in the classical past, while the other moved toward the future. (Courtesy of L. H. Bober)

The mountains surrounding Monticello, showing the garden pavilion. (Courtesy of L. H. Bober)

the Southwest Mountains and looks toward the wilderness, while the east front looks toward Rome. Thus Jefferson maintained one foot firmly planted in the classical past, and the other turned toward the future. In time the entrance hall became a museum that reflected the broad scope of Jefferson's interests and included one of the most important private collections of natural history specimens and American Indian artifacts in America at that time. He had designed the entrance hall to educate his visitors. The elk antlers, the jaw of a mastodon, the horn of a buffalo, and the musk ox skull hanging there all revealed his interest in natural history.

Most houses of the time had family portraits on the walls. The portraits that Thomas Jefferson hung in his parlor represented the patriarchy of the country. High above the founding fathers—George Washington and John Adams, among others—and looking down on them, were the portraits of Isaac Newton, Francis Bacon, and John Locke, icons of Jefferson's humanism. He hung art that he had sent home from France on the walls of his parlor to act as objects of learning. And he hung maps to bring the larger world to Monticello. Jefferson's parlor told the story of the forces that had shaped America.[6]

The dining room, where the entire family gathered for dinner at three thirty every afternoon, perhaps best exemplifies life at Monticello in the later years of Jefferson's life. The Wedgwood inserts on the mantel and the silver candlesticks on the Chippendale dining table, a gift from his old friend George Wythe, impart a sense of quiet elegance. The small

The parlor at Monticello. The musical life at Monticello took place in the parlor. Here Jefferson hung portraits of the founding fathers and of his "trinity of immortals." (Courtesy of Robert C. Lautman/ Thomas Jefferson Foundation, Inc.)

candle stand and chair* near the fireplace and the selection of books on the mantel attest to Jefferson's habit of reading while waiting for the family to assemble for dinner. This was a man who never wasted a minute.

Mechanical dumbwaiters on either side of the mantel allowed wine and fruit to be sent up from the cellar below. Small rectangular tables, also called dumbwaiters, placed between guests enabled them to serve themselves, reducing the number of servants necessary in the room. This allowed for more privacy for conversation during dinner.

Jefferson's deep need for privacy is reflected in his own suite of rooms, which included his bedroom; his cabinet, or study, where he did all his writing; and his library, which he called his "bookroom." A greenhouse adjoined. This wing was always locked and was considered his private sanctuary, his "sanctum sanctorum." No one entered without an invitation. It was the only place at Monticello where he could escape from the incessant swarm of visitors, to read and to carry on his voluminous correspondence.† It was, in fact, the heart of his private world. His books, his telescope, his measuring devices were all there, centered around his

*The last chair Jefferson ever sat in. After Jefferson died, his grandson-in-law had Jefferson's initials carved into it.
†It is estimated that in his lifetime Thomas Jefferson wrote some 18,000 letters and maintained a 656-page index of every letter written and received from 1783 until his death in 1826.

chair with candlesticks in its arms for light and a chaise longue to accommodate his long legs. A desk drawn up over the chair held his writing materials and the polygraph, purchased in England, that he used to make file copies of his letters. The little portable desk on which he had written the Declaration of Independence was kept on a shelf in the study, at just the proper height for writing while standing.

His bed, set in an alcove in the French style, was open on both sides, providing ventilation and allowing him to rise on either side—his bedroom or his cabinet. Making things with his hands was always a relaxing hobby for Jefferson, so a nearby room was equipped with a carpenter's workbench and a large assortment of tools. But perhaps the greatest convenience that Monticello could boast were the indoor privies (bathrooms) that he had seen in France. Beauty and function were always inseparable in his mind.

So Thomas Jefferson made use of all he had learned in France to create a home that met his family's practical, social, and emotional needs, as well as a house that reflected the same human dignity and scholarship that he strove for throughout his life. It became a symbol of his ideal for the country he helped to build.

Thomas Jefferson was a very private person who "possessed an inner

The fireplace and mantel in the dining room at Monticello, where the family gathered for dinner. Wine was sent up from the cellar in the dumbwaiters on either side of the mantle. (Courtesy of L. H. Bober)

Thomas Jefferson's cabinet, or study, his "sanctum sanctorum," showing his chaise longue. Note his polygraph, which allowed him to make copies of everything he wrote, and his revolving book stand, which made it possible for him to consult five books at a time. (Courtesy of L. H. Bober)

core of personal privacy that no one has ever breached." One historian has mused that this privacy was "a symptom of the supreme value he placed on individual freedom. . . . The Revolution he fought was for the right of the individual to manage his own life with the minimum of interference from governments."[7]

When Jefferson had first begun building Monticello, he was just beginning to acquire an understanding of the art and craft of architecture. As he continued to read and study the subject and to watch his house taking shape, his knowledge and his skills increased. Eventually he became "a knowledgeable architect and builder who sought out the best craftsmen he could lure to Virginia and insisted that they comply with his most exacting wishes."[8]

Essential to the building of Monticello was the use of slave labor, and an integral aspect of the five-thousand-acre plantation on which the house was situated was the slave community.

Before he left for France, Jefferson had had some of his domestic servants trained in a second trade so that they could be productive while he was gone. Jupiter learned stonecutting and was hired out to a local white stonemason, earning twenty-five pounds a year for his master. When Jefferson returned, Jupiter was put to work building the four Doric columns of the entrance portico of Monticello. In 1793, Jefferson's son-in-law reported, Jupiter was given the arduous task of blasting and hauling a thousand pounds of limestone and was entrusted with the job of using gunpowder for digging a canal.[9]

Every day Jefferson was confronted by his slaves busily engaged in all the activities that kept Monticello running smoothly and efficiently. He had come to recognize the possibility that America might some day be excluded from trade with other nations, and he understood, as he wrote years later, that "to be independent for the comforts of life we must fabricate them ourselves. We must now place the manufacturer by the side of the agriculturist."[10] He would ensure that Monticello became self-sustaining. His farms, left in the care of overseers, had been neglected during the years he had been in France, and his debts ran to many thousands of pounds. It was essential now that he attempt to make his plantation an income-producing operation—one more reason that he couldn't afford to free his slaves.

When the Duc de la Rochefoucauld-Liancourt, whose family Jefferson had come to know in France, visited Monticello in 1796, he found the plantation humming with activity, and Mr. Jefferson actively involved in every aspect of it.

> He orders, directs and pursues in the minutest detail every branch of business relative to [the management of his farms and buildings]. I found him in the midst of the harvest, from which the scorching heat of the sun does not prevent his attendance. His negroes are nourished, clothed and treated as well as white servants could be. . . . Every article is made on his farm; his negroes are cabinet-makers, carpenters, masons, bricklayers, smiths, &c. The children he employs in a nail-manufactory, which yields already a considerable profit. The young and old negresses spin for the clothing of the rest. He animates them by rewards and distinctions; in fine, his superior mind directs the management of his domestic concerns with the same abilities, activity, and regularity, which he evinced in the conduct of public affairs.[11]

Mulberry Row, a thousand-foot-long road just south of the main house and named by Jefferson after the mulberry trees that lined it, was the home of Monticello's laboring community and the hub of all these activities. By the time La Rochefoucauld-Liancourt arrived, seventeen structures had been built along the road, including log dwellings for the slaves, a stone house for free resident workmen, a stable that housed Jefferson's carriage horses and his saddle, a wash house, a weaving room, a smokehouse and dairy, a blacksmith shop and nail factory, two woodworking shops—the carpenter's shop and the joinery where much of the fine architectural woodwork for the house was crafted—and storage sheds for charcoal, which was used to fuel the blacksmith's forge and the fires of the nail makers.[12]

Mulberry Row was often a noisy place, the hammers of the nail makers ringing on the anvils adding to the din of carpenters sawing wood, milk pans clattering in the dairy, and mule-drawn carts rattling up and down the street carrying barrels of water, firewood for the kitchens, and charcoal for the forges. It was only as daylight faded that the shops grew silent and the workers returned to their cabins.[13]

A talented blacksmith was essential to every working plantation, because the blacksmith shod horses, repaired wagons, coaches, and carriages, and made hoops for barrels. Indeed, he could manufacture anything made of metal.

Moment on Mulberry Row, painting by Nathaniel Gibbs. (Courtesy of Monticello/ Thomas Jefferson Foundation, Inc.)

Nails, which were made by hand using blacksmith's tools, were an item that every farmer needed. They were an extremely important income-producing material. In 1794 Jefferson installed a nail factory in the same building as the blacksmith's shop. Here, nails were shaped into different sizes from rods of iron. Jefferson found that he was able to produce them more cheaply in his nailery than they could be purchased from England. And he could sell them to merchants in the area.[14]

Twelve boys, ages ten to sixteen, worked in the nail factory from dawn to dusk every day. They "stood at their anvils around four fires, pointing and heading nails with heavy hammers until they had completed their appointed tasks." Jefferson was at the nailery every day at dawn to weigh out the nailrods given to the boys, and returned every evening to weigh the nails they had produced, keeping a careful account of the amount of iron wasted and the relative efficiency of each of the boys. He described himself as spending "half the day . . . counting and measuring nails." The blacksmith oversaw their work during the day, but Jefferson's presence helped to keep the nailery peaceful and productive. He was able to instill in the boys a sense of pride in their work.[15]

Years later, while he was president, Jefferson learned that his overseer was whipping some of the boys in the nailery. He immediately wrote to his son-in-law Thomas Mann Randolph, asking him to speak to the overseer and put a stop to it: "It would destroy their value, in my estimation, to degrade them in their own eyes by the whip. This, therefore, must not be resorted to but in extremities. As they will be again under my government, I would chuse they should retain the stimulus of character."[16] He hoped to convince his overseer that more could be accomplished through a congenial relationship than through fear. He wanted his slaves managed "on a rational and humane plan."

During the summer of 1795 Jefferson wrote that "a nailery which I have established with my own negro boys now provides completely for the maintenance of my family."[17] His pride was evident. Girls of the same age as the boys in the nailery were set to spinning. Young girls below the age of ten were "nurses" (babysitters) while their mothers worked, and were overseen by women too old to work in the fields. Slave cabins were built close together so that this was possible.[18]

Isaac, a young son of the slaves Ursula and George, who had come to Monticello at Martha Jefferson's request in 1773, was one of the boys who worked in the nailery. His father, nicknamed "Great George" or sometimes "King George," became the first manager of the nailery. Earlier, while Jefferson was in France, this trusted slave was in charge of Monticello's orchards and grounds; and from 1797 until his death he was overseer at Monticello. When Great George's oldest son, named Little George, later became manager of the nailery, Jefferson paid him a percentage of its profits.

Isaac reminisced many years later: "Mr. Jefferson bowed to everybody he meet; talked wid his arms folded. Gave the boys in the nail factory a pound of meat a week, a dozen herrings, a quart of molasses, and a peck of meal. Give them what wukked the best a suit of red or blue; encouraged them mightily."[19] Isaac told the story that Mrs. Jefferson "would come out [to the kitchen] with a cookery book in her hand and read out of it to Isaac's mother how to make cakes, tarts, and so on."

Isaac told a different kind of story about Archibald Cary, who would come to Monticello periodically to visit his friend Thomas Jefferson. (It was Archibald Cary who had invited Jefferson to bring his own and

Isaac Jefferson took the Jefferson surname when he became free. His many recollections of Jefferson and life at Monticello are much valued because they are told from the black perspective. (Daguerreotype, MSS 2041. Courtesy of the Tracy W. McGregor Library, Special Collections, University of Virginia Library)

The cook's room, one of the dependencies under the south terrace, next to the kitchen. Edie Fossett, who had learned French cooking and was Jefferson's cook at the President's House in Washington, D.C., became head cook at Monticello in 1809 and lived there with her family. (Courtesy of L. H. Bober)

the Carr children to his home, Ampthill, to have them inoculated against smallpox in 1782.) When Isaac was about nine years old, it was his job to open the gates in the road leading up the mountain for visitors.

> [Colonel Cary] has given Isaac more whippings than he has fingers and toes. . . . There was three gates to open: the furst bout a mile from the house: tother one three quarters; then the yard gate at the stable three hundred yards from the house. . . . Colonel Cary would write to Old Master what day he was coming. Whenever Isaac missed opening them gates in time, the Colonel soon as he git to the house look about for him and whip him with his horse-whip. Old Master used to keep dinner for Colonel Cary. The Colonel . . . walk right straight into the kitchen and ax the cooks what they hab for dinner. If they didn't have what he wanted, bleeged to wait dinner till it was cooked. Colonel Cary made freer at Monticello than he did at home; whip anybody. Would stay several weeks; give servants money, sometimes five or six dollars among 'em.[20]

Jefferson, on the other hand, tried to develop honesty, industry, and trust in his slaves. His sensitivity to them is revealed time and again in his letters. When the slave Hercules attempted to run away, he was caught and briefly imprisoned. Jefferson suggested to his overseer that since "it is his first folly in this way," further punishment was inappropriate. But Jefferson cautioned the overseer to let Hercules "receive the pardon as from yourself alone, and not by my interference, for this is what I would have none of them to suppose." But they did know. First-time offenders frequently turned to him for leniency.

Yet there were times when Jefferson himself ordered whippings, generally for the benefit of those watching. He had the chronic runaway Jame Hubbard brought to Monticello in irons and "severely flogged in the presence of his old companions." For the most part, however, if a slave could not be disciplined by words alone, he was simply sold.[21]

Sunday on the plantation was the one day that slaves could spend as they liked. Many of the men, women, and children from Jefferson's surrounding farms came to Monticello on Sundays to offer something to buy or to ask for something. Every family had a poultry yard, and most cultivated a vegetable garden. They regularly sold to Jefferson "chicken and eggs, cabbages and lettuce, cucumbers and melons." That they also sold "fish, fruit, animal skins, beeswax, and walnuts" indicates that they "took advantage of the natural bounty of their surroundings, fishing in the Rivanna River and hunting or gathering nuts in the woodlands." At times, with their master's permission, they took surplus provisions to the Sunday market in Charlottesville.[22]

Many also continued to work after they had finished their assigned jobs, to supplement their own allotments of food, clothing, furniture, or household items. Jefferson paid them for work that he considered particularly difficult or unpleasant. Two young slaves spent their Sundays cleaning Monticello's privies, which earned them an extra dollar each month. Sundays were also the time to visit their families on neighboring plantations (some men walked miles to see them), or to come together with others from Monticello for songs, stories, and prayer.[23]

## 30

# "I Have No Ambition to Govern Men"

WHEN THOMAS JEFFERSON retired to Monticello in January 1794, he anticipated that this would be a permanent retirement for him. But world events intervened.

The French Revolution had entered an ominous phase in 1792, when France declared war on Austria and then, later that year, declared itself a republic. Soon the guillotine was set up, and in January 1793 King Louis XVI was beheaded; in February, France declared war on England and Holland, and just one month later on Spain. The Reign of Terror had begun.[1] With Great Britain pulled into the conflict, effects of the war were soon felt across the Atlantic Ocean. Many Jeffersonian Republicans were eager to enter the battle against Britain on the side of France.

Although the Treaty of Paris, signed in 1783, had ended the American War of Independence, the years that followed saw relations between America and England continue to deteriorate. England refused to relinquish the frontier forts in the Northwest Territory, and it seized American ships, forcing American sailors to serve on British ships in the war against France. The United States passed navigation laws that were potentially damaging to Great Britain.

But President Washington understood that war had to be avoided at all costs. The United States was not yet strong enough to enter into a war. So in 1793, shortly after the outbreak of the conflict between Britain and France, Washington boldly issued his Neutrality Proclamation. Then, in a last desperate gamble, in 1794 he sent Supreme Court Justice John Jay, who, like Alexander Hamilton, was a staunch Federalist and an admirer of Great Britain, to London to negotiate the disagreements between the United States and Great Britain. On November 19, 1794, Jay's Treaty was signed. While the treaty provided for the British evacuation of the forts in the Northwest Territory, it made no provision to stop the British from boarding American ships and impressing American seamen. And the treaty was silent about compensation for slaves carried off by the British in 1783 and about Indian affairs on the northwestern boundary.[2]

After much consideration, Washington approved the treaty, causing an uproar in the country. Although still admired, Washington came under sharp attack. An angry crowd in New York threw stones at Hamilton, and John Jay resigned from the Supreme Court and was burned in effigy all across the country.

Jefferson had often urged George Washington to maintain American neutrality as national policy. Now he defended him for seeming to align the country with England: "He errs as other men do," he wrote to an angry neighbor in Virginia, "but he errs with integrity."[3]

But the treaty was enough to shake Jefferson "out of his political slumber at Monticello." He characterized it as "nothing more than a treaty of alliance between England and the Anglomen of this country against . . . the people of the United States."[4]

The fight over Jay's Treaty has been called the opening round in the presidential campaign of 1796. When an exhausted George Washington determined not to run for a third term, the Republicans made Jefferson their candidate against his old friend John Adams. Jefferson had already expressed his hope of seeing James Madison elected president, telling him that "there is not another person in the U.S. who, being placed at the helm of our affairs, my mind would be so completely at rest for the fortune of our political bark." For his part, Jefferson said that he had "thoroughly weighed and decided on . . . my retirement from . . . all office high or low, without exception. . . . The little spice of ambition, which I had in my younger days, has long since evaporated. . . . The question is forever closed with me."[5]

Now, almost two years later, Jefferson reluctantly agreed to run. But he would do nothing to aid the campaign. Using a metaphor of the sea to express his sentiments, as he frequently did, he told Madison that he would be willing to go into the presidency for a while, in order "to put our vessel on her republican tack before she should be thrown too much to leeward of her true principles."[6] But he remained on his mountaintop—a silent candidate.

"I have no ambition to govern men," he had written to John Adams just a few days before, concluding his letter by describing himself as "one who tho', in the course of our voyage thro' life, various little incidents have happened or been contrived to separate us [Adams, like Hamilton, was a Federalist], retains still for you the solid esteem of the moments when we were working for our independence, and sentiments of respect and affectionate attachment."[7]

Jefferson had already indicated his hope that Adams would be elected president. He would be satisfied with second place, he said, although he would prefer third—his rejection—since then he would be free to remain at home. In the case of a tie, it was important, he cautioned Madison, that he request, on Jefferson's behalf, that Adams be preferred. Mr. Adams, he told him, had always been his senior and had always "ranked" him in public life, both in France and in America. "I am his junior in life, was his junior in Congress, his junior in the diplomatic line, his junior lately in our civil government."[8]

Word soon reached Jefferson that Adams had received three more votes than he in the Electoral College, thereby designating John Adams president and Thomas Jefferson vice president. Never anticipating that the president and the vice president might represent antagonistic points of view—as noted above, the Constitution made no provision for organized political parties—the framers of the Constitution had provided simply that the man who received the highest number of votes would become president, and the one who received the second highest number of votes would be vice president.

During the previous eight years there had been serious disagreements over the balance of liberty and authority in the government, and as a result two great political parties had come into being. The line between these parties had gradually hardened, and now the Republican Party was welded together on a platform of states' rights, whereas the Federalists favored the increasing power of the federal government.

This was not the only difficult issue presented by the Constitution. The U.S. Constitution had been drafted as a bundle of compromises, in an effort to surmount serious regional differences and jealousies. One crucial question was how to apportion the votes of the states in Congress. The small states wanted an equal vote; the large states, for obvious reasons, preferred a proportional one. Debate on the issue provoked much bitterness.

The question was also raised whether a slave, who had no vote, should be counted as a "person" in apportioning both taxes and representation in the House of Representatives. The South, with a lot of slaves, said yes; the North said no. "Blacks are property," said Eldridge Gerry, a delegate from Massachusetts, "and are used to the southward as horses and cattle to the northward."[9]

As a compromise between total representation and none at all, it was decided that a slave would count as three-fifths of a person. The vote would tally the whole number of white and free citizens and three-fifths of "all other Persons," excluding Indians, not taxed. "All other Persons" were, of course, slaves, a word carefully excluded from the Constitution. (This ratio of three slaves to five free citizens—the "Great Compromise"—had actually been worked out five years before, when the Confederation Congress sought a new base for national taxes.)

In this way the three-fifths clause determined how many congressmen a state would send to the House of Representatives, and it specified the amount of direct taxes the state would pay to the national government. As an appeasement to the small states, it was agreed that in the second branch of the Congress—the Senate—each state, regardless of its size or population, would have two senators.

The election of a president was also affected by the three-fifths clause because it is the members of the Electoral College who actually cast ballots for the president and the vice president, and the number of electors from each state equaled the total number of its representatives and senators.[10] The establishment of the Electoral College was agreed to after the three-fifths principle had been approved.

The three-fifths rule, or *federal ratio,* remained the law until the Fourteenth Amendment to the Constitution was passed in 1866, eight months after the Civil War ended.* Alexander Hamilton said that without the federal ratio "no union could possibly have been formed," and approval of it was an essential condition for joining the Union in 1787.[11] While it was not a specific endorsement of slavery, it has been described as the major instrument in uniting slave and nonslave states in a national legislature. Although the South was terrified of a slave rebellion, southern plantation owners had no desire to limit the number of slaves in their society. Slavery made the South—economically and politically.[12]

꧁ Jefferson, wishing to avoid the elaborate ceremonies planned for the inauguration in Philadelphia, looked up the Constitution and de-

---

*Amendment Thirteen, which prohibits slavery, is the only explicit mention of slavery in the Constitution.

cided that the oath of office could be administered anywhere—at Char-lottesville, even at Monticello. But he finally decided to brave the long winter journey over muddy roads out of respect for the American people. This time the delicate Maria did not accompany him. More and more, Maria reminded Jefferson of her mother, and he was fearful that the trip at this time of year would prove too strenuous for her.

Jefferson, who hated the cold, traveled ten days to Philadelphia in weather so severe that the ink froze in his pen. Jupiter accompanied him for part of the way, but his master soon sent him home in order to spare him and the horses the hard trip. Jefferson completed the journey by stage. His fellow passengers might have been surprised to learn that the bag he carried with him contained the fossilized bones of a prehistoric mastodon that had once roamed the western part of Virginia. They had been given to him by an Indian chief, and now he planned to present them to the American Philosophical Society, which met in Philadel-phia.

Jefferson had hoped to arrive in the capital unnoticed, but he was met by a military delegation carrying a banner inscribed: JEFFERSON, THE FRIEND OF THE PEOPLE.

On March 4, 1797, Thomas Jefferson was inaugurated as the second vice president of the United States.

The evening before, he had been installed as president of the Amer-ican Philosophical Society. He succeeded the noted astronomer and mathematician David Rittenhouse, who had succeeded Benjamin Franklin. The society's meetings, and Jefferson's contacts with its mem-bers, would help considerably to diminish his loneliness in Philadelphia. His election as president of the society attested to his national recogni-tion as a man of science—or knowledge, the broad sense in which the word *science* was used at the time. He later referred to his installation as president of the society as the "most flattering incident" of his life.

 The vice presidency provided Jefferson with relative leisure and enabled him to divide his time between Monticello and Philadelphia. He played no part in the conduct of the administration—President Adams ignored him in all political matters—although he was frequently the target of the Federalist press, which had attacked him during the campaign and continued to target him and his Republican beliefs. He kept a remarkably cool head in the midst of the turmoil swirling around him, hopeful that his country would not be drawn into the hazards of a war with France. But the differences between Adams and Jefferson continued, by painful degrees, to undermine their old friendship.

In the fall of 1797, in an attempt to resolve existing differences between the United States and France, John Adams appointed three ministers to France. When the men reached Paris they expected to meet with Charles Maurice de Talleyrand, the crafty French foreign minister. Instead, they were secretly approached by three go-betweens, referred to only as X, Y, and Z, who demanded a large bribe for the privilege of merely talking to Talleyrand. The terms were unacceptable to the American envoys.

It was the following March before dispatches from the ministers finally arrived in Philadelphia. These indicated that war with France seemed inevitable. Frenchmen were infuriated by Jay's Treaty, condemning it as the first step of the United States toward an alliance with England and as a violation of the Franco-American Treaty of 1778. In retaliation, French warships began to seize defenseless American merchant vessels.

When the dispatches from France were published in the newspapers, public opinion rallied in support of President Adams. War hysteria swept the country, and the slogan of the hour was "Millions for defense, but not one cent for tribute." But neither Adams nor Congress was prepared to declare war. Instead, they concentrated on strengthening the United States' military defenses. The Navy Department was created, and the three-ship navy expanded. John Adams was particularly anxious to create a strong navy, what he called "wooden walls," to defend the country's coastline and protect its shipping. Between 1798 and 1800 the U.S. navy captured more than eighty French ships, although neither country officially declared war. The period has been called the "Quasi War."

In France, Talleyrand realized that he had been outwitted, and let it be known that if the American government sent a new minister, he would be received with proper respect.

It wasn't long, however, before Republican criticism of Federalist anti-French policies reached unprecedented heights. Verbal violence in the press was unrestrained. John Adams determined to silence these attacks, and the Federalists drove through Congress the Alien and Sedition Acts.[13]

The Alien Acts were aimed at the European immigrants, who, lacking wealth, were scorned by the aristocratic Federalists, yet welcomed as voters by the less prosperous and more democratic Jeffersonians. The acts extended the term of residence required for immigrants who desired to become citizens from five to fourteen years. This was a drastic change that violated the American policy of open-door hospitality and speedy assimilation. Further, the president was granted the right to expel or imprison any foreigner whose presence he considered dangerous and to expel the nationals of any state with which the United States was at war.

The Sedition Act, passed on July 14, 1798, was an attempt by the Federalists to limit free speech and silence the opposition party. It was a direct slap at two freedoms guaranteed by the Bill of Rights: freedom of speech and freedom of the press. The act made it a federal crime "to write, print, utter or publish . . . any false, scandalous or malicious writings" against the government, the president, or Congress, or to stir up hatred or disrespect for them.[14]

The Alien and Sedition Acts, despite outcries from the Jeffersonians, commanded widespread popular support. Anti-French hysteria played directly into the hands of conservatives looking for a campaign issue. In the congressional elections of 1798–99 the Federalists, riding a wave of popularity, scored a sweeping victory.[15]

Jefferson regarded these acts as "an experiment on the American mind to see how far it will bear an avowed violation of the constitution."[16] Even as vice president, he was powerless to act against them, since he too could be prosecuted for sedition if he publicly criticized them. Yet he recognized that if the Federalists managed to stifle free speech, the country might well become a dangerous one-party monarchy.

Ten years before, referring to Shays's Rebellion in Massachusetts, he had said, "The people are the only censors of their governors . . . and were it left to me to decide whether we should have a government without newspapers or newspapers without a government, I should not hesitate to choose the latter. But I should mean that every man should receive those papers and be capable of reading them."[17] He was saying that the mind of man must be left free. There must be freedom of discussion. The security of society is dependent on the free dissemination of knowledge. To Thomas Jefferson, a free press was an essential feature of a republican government. This was one of his deepest convictions.

So he and James Madison secretly collaborated on a counterattack. They wrote the Kentucky (Jefferson) and Virginia (Madison) resolutions that declared that individual states had the right to reject federal laws that they saw as unconstitutional. The resolutions reaffirmed natural rights and states' rights and challenged the constitutionality of the Alien and Sedition Acts. Freedom of speech would become an important issue in the next campaign.

The first duty of the vice president is to preside over the Senate, but Jefferson's recollection of the rules of parliamentary procedure had grown rusty over the years. As a young lawyer and member of the Virginia legislature he had prepared a *Parliamentary Pocket Book,* and this he now studied and then revised and expanded. *A Manual of Parliamentary Practice* remains today the standard book of rules that govern American deliberative bodies.

In June of 1797 Jefferson received news that couldn't have surprised him but must surely have delighted him. Maria was engaged to marry Jack Eppes. Over the years, and particularly in Philadelphia, Jefferson had watched as friendship blossomed into love. He was "inexpressibly" pleased, he confided to Martha, and said he couldn't have found a better person "if I had the whole earth free to have chosen a partner for her."[18]

Later he would advise his young daughter, "Harmony in the married state is the very first object to be aimed at . . . a determination in each to consider the love of the other as of more value than any object whatever."[19]

Maria and Jack were married at Monticello on a glorious autumn day, the brilliant fall foliage a foil for her delicate beauty. Tradition says that she wore her mother's white satin wedding gown. Her Uncle Eppes nearly drowned attempting to pick pond lilies for her bridal bouquet.

Maria Jefferson had finally become an Eppes in name—as she had long been in spirit.

〜 Jefferson continued to divide his time between Philadelphia and Monticello, but his time away from his family always made him homesick. He counted the days until he could return to his mountain and his family. During the intervals when he was at Monticello, his joy was lessened if his daughters weren't there to share it. "The bloom of Monticello is chilled by my solitude. It makes me wish the more that yourself and sister were here to enjoy it," he wrote to Martha.[20]

Waiting impatiently for Maria and Jack's arrival when he was home for a holiday during the summer of 1798, he wrote, "We have been . . . imagining that every sound we heard was that of the carriage which was once more to bring us together." But when he learned that Maria was ill and unable to travel, he cautioned her not to undertake the journey until she was strong enough and then only by very short stages. "Nurse yourself, therefore, with all possible care for your own sake, for mine, and that of all those who love you," he entreated her. He would be uneasy, he told her in another letter the next day, until he knew the "truth of your situation."[21]

Maria came as soon as she recovered.

〜 31 〜

# "We Are All Republicans, We Are All Federalists"

DURING JEFFERSON'S TENURE as secretary of state, he had worked closely with George Washington in planning Federal City, the new national capital on the Potomac River. In June of 1800, the government was moved there, and President and Mrs. John Adams took up residence in the half-finished President's House. Jefferson returned to Monticello and tried to remain aloof from the "tumult of the world."

By now, three new states had been added to the original thirteen:

Vermont, Kentucky, and Tennessee. The population of the United States was 5,308,000, more than 1,000,000 of whom were enslaved.

By late fall of 1800 Jefferson found himself nominated for the presidency as the Republican Party candidate. Aaron Burr of New York would be his running mate for vice president. The Federalists nominated John Adams for a second term, with Charles Coatsworth Pinckney of South Carolina for vice president.

Jefferson immediately wrote to John Adams, assuring him that the presidential contest had nothing to do with their personalities and everything to do with their conflicting political principles. "Were we both to die today," Jefferson told Adams, "tomorrow two other names would be put in the place of ours, without any change in the motion of the machinery."[1]

Nonetheless, a bitter campaign was soon underway. It quickly became clear to Jefferson and the Republicans exactly what the Sedition Act was meant to accomplish. The Federalists were attempting to close off the Republicans' ability to criticize the government and hold it accountable to the people. They were also controlling what newspapers would write about the candidates and the parties just before the coming presidential election. The Republicans knew that if they were silenced, they could not win.

At the same time, fierce invectives were being hurled at Thomas Jefferson by the clergy. In some states, they denounced him as an atheist. They hoped to see the formation of an established church in the United States as in England. To Jefferson, this would undermine the freedom of religion guaranteed by the Bill of Rights. In his view, the Sedition Act had already attempted to crush free speech and to suppress public criticism of Federalist policies. He couldn't allow this to happen to freedom of religion.

The Sedition Act negated one of Jefferson's sacred beliefs: freedom of the human mind. But he stubbornly refused to make any public statement in reply to the attacks. He outlined his views in a letter to his friend Dr. Benjamin Rush, a Philadelphia physician and fellow member of the American Philosophical Society. The law, Jefferson wrote, had "given to the clergy a very favorite hope of obtaining an establishment of a particular form of Christianity thro' the U. S.; and as every sect believes its own form the true one, every one perhaps hoped for its own, but especially the Episcopalians & Congregationalists. . . . They believe that any portion of power confided to me, will be exerted in opposition to their schemes. . . . And they believe rightly; for I have sworn upon the altar of god, eternal hostility against every form of tyranny over the mind of man."[2]

December 3, 1800, was designated election "day," but it would take two and a half months for the results of the election to be final. Actually, December 3 was the day on which *electors* were to cast their votes. The electors themselves had been chosen by the legislatures in their respective states over a period of months.

Jefferson knew that in his own state of Virginia the voters supported him solidly. From the time that he had first been elected a burgess for the county of Albemarle more than thirty years before, he had never suffered defeat at the Virginia polls. He expected that he would carry most of the southern states, while the Federalists would carry New England. Thus the "middle states" were critical, and none more so than New York.

New York had twelve votes. The Federalists currently controlled the legislature in that state, but a new legislature would be elected in April, and it was the new one that would name the presidential electors. It was crucial, therefore, that Republicans win the legislative elections. Aaron Burr of New York, who had lost his seat in the U.S. Senate, campaigned skillfully, tirelessly, ceaselessly for the Republicans. The prize, he was certain, would be a place for himself on the Republican national ticket. After three days of balloting in New York, at midnight on May 1, a newspaper headline there announced a stunning victory: REPUBLICANISM TRIUMPHANT.[3]

In November the government had moved from Philadelphia to Federal City,* which had been carved out of a small piece of the Mary-

---

*Soon to be named Washington, in honor of George Washington, who died on December 14, 1799, just seventeen days before the start of the new century.

land woods on the shore of the Potomac River. When Jefferson arrived there at the end of the month, he took lodgings at the boardinghouse of Conrad and McMunn, often called simply Conrad's. Here he took his meals at a common table with anywhere from twenty-four to thirty people, all of them political friends. From Conrad's, he could walk to the new and still unfinished Capitol building, where, as vice president, he presided over the Senate.

Within two weeks of his arrival, Jefferson knew that his party was victorious. The Republicans had a clear victory over John Adams and the Federalist Party. But Jefferson's own victory was not assured. When as vice president presiding over a joint session of Congress, he calmly opened the electors' certificates, he realized that there was a tie between him and his running mate, Aaron Burr. Each man had received 73 electoral votes against 65 for Adams, 64 for Pinckney. In accordance with the Constitution, the person receiving the highest number of electoral votes would become president, while the second highest would become vice president.

This sort of tie within the same party had never been foreseen. It could be broken only by a vote in the House of Representatives, where each state had just one vote. A majority vote of nine of the sixteen states would be necessary for election. The two parties agreed that the representatives would meet and vote in continuous session until a winner was declared.

John Adams was horrified at the thought that Aaron Burr might become the next president of the United States. "All the old patriots, all the splendid talents, the long experience, both of federalists and anti-federalists must be subjected to the humiliation of seeing this dexterous gentleman rise, like a balloon, filled with inflammable air, over their heads," he wrote to Elbridge Gerry. "What a discouragement to all virtuous exertion, and what an encouragement to party intrigue, and corruption!"[4]

Jefferson had won eight of the sixteen states, and needed only one more state to reach a majority. Burr had received six. One bloc of six states was firmly Federalist. Two states, Vermont and Maryland, were equally divided, Federalist and Republican. The House remained in session throughout the night, until eight o'clock the next morning, taking twenty-seven ballots. At each new balloting the results remained the same. Members of the House dozed between ballots. Some went home for blankets and pillows. Candles were brought in. One of the delegates, Republican Joseph Nicholson of Maryland, although ill and running a high fever, was brought to the House with his bed in spite of the whirling snowstorm that was blanketing the city. With his wife sitting beside him, periodically giving him medicine, he rested in a little ante-room off the House Chamber, voting at each ballot. He knew his vote was crucial.

Through it all, both sides were attempting to sway the needed votes. Describing the situation, Jefferson wrote to his daughter Martha, "[T]here is such a mixture of bad passions in the heart that one feels themselves in an enemy's territory."[5]

Approached by the Federalist Gouverneur Morris as he was coming out of the Senate Chamber, Jefferson was told that Morris would influence one vote provided Jefferson would make certain promises. Jefferson answered that he would not make any such declaration. In a letter to James Monroe, Jefferson wrote: "Many attempts have been made to obtain terms and promises from me. I have declared to them unequivocally, that I would not receive the government on capitulation, that I would not go into it with my hands tied."[6]

The deadlock continued. Passions raged. A chain of express riders carried messages back and forth between Washington and the capitals of the states to keep the people informed of events in Washington. Jefferson continued to hold out hope.

Neither John Adams nor Alexander Hamilton trusted Aaron Burr. Now no longer in the running himself, Adams—and Hamilton—decided to support Jefferson, and urged their colleagues to do the same. Despite this, the deadlock continued in the Federalist-dominated House of Representatives through thirty-five ballots, over a tense period of six days. Throughout, Thomas Jefferson maintained his traditional calm and dignity.

Finally, the Federalists realized they had to surrender. Staunch Federalist James A. Bayard, a strong Burr supporter and Delaware's sole representative, in an act of pure patriotism, courageously indicated that he would defer to the will of the people by withholding his vote from

Burr. He would do so, he said, because he was "perfectly resolved not to risk the Constitution or a civil war."[7]

On February 17, on the thirty-sixth ballot, Bayard entered a blank piece of paper, as did Federalist delegates from South Carolina, thereby reducing Burr's total to four states and giving Jefferson a majority of the votes cast. Vermont and Maryland also submitted blank ballots, thus effectively delivering those states to Jefferson.[8]

On February 28, 1801, Thomas Jefferson resigned from the chair of the Senate and prepared for his inauguration as the third president of the United States. The fragile union had been preserved.[9]

During the weeks in which the outcome of the election had remained uncertain, President Adams had filled every office under his control with Federalists loyal to him. By March 3 he had appointed 216 new officials in what came to be known as the "midnight appointments." The most distressing of these to Jefferson was Adams's appointment, for life, of John Marshall—Jefferson's distant cousin and bitter political foe—as chief justice of the Supreme Court. Adams had initially offered the chief justiceship to New York's governor, John Jay, but Jay had declined. As chief justice, the forty-five-year-old Marshall, a moderate Federalist loyal to President Adams, would be able to defeat many of Jefferson's cherished aims.

On the eve of the inauguration, at four o'clock in the morning, John Adams quietly left Washington by stagecoach and went home to Quincy, Massachusetts.

Later the "federal ratio"—the three-fifths rule—would prompt the accusation that Thomas Jefferson had stolen the election from John Adams. There were many who felt that Adams was ejected from Washington only because Southerners, who owned the most slaves, supported Jefferson. Some were heard to say that Jefferson rode into the presidency on the backs of his slaves. Soon he was branded with the epithet "Negro President."[10]

Jefferson saw it differently. "The storm we have passed through proves our vessel indestructible," he wrote to his old friend the Marquis de Lafayette.[11] Power had been transferred peacefully from one party to another. American voters had brought about a bloodless transfer of power that Jefferson called "The Revolution of 1800." This was the first time in the history of the world that an election had brought about the move from one political philosophy to another without bloodshed. To Thomas Jefferson, the momentous change of government was "as real a revolution in the principles of our government as that of 1776 was in its form; not effected indeed by the sword . . . but by the rational and peaceful instrument of reform, the suffrage of the people." The point of his "revolution" was to banish forever the possibility that the power of the central government would jeopardize the rights of states or citizens. Acutely conscious of the "fragility of the American experiment," his revolutionary optimism was predicated on the restraint of power. He had no desire to exterminate his enemies when he gained power.[12]

Jefferson had won without a single Federalist vote being cast for him. James Bayard and the others had simply abstained from voting.[13] But the Federalist Party of George Washington and many of the founding fathers had been crushed.

During the three weeks that separated the voting from the inauguration, Jefferson bent all his efforts toward repairing old differences. He made it clear that the Federalists would be welcomed into the Republican Party with open arms, for "if we can once more get social intercourse restored to its pristine harmony, I shall believe we have not lived in vain; and that it may, by rallying them to true Republican principles, which few of them had thrown off, I sanguinely hope."[14]

On March 2 Thomas Jefferson wrote to Chief Justice John Marshall, "I propose to take the oath of office as President of the U. S. on Wednesday the 4th [of March] at 12. o'clock in the Senate chamber. May I hope the favor of your attendance to administer the oath?"

"I shall with much pleasure attend to administer the oath of office on the 4th," Marshall replied the same day, "& shall make a point of being punctual."

On March 4, 1801, at ten o'clock in the morning, a detachment of Alexandria militia officers and marshals of the District of Columbia paraded by Conrad and McMunn's boarding house. Just before noon, a tall and lanky Thomas Jefferson, dressed simply in clothes that were, "as usual, that of a plain citizen, without any distinctive badge of office," and accompanied by the secretaries of the Navy and the Treasury and a small number of his political friends in the House of Representatives, left the house to walk along the mud streets, past unfinished buildings and a few scattered houses, to the Capitol building, on New Jersey Avenue at C Street, a few blocks away. Streaming along behind him came exuberant Republicans, eager to be part of the excitement of the day. The scene was in sharp contrast to the inaugurations of Jefferson's predecessors, George Washington and John Adams, both of whom had dressed elegantly, Adams in a splendid new suit of pearl-gray broadcloth, a cockaded hat, and a full sword at his side. Both had arrived in ornate carriages.[15]

As Jefferson approached the north wing of the Capitol, the only section of the building that had thus far been completed, the Alexandria rifle company posted outside the door opened ranks, and as Jefferson entered, they presented arms. Thomas Jefferson was about to become the first president of the United States to take the oath of office in Washington, D.C. George Washington and John Adams had been inaugurated in New York and Philadelphia, respectively.[16]

When the door to the tiny Senate Chamber opened, the crowd inside arose as one as the president-elect entered. "The Senate chamber was so crowded that, I believe, not another creature could enter," Margaret Bayard Smith wrote. She was the young wife of Samuel Harrison Smith, editor of the *National Intelligencer,* the capital city's major newspaper, and was describing it to her sister-in-law Susan. "On one side of the House the Senate sat, the other was assigned by the Representatives to the ladies. The roof is arched, the room half circle; every inch of ground was occupied. It has been conjectured by several gentlemen whom I asked that there were a thousand persons within the walls."[17]

Now Aaron Burr, newly inaugurated as vice president, left the presiding officer's chair. Jefferson took this seat, with Burr on his right hand and John Marshall on his left—three men, all of whom had never trusted one another. Only a few years later Aaron Burr would be arrested for treason at Jefferson's order and tried for his life, with John Marshall presiding at the trial.[18]

Thomas Jefferson sat for a few moments in silence. Then he rose and quietly began to speak. Although his voice was barely audible and only those fortunate enough to be seated in the front rows could hear him, he delivered an address that has resounded through the generations. He seems to have known that posterity would be listening. Once again, Jefferson recognized the power of the word, as he had twenty-five years earlier in the Declaration of Independence. With only fifteen days in which to prepare, he had chosen his words carefully, making three different drafts. He had managed to compress his address to fit on two sheets of paper written on both sides in his tiny and precise handwriting. It was a literary composition more than a speech and must be considered one of his greatest documents.

Speaking of a "rising nation, spread over a wide and fruitful land, traversing all the seas with the rich productions of their industry, engaged in commerce with nations who feel power and forget right, advancing rapidly to destinies beyond the reach of mortal eye," he committed to the "auspices of this day . . . the honor, the happiness, and the hopes of this beloved country." Then, with an appeal for national unity, he asked for guidance and support from the members of the legislature "which may enable us to steer with safety the vessel in which we are all embarked amidst the conflicting elements of a troubled world."

Jefferson understood full well the fragility of the American experiment. He knew that it was imperative that the "passions raised by the violent agitations" of the past eight years be quieted.[19] The anger that had raged throughout the campaign must be calmed. With a charm of style peculiarly his own and a choice of words calculated to please the ear of his and later generations, he turned the anger of the campaign into "the animation of discussions . . . which might impose on strangers unused to think freely and to speak and to write what they think." Here Jefferson was alluding to the Roman historian Tacitus, who in his *Historiae* had described the privilege of Roman citizens, in a happy time, to "think as we please, and speak as we think." Jefferson regarded Tacitus as the "first writer in the world, without a single exception."[20]

He continued with another deftly crafted sentence: "All, too, will bear in mind this sacred principle, that though the will of the majority is in all cases to prevail, that will to be rightful must be reasonable; that the minority possess their equal rights, which equal law must protect, and to violate would be oppression."

Having been carried into office on a great tide of public feeling, he resolved that the policy of his administration would not be one of reprisals. Jefferson was a pacifier and a harmonizer; he was not vindictive. Thus, he would use this opportunity as an attempt to unite the country behind the Republican leaders.[21] "Let us, then, fellow-citizens, unite with one heart and one mind," he pleaded.

> Let us restore to social intercourse that harmony and affection without which liberty and even life itself are dreary things. And let us reflect that, having banished from our land that religious intolerance under which mankind so long bled and suffered, we have gained little if we countenance a political intolerance as despotic, as wicked, and capable of as bitter and bloody persecutions. . . . But every difference of opinion is not a difference of principle. We have called by different names brethren of the same principle. We are all republicans, we are all federalists. If there be any among us who would wish to dissolve this Union or to change its republican form, let them stand undisturbed as monuments of the safety with which error of opinion may be tolerated where reason is left free to combat it.

He went on to affirm his belief in this country as "the strongest Government on earth. . . . [and] the only one where every man, at the call of the law, would fly to the standard of the law, and would meet invasions of the public order as his own personal concern. Sometimes it is said that man can not be trusted with the government of himself. Can he, then, be trusted with the government of others? Or have we found angels in the forms of kings to govern him? Let history answer this question."

He reminded his listeners that they possessed a "chosen country, with room enough for our descendents to the thousandth and thousandth generation," that they were "enlightened by a benign religion," and "adoring an overruling Providence." He then asked, "[W]hat more is necessary to make us a happy and a prosperous people?" "Still one thing more," he answered, "a wise and frugal Government, which shall restrain men from injuring one another, shall leave them otherwise free to regulate their own pursuits of industry and improvement, and shall not take from the mouth of labor the bread it has earned."

"It is proper," he told his fellow citizens, "you should understand what I deem the essential principles of our Government":

> Equal and exact justice to all men, of whatever state or persuasion, religious or political. . . .
> peace, commerce, and honest friendship with all nations, entangling alliances with none. . . .
> the support of all the State governments in all their rights. . . .
> the preservation of the General Government in its whole constitutional vigor, as the sheet anchor of our peace at home and safety abroad. . . .
> a jealous care of the right of election by the people. . . .
> absolute acquiescence in the decisions of the majority. . . .
> the supremacy of the civil over the military authority. . . .
> economy in the public expense, that labor may be lightly burthened. . . .
> the honest payment of our debts and sacred preservation of the public faith. . . .
> the diffusion of information, and the arraignment of all abuses at the bar of the public reason. . . .
> freedom of religion; freedom of the press; and freedom of person under the protection of the habeas corpus, and trial by juries impartially selected.

"Relying, then, on the patronage of your good will," he concluded, "I advance with obedience to the work, ready to retire from it whenever you become sensible how much better choice it is in your power to make. And may that Infinite Power which rules the destinies of the universe lead our councils to what is best, and give them a favorable issue for your peace and prosperity."[22]

At the conclusion of his address, Thomas Jefferson turned toward Chief Justice Marshall, who administered the oath of office.

After another volley of artillery, President Jefferson left the chamber and strolled back to Conrad's, accompanied by Burr, Marshall, and some of his friends. He took his usual seat at the dinner table far from the fire, at the coldest end of the table.

That morning Jefferson had sent a copy of his address to Samuel Smith, editor of the *National Intelligencer*. That enterprising young man had it printed and available for distribution as visitors left the Capitol.

Reading the speech in Philadelphia a few days later, and fully approving the maxims of republicanism that his friend Thomas Jefferson had set down, Benjamin Rush wrote to him: "You have concentrated whole chapters into a few aphorisms in defense of the principles and form of our government." Rush went on to say that the speech had opened a new era, then summed things up by saying, "I consider it as a solemn and affecting address to your fellow citizens, to the nations of Europe, to all the inhabitants of the globe, and to posterity to the latest generation, upon the great subject of political order and happiness."[23]

In contrast, Boston's *Columbian Centinel* of March 4, 1801, published a eulogy for the nation—encased in a black border—that mourned the passing of twelve exemplary years of Federalist government, "animated by a Washington, an Adams."[24]

On the evening of the inauguration, in their home just a short distance from where the new president resided, with candles blazing in all the windows of the houses along New Jersey Avenue in honor of President Thomas Jefferson, Margaret Bayard Smith continued her letter to her husband's sister, describing her emotions:

> I have this morning witnessed one of the most interesting scenes a free people can ever witness. The changes of administration, which in every government and in every age, have most generally been epochs of confusion, villainy and bloodshed, in this our happy country take place without any species of distraction or disorder. This day, has one of the most amiable and worthy men taken that seat to which he was called by the voice of his country. I listened to an address, containing principles the most correct and sentiments the most liberal, and wishes the most benevolent, conveyed in the most appropriate and elegant language and in a manner mild as it was firm. If doubts of the integrity and talents of Mr. Jefferson ever existed in the minds of anyone, methinks this address must forever eradicate them.[25]

Her husband echoed her sentiments: "Truly, these are strange times. But they are glorious ones, and they promise perpetuity."[26]

# Architect of American Expansion

THE CITY OF WASHINGTON at this time, was little more than a swamp, with a few shapeless, unfinished buildings. There were only a very few shops, including a tavern, some boardinghouses, a grocery and dry goods store, and a bookstore. There were, as well, the homes of a tailor, a shoemaker, and a washerwoman, but no amusements of any kind. Homes were being built, including the Smiths' home and the printing shop and office of Samuel Smith's newspaper.

But the members of Congress who came exhibited a faith in government and in a way of life they were building. Thomas Jefferson had the distinction of being the first president to be inaugurated in the new capital, in the first year of the new century.

Politically, Jefferson's first term as president was a brilliant success. He had surrounding him men of extraordinary intellect and loyalty. Among these, he had named as secretary of state James Madison, his closest political colleague and personal friend. Albert Gallatin, who combined financial and administrative talent with political wisdom, was his secretary of the treasury. In Gallatin, Jefferson had found a financial mind that could challenge Alexander Hamilton. All his Cabinet members recognized that harmony was important to their leader, and they made a particular effort to cooperate. At Jefferson's request, they avoided argumentative debates within the cabinet by resorting to "separate consultations" before the meetings, which, Jefferson felt, prevented "disagreeable collisions" at the full meetings.[1] Jefferson, in turn, frequently sought their advice and was willing to alter his own views when he was presented with a better argument.

By the end of 1803, most of his party's political program had been accomplished. In close collaboration with Congress, Jefferson had begun to pay off the national debt, and he had cut taxes, reduced the standing army, and ensured that the oceans were safe for American shipping.

During his presidency, he refused to sanction any alterations in the Constitution. The only change he would endorse was the Twelfth

Amendment, which corrected the irregularities that had occurred in the elections of 1796 and 1800 by providing that separate electoral ballots be cast for president and vice president.

The hated Alien and Sedition Acts had already expired, and Jefferson pardoned the "martyrs" serving sentences under the Sedition Act; the government also returned many fines. In 1802 a new naturalization law was enacted, reducing the requirement of fourteen years of residence to the original five.

Jefferson had determined as soon as he took office that he would change the formal social practices that had been favored by the Federalists. In keeping with his new policy, he shocked a visiting minister from Great Britain when he received him in his "usual morning-attire" and wearing slippers. The minister was in "full dress." Nor did Jefferson ever observe any formality at his table. He seated his guests indiscriminately and denied that there was ever a guest of honor. And he abolished the formal receptions that President Washington had instituted. When a group of ladies called on him despite this, the president, who had just returned from his morning ride, greeted them in his muddy riding boots. But he was never rude. His manners were easy, if not polished, and his simplicity was the naturalness of one who had achieved enough to dare to be himself.

Most dramatic of all, his long-standing fascination with the western wilderness inspired his brilliant purchase of the vast Louisiana Territory from France in 1803. This territory contained 828,000 square miles of virgin land west from the Mississippi River to the Rocky Mountains, including the strategic port of New Orleans.

The territory had recently been ceded to Napoléon and France by Spain, a cause for concern. As the United States was expanding westward, navigation of the Mississippi River and access to the port of New Orleans, with its vital outlet to the Gulf of Mexico, had become critical to American commerce. After Spain transferred the territory to France, American merchandise could no longer be stored in New Orleans warehouses duty free, and the entire economy of America's western territories was placed in jeopardy. It was crucial, Jefferson believed, that the port of New Orleans remain open and free for American shipping, particularly the goods coming down the Mississippi River. Jefferson "had a vision of America as an empire of liberty, and he saw the Mississippi River not as the western edge of the country, but as the great spine that would hold the continent together."[2]

"There is on the globe one single spot, the possessor of which is our natural and habitual enemy. It is New Orleans," he wrote to Robert Livingston, U.S. minister to France. "France placing herself in that door assumes to us the attitude of defiance." Despite his personal feelings for France, Jefferson understood that this must not be allowed to happen. "Perhaps nothing since the revolutionary war has produced more uneasy sensations through the body of the nation," he continued.[3]

In January 1803 Jefferson asked James Monroe to join Robert Livingston in Paris as minister extraordinary. Monroe's charge was to obtain land east of the Mississippi, and he was allocated $10 million for the purchase of New Orleans and all or part of the Floridas. "All eyes, all hopes, are now fixed on you," Jefferson told Monroe, "for on the event of this mission depends the future destinies of this republic."[4]

When Monroe arrived in Paris in April, he learned that Napoléon had decided to sell the entire Louisiana Territory to the United States for $22.5 million. On April 29, after brief negotiations, the price was lowered to $15 million.

Not only would this purchase open up the port of New Orleans, "through which the produce of three-eighths of our territory must pass to market,"[5] but it would double the size of the United States at less than three cents an acre.

When news of the opportunity to strike this magnificent real estate bargain reached Jefferson, he was in a quandary. He was determined to maintain free navigation of the Mississippi River, so crucial to the economic life of the trans-Appalachian states and territories. Now, this strict constructionist—this literal interpreter of the Constitution—wrestled with the realist and public servant that he was. He knew the Constitution did not authorize the president to negotiate treaties for acquiring new land. But he also knew that it was a wise move, best taken advantage of quickly. So a conscience-stricken Jefferson decided to submit the treaties to the Senate, which promptly and enthusiastically approved them. The Louisiana Purchase is considered the single greatest achievement of his presidency.[6] But "this vast addition to American territory, Jefferson's great diplomatic triumph, made possible the vast expansion and entrenchment of a brutal regime of plantation slavery."[7] The entire region ultimately became a new source of conflict between the North and the South.

Even before the Louisiana Purchase was complete, Jefferson had asked Congress to fund an expedition that would cross the Louisiana Territory, regardless of who controlled it.

On June 20, 1803, President Jefferson sent a letter to Meriwether Lewis, his private secretary and son of an old family friend. Jefferson's father and Lewis's grandfather had mapped Virginia together many years before. The letter contained secret instructions that Lewis was to follow as he fulfilled Jefferson's dream of an expedition across the Far West to map the Missouri River and to explore the land of the "Western country," over the Rocky Mountains and "even to the Western [Pacific] Ocean." It was to be Jefferson's great scientific contribution to his country and one of his greatest Enlightenment experiments— indeed, one of the glories of his administration. The letter's interest lies not least in the fact that Jefferson's instructions encompassed all the subjects that interested *him,* that would make it possible for *him* to acquire more knowledge and then to diffuse that knowledge in order to improve the world:

> The object of your mission is to explore the Missouri River, & such principal stream of it, as, by its course & communication with the water of the Pacific Ocean may offer the most direct and practicable water communication across this continent, for the purposes of commerce.
>
> Beginning at the mouth of the Missouri, you will take observations of latitude and longitude at all remarkable points on the river, & especially at the mouths of rivers, at rapids, at islands & other places & objects distinguished by such natural marks & characters of a durable kind, as that they may with certainty be recognized hereafter. The courses of the river between these points of observation may be supplied by the compass, the log-line & by time, corrected by the observations themselves. The variations of the compass too, in different places should be noticed. Your observations are to be taken with great pains & accuracy.

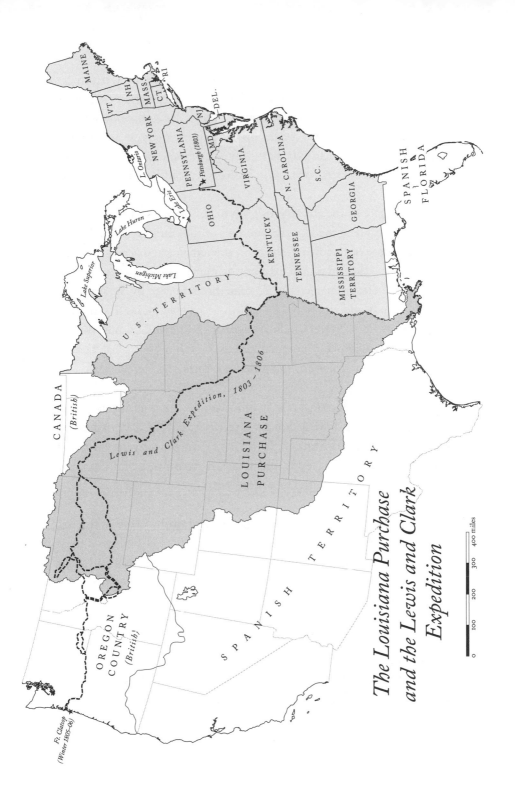

The Louisiana Purchase and the Lewis and Clark Expedition

MAINE

NH

VT

MASS.

CT

RI

NEW YORK

L. Ontario

Lake Erie

PENNSYLVANIA

Pittsburg (1803)

NJ

MD

DEL.

VIRGINIA

N. CAROLINA

S.C.

SPANISH FLORIDA

OHIO

KENTUCKY

TENNESSEE

GEORGIA

MISSISSIPPI TERRITORY

Lake Huron

Lake Michigan

Lake Superior

U. S.  T E R R I T O R Y

Lewis and Clark Expedition, 1803–1806

CANADA (British)

LOUISIANA PURCHASE

S P A N I S H   T E R R I T O R Y

OREGON COUNTRY (British)

Ft. Clatsop (Winter 1805–06)

0    100    200    300    400 miles

Jefferson went on to suggest that "one of these copies be written on the paper of the birch, as less liable to injury from damp than common paper." He may have remembered that twelve years before, when he and James Madison were on their tour up the Hudson River, he had written a letter to his twelve-year-old daughter Maria on a piece of birch bark.

"Other objects worthy of notice," Jefferson told Lewis, were

> the soil and face of the country, its growth and vegetable productions; especially those not of the U.S., the animals of the country generally, and especially those not known in the U.S., the remains and accounts of any which may be deemed rare or extinct; the mineral productions of every kind; . . . climate as characterized by the thermometer, by the proportion of rainy, cloudy and clear days, by lightning, hail, snow, ice, by the access and recess of frost, by the winds, prevailing at different seasons, the dates at which particular plants put forth or lose their flowers, or leaf, times of appearance of particular birds, reptiles or insects.[8]

Not only was Jefferson seeking knowledge, he was intent on tying together the east and west coasts, thereby creating a continent-wide empire for the United States. He was well on his way toward accomplishing that goal. The Lewis and Clark expedition became a brilliant consummation of his westward vision.

Jefferson continued to hunger for his family. "It is in the love of one's family only that heartfelt happiness is known. I feel it . . . beyond what can be imagined. . . . I count from one meeting to another as we do between port and port at sea: and I long for the moment with the same earnestness," he wrote to Maria.[9]

During the autumn of 1799, Maria and Jack had told him that Maria was expecting a baby. By this time Martha already had four children and seemed to have no difficulty bearing them. But Maria was so like her mother that Jefferson was filled with dread at the thought of what might be in store for her. His fear was justified. Maria's baby was born prematurely at Eppington on New Year's Eve and died less than a month later. The grief-stricken Maria had a long and painful convalescence.

"How deeply I feel it in all its bearings I shall not say—nor attempt consolation when I know that time and silence are the only medicines. I shall only observe, as a source of hope to us all, that you are young, and will not fail to possess enough of these dear pledges which bind us to one another and to life itself," her distraught father wrote to her. In the same letter he told her of the untimely death of Jupiter, his faithful servant and traveling companion, whom Martha's little daughter Ellen lovingly referred to as "Uckin [Uncle] Juba." "You have perhaps heard of the loss of Jupiter. With all his defects, he leaves a void in my domestic arrangements which cannot be filled."[10]

In an uncharacteristically detailed and sympathetic letter to his son-in-law Thomas Mann Randolph, Jefferson described the circumstances leading up to Jupiter's death and ended, "I am sorry for him."

The relationship between Jefferson and Jupiter reflects the cruel conflicts of the slave system and is difficult to understand completely. Jupiter was valuable property to Jefferson, as well as a human being— and a childhood friend.[11] A story is told that offers some insight into this relationship. It suggests Jupiter's fierce pride in his position was juxtaposed against Jefferson's refusal to allow Jupiter to "cross an invisible line" and challenge an established pattern of authority.

Jefferson, whose "unruffled temper was legendary," sent a young slave to the stable to take one of the carriage horses to the post office. Jupiter refused, telling the boy that these horses could not be used for any such purpose. The boy returned to Jefferson with the message. Jefferson, thinking Jupiter was playing a joke on the boy, sent him back with the same order. He must tell Jupiter that Mr. Jefferson was awaiting important letters. The boy returned to Jefferson with the same message: "Neither of his horses should go for anybody." Jefferson, visibly angry, ordered the boy to tell Jupiter that he must come to Mr. Jefferson at once. Jupiter came, and met a look and tone "which neither he nor the terrified bystanders ever forgot," but he "firmly declared that he must not be expected to keep the carriage horses in the desired condition if they were to be 'ridden round by boys.'" Jefferson agreed with his concern, but Jupiter was never again to use "so blunt a method of telling his mind."[12]

Two years after Maria lost her baby, she did have another of "these dear pledges." Francis Wayles Eppes, named for his paternal grandfather, was born at Monticello while his maternal grandfather was there enjoying a long summer vacation from the presidency.

Jefferson always made it a practice to spend the two sickly months of August and September on his mountain, where the air was free of infection. This summer he had immunized the members of his family and slaves who had not previously been inoculated against smallpox and also brought vaccine from Washington to Albemarle for the use of his neighbors. In this way he unofficially established vaccination as a public health procedure in Virginia.

Martha had also given birth at Monticello, to her fifth child, Virginia, just a month before. This newest daughter proved to be the largest and healthiest Martha ever had. She had a total of twelve children, all but one of whom survived. Martha herself remained amazingly strong and healthy throughout her life.

She was content to move between her own homes and Monticello—to spend, in fact, the greater portion of her time at her father's house. Jefferson had also helped his son-in-law Thomas Randolph purchase Edgehill, just a few miles from Monticello, from his father, Randolph

Martha Jefferson Randolph. (Courtesy of Monticello/ Thomas Jefferson Foundation, Inc.)

Sr. "It is essential to my happiness, our living near together," the president explained to his son-in-law. Martha's husband apparently had no objections to this, moving easily between the houses. When he was elected to the House of Representatives, he willingly added the trip to Washington to his itinerary as well.

During the winter of 1802 to 1803, Maria's strength returned, and she and Martha, together with some of the older children, were able to make the arduous journey from Virginia to Washington to visit their father and their husbands.* This was the only time Jefferson had both his daughters together with him in Washington. The solicitous president was happy to pay all their traveling expenses and delighted in taking them to the new shops for the latest fashions. His generosity to his daughters and their husbands and children never ceased.

He was overjoyed to have them all together in the presidential mansion, despite the lack of plaster on some of the ceilings and the cold. Thirteen fires had to be kept going in order to provide even minimum warmth, and the children were bundled up in coats as though they were out-of-doors.

All of Washington was charmed by the president's daughters. Martha's friendliness and intelligence and Maria's beauty and sweetness were frequently remarked upon. But the modest Maria hated allusions to her beauty. She wished for the kind of intelligence her sister had, in order—she told her father—to be more worthy of his love. In spite of her father's reassurances that there could never be a difference in his feelings for them, Maria was not convinced.

Jefferson doted on his grandchildren, and in Washington he served them ice cream for the first time; he had brought the recipe from France. In fact, to Thomas Jefferson goes the credit for introducing to America not only ice cream but also macaroni and waffles.

An official caller who found the president of the United States on the floor, playing with his grandchildren, was disarmed when Jefferson asked if he too was a father. "If so," said the president, "I need offer no apology."

As Jefferson's first term of office was drawing to a close, his popular-

---

*Jack Eppes, like his brother-in-law, had been elected to the House of Representatives.

ity was as its highest peak, and the nation was prospering. In fact, after his reelection to the presidency in 1805, it was said, half in jest, that he had a "prospect of reelection for life." None but his closest friends knew that he was determined that his second term would be his last.

His daughters had been temporarily living together in Albemarle while their husbands and father were in Washington, waiting for Congress "to rise." Martha had had a sixth child, and Maria, ill once again, was fearfully awaiting the birth of her third. The baby, a girl whom they named Maria, was born on February 15, 1804—before the arrival of her father or her grandfather. Jefferson sent "A thousand joys to you, My dear Maria, on the happy accession to your family."[13]

But their joy was short-lived. Jefferson soon learned from Martha that her fragile sister was dangerously ill. When Maria's milk dried up as a result, Martha simply took over the job of nursing the infant along with her own. "Nothing but the impossibility of Congress proceeding a single step in my absence" prevented an "instant departure to join you," the president wrote to his daughter. "God bless you my ever dear daughter and preserve you safe to be the blessing of us all."[14]

By the time Jefferson arrived at Monticello—where, at his suggestion, Maria had been gently carried by hand on a litter in the hope that the change of air would do her some good—he found her "so weak as to be barely able to stand, her stomach so disordered as to reject almost every thing she took into it, a constant small fever, & an imposthume [abscess] rising in her breast."[15] She grew steadily weaker.

Four days after his own sixty-first birthday, when the first bloom of spring was just beginning on the mountainside, Thomas Jefferson entered in his Account Book: "This morning between 8 & 9 o'clock my dear daughter Maria Eppes died." She was not yet twenty-six.

While Jefferson may never have fully acknowledged the clash of loyalties that constantly beset Maria, she was, in fact, more an Eppes than a Jefferson. But in death he claimed her as his own. He buried her in the lonely hillside graveyard at Monticello, near her mother and the tiny children they had lost.

"On the 17th instant our hopes and fears took their ultimate form," he wrote to James Madison, adding that he was not able to leave Monticello. A "desire to see my family in a state of more composure before we separate, will keep me somewhat longer."[16]

His grief, he said, was "inexpressible." Replying to a letter of condolence from his old friend John Page, he wrote, "Others may lose of their abundance, but I, of my want, have lost even the half of all I had. My evening prospects now hang on the slender thread of a single life."[17] Jefferson was never quite the same after Maria died. He lost his joie de vivre, his exuberance.

Abigail Adams, who never quite forgave Jefferson for what she considered his political offenses against her husband, read of Maria's death in the Quincy, Massachusetts, newspapers. Poignant memories of the tearful little girl who had clung to her in London prompted her to write to her old friend, "The powerful feelings of my heart burst through the restraint, and called upon me to shed the tear of sorrow over the departed remains of your beloved and deserving daughter."[18]

Francis and Elizabeth Eppes took the little Maria and Francis—all they had left of their precious Polly—back to Eppington to care for them there. Little Maria's life, too, was brief; she lived only three and a half years. But Francis grew up to be a source of pride and joy to his grandfather and remained a living link with this cherished daughter.

Throughout his presidency, Jefferson delivered only two public speeches, his two inaugural addresses. Even his Annual Messages to Congress were presented in written form, which he described as more efficient. He governed almost entirely by writing. "In his first year as president he received 1,881 letters, not including internal correspondence from his cabinet, and sent out 677 letters of his own." His tenure as executive has been described as "the textual presidency. The art of making decisions was synonymous with the art of drafting and revising texts."[19]

Politically, Jefferson's second term in office did not end on the same optimistic note as his first. The last years of his presidency were dominated by the problem of maintaining American neutrality in the face of a war between France and Great Britain. Both countries interfered with American trade. England had continued to seize American seamen and had attacked the American naval frigate *Chesapeake* off the coast of Norfolk, Virginia, claiming that it harbored four British deserters. When the British fired at the ship at close range, three Americans were killed and eighteen wounded.

Determined to avoid war, Jefferson recommended, and Congress speedily adopted, an embargo on foreign trade. It has been described as an original and daring act of statesmanship but a practical failure. While it did avoid war and encourage American manufacturing, there was widespread opposition to it, particularly in New England and in parts of the Middle Atlantic states, where shipping was an important industry. Merchants and ship owners found ways to evade it.

At first, Jefferson did not realize the full extent of the economic distress the embargo was causing. When he did, he acceded to the will of the people and lifted it. He signed the law repealing it during his last days in office. But he left the presidency disheartened.

Jefferson described himself as a wave-worn mariner approaching the shore and as a prisoner emerging from shackles. In a letter to a friend he wrote, "Nature intended me for the tranquil pursuits of science, by rendering them my supreme delight. But the enormities of the times in which I have lived have forced me to take a part in resisting them, and to commit myself on the boisterous ocean of political passions. I thank God for the opportunity of retiring from them without censure, and carrying with me the most consoling proofs of public approbation."[20]

Indeed, he received from the citizens of Washington an address that, while acknowledging his public service, expressed their gratitude and "appreciation for the mild and endearing virtues" that had made every one of them his friend. His reply, in language matched by no successor until Abraham Lincoln, expressed his hope that their country, "this solitary republic of the world, the only monument of human rights, and the sole depository of the sacred fire of freedom and self-government" would extend "its benign influence" to "other regions of the earth." In conclusion, he urged his fellow citizens "to maintain harmony and union among ourselves and to preserve from all danger this hallowed ark of human hope and happiness."[21]

In keeping with his republican beliefs, he rode down Pennsylvania Avenue to James Madison's inauguration as the fourth president of the

United States accompanied only by his grandson Thomas Jefferson Randolph.[22]

As he prepared for the trip home, he packed a trunk with papers pertaining to the American Indian to be shipped from Washington to Monticello. Jefferson's interest in the Native Americans was long-standing. He had grappled with their problems and studied their languages. Over the years, he had collected fifty Native American vocabularies, which he planned to have printed side by side in columns, in order to compare them with each other and with the Russian language, which he found similar. He had hoped to discover a common origin. But some wharf hands, thinking the trunk heavy enough that it might contain gold, made off with it. When they opened it and discovered that it contained nothing but papers, they were so angry they ripped the sheets and tossed them into the James River. A few of the papers were later found soaked and muddy and completely useless. It was an irreparable loss.

# PART V

# Patriarch of Monticello

# Octagonal Retreat

JEFFERSON'S PERPETUAL LONGING for Monticello—and all that it symbolized for him—the pull that existed throughout most of his life between what he saw as his duty to his country and the domestic peace and tranquillity he found with his family—finally ended with his retirement from the presidency and his return to Monticello in 1809.

He was now able to give free rein to his plans to revitalize his gardens, and in this his eighteen-year-old granddaughter Anne, whom he once compared to a gleam of sunshine, was his enthusiastic assistant, his keeper of the flowers. All the time he was in Washington, letters had flowed between them filled with talk of flowers. When Anne married in September 1808, her younger sister Ellen took over the job.

Jefferson was always essentially a scientist, and his gardens and groves were his laboratory. If they proved suitable, he passed cuttings on to interested neighbors and friends. The greatest service one could render any country was to add a useful plant to its culture, he had said some years before. Now he planted 250 varieties of vegetables and 150 varieties of fruit trees. Peas were his favorite food, and he grew 22 varieties. In a radical departure from the customs of the times, when southern houses had their lawns swept clean, he planted trees close to the house.

The weather continued to interest him, so he made careful note of the amount of rainfall, the severity of the winds, the dates of the first and last killing frosts, and the range in temperature. That he found the time to make such an enormous number of observations in his Garden Book shows that observing nature was something he loved to do.

"No occupation is so delightful to me as the culture of the earth, and no culture comparable to that of the garden. . . . But though an old man, I am but a young gardener."[1] His usual cheerfulness manifested itself most visibly here. The setting of his house on his mountaintop, with its unobstructed spectacular views in all directions, further attests to the

Jefferson's granddaughter Anne Cary Randolph, his "keeper of the flowers," whom he once described as a "gleam of sunshine." (Courtesy of Monticello/ Thomas Jefferson Foundation, Inc.)

importance of nature in his thinking. The changing moods and seasons of nature served as a constant spark for his imagination.

In the greenhouse off his suite of rooms he kept his favorite bird, a mockingbird, in a cage suspended over his flowers. He often allowed it to fly free, and it would at times sit on his table and sing for him or perch on his shoulder and take food from his lips. His grandchildren loved to watch it hop up the stairs after him.

Jefferson had at one time planned to build a home for Maria at Pantops, near Monticello. When she died, he abandoned the plan and decided instead to build in Bedford County, a three-day carriage ride away, on land he had inherited from his wife. It would be his legacy to Maria's son, Francis.

He named the house Poplar Forest for the 190 tulip poplar trees growing in the uncleared woodlands when Jefferson inherited the property. A beautiful relative of the magnolia tree, the tulip poplar grows tall and full in the Virginia woods. The dwelling at Poplar Forest became the first octagonal house in the New World, and one of the most imaginative. Jefferson believed then, and architects have since confirmed, that the octagonal floor plan uses space economically and allows maximum flow of light and air. In both Poplar Forest and Monticello he was particularly concerned that there be large rooms and large windows.

It was only at Poplar Forest that Jefferson, always accompanied by one or two grandchildren, could escape the steady stream of visitors at Monticello, exchanging it for "his favorite pursuits—to think, to study, to read—whilst the presence of his family took away all the character of solitude from his retreat."[2] He made at least three visits there annually, and the grandchildren who were chosen to accompany him considered it a special treat.

In the fall of 1818, when Jefferson realized that he was not well enough to make the trip to Poplar Forest, he wrote to Yancey, his overseer there, directing him to "act in all things for the best according to your own judgment." He did, however, send along certain instructions, including a list of slaves who were to be given blankets that winter and those who were to be given beds. Then he added: "Maria [a slave] having now a child, I promised her a house to be built this winter. Be so

Poplar Forest, Jefferson's octagonal retreat, of which he said in 1812, "When finished, it will be the best dwelling house in the state, except that of Monticello; perhaps preferable to that, as more proportioned to the faculties of a private citizen." (Courtesy of Thomas Jefferson's Poplar Forest, Les Schofer, photographer)

good as to have it done. Place it along the garden fence on the road east-ward from Hanah's house."[3]

When Hanah, or Hannah as she spelled her name, heard of her mas-ter's illness, she sent him a note: "Master, I write you a few lines to let you know that your house and furniture are all safe as I expect you would be glad to know. I heard that you did not expect to come up this fall. I was sorry to hear that you was so unwell you could not come. It grieve me many time but I hope as you have been so blessed in this [life] that you considered it was God that done it. . . . Your humble servant, Hannah."[4]

Hannah was one of several of Jefferson's slaves who were literate. Jefferson preserved the letter.

# 34

## "A Fire Bell in the Night"

"I THANK YOU for your information on the progress and prospects of the Missouri question. It is the most portentous one which ever yet threatened our Union. In the gloomiest moment of the revolutionary war I never had any apprehensions equal to what I feel from this source."[1]

So Thomas Jefferson began a letter to a correspondent in February 1820. Sectional tensions had reemerged in 1819 when the territory of Missouri appealed to Congress for admission to the Union as a slave state. The North protested, and abolitionists sought to make Missouri a free state. By this time, free and slave states were equally balanced—eleven of each—giving each side equal representation in the Senate. The South wanted to keep it that way, but the North was becoming wealthier and more populated, thereby giving them a majority in the House of Representatives. Now a bill to admit Maine to the Union as a free state had passed the House. The South refused to allow Maine entry into the Union if Missouri could not enter as a slave state.

Jefferson had already expressed his fears that the country might revolt in a letter to his old friend John Adams: "From the battle of Bunker's Hill to the Treaty of Paris, we never had so ominous a question. . . . I thank God I shall not live to witness its issue." In his reply, Adams voiced his own fear that "this mighty Fabric," the nation, might be torn apart and "produce as many Nations in North America as there are in Europe."[2]

Missouri was the first state entirely west of the Mississippi River to be carved out of the Louisiana Purchase. Southerners feared that if Missouri were allowed to enter as a free state, a precedent would be set for the rest of the territory. Indeed, a bloc of Northern representatives and senators proposed to stop the westward advance of slavery by making the Mississippi River above the southern boundary of the state of Missouri (latitude 36°30′ north) the line of demarcation of slavery. This "containment policy" would have made most of the Louisiana Purchase free soil. Thirty-five years before, Jefferson had tried, unsuccessfully, to exclude slavery from all the territories of the United States east of the Mississippi. Now, the North and South were locked in a struggle for control of the West.[3]

Jefferson was certain that drawing an artificial geographical line that would become a line of separation between free and slave states would tear the country asunder:

> But this momentous question, like a fire bell in the night, awakened and filled me with terror. I considered it at once as the knell of the Union. . . . A geographical line, coinciding with a marked principle, moral and political, once conceived and held up to the angry passions of men, will never be obliterated; and every new irritation will mark it deeper and deeper. I can say, with conscious truth, that there is not a man on earth who would sacrifice more than I would to relieve us from this heavy reproach, in a *practicable* way. . . . But as it is, we have the wolf by the ear, and we can neither hold him, nor safely let him go. Justice is in one scale, and self-preservation in the other.

He concluded sadly: "I regret that I am now to die in the belief, that the useless sacrifice of themselves by the generation of 1776, to acquire self-government and happiness to their country, is to be thrown away by the unwise and unworthy passions of their sons, and that my only consolation is to be, that I live not to weep over it."[4]

A compromise was essential. Henry Clay of Kentucky, Speaker of the House of Representatives, played a leading role in effecting it. Missouri would be admitted as a slave state if, at the same time, Maine, a free-soil state that until then had been a part of Massachusetts, was admitted as a separate state. The balance would be maintained at twelve states each (which it would remain for the next fifteen years).

Compromise had made the Union in 1789. Now compromise saved the Union—at least until 1860, when Adams's and Jefferson's worst fears would be realized.

## ⤳ 35 ⤲

## Scandal

O N SEPTEMBER 1, 1802, during the first term of Jefferson's presidency, a feature article appeared in the Richmond *Recorder,* a weekly newspaper, that kindled a scandal that would haunt Thomas Jefferson for the rest of his life and that has not died out even in our own day.

> It is well known that [Thomas Jefferson] the man, whom it delighteth the people to honor, keeps and for many years past has kept, as his concubine, one of his slaves. Her name is SALLY. The name of her eldest son is Tom.* His features are said to bear a striking although sable resemblance to those of the president himself. The boy is ten or twelve years of age. His mother went to France in the same vessel with Mr. Jefferson and his two daughters.† The delicacy of this arrangement must strike every person of common sensibility. . . .

---

*Sally did not have a son named Tom.
†Callender later admitted that this accusation was not true.

By this wench Sally, our president has had several children. . . .

The AFRICAN VENUS is said to officiate, as housekeeper at Monticello.

The "Dusky Sally" story, as it came to be called, was written by James Callender, the notoriously unscrupulous editor of the *Recorder*, whom Thomas Jefferson had previously—unwisely—befriended. Its motive was clear: Callender wanted revenge.

Callender was a Scot who had fled his native country in 1793 to escape a jail sentence for sedition and libel. In the United States he used his literary talents in the newspaper battle being waged between the Federalists and the Republicans during the elections of 1796 and 1800. Jefferson, unaware of Callender's lack of scruples, at first welcomed his support, never anticipating that Callender might try to blackmail him.

In 1798 Callender was tried and convicted under the Sedition Act for defaming President John Adams. He was sentenced to nine months in jail and fined two hundred dollars. Three years later, when Thomas Jefferson became president, Callender was one of the "martyrs" he pardoned. When the government was unable to refund Callender's fine immediately, Jefferson paid part of it out of his own pocket. But Callender was not satisfied.

Now he demanded an appointment as postmaster in Richmond as a reward for his previous political support. Jefferson refused, and Callender took his revenge in the stinging attack in the *Recorder.* Its accusations have echoed down through the centuries.

Jefferson, Callender claimed, had seduced Sally Hemings, his young slave, in Paris when she was just fifteen years old, and Sally was pregnant when she returned to America with him and his two daughters. Callender further alleged that Jefferson kept Sally as his mistress—having six children by her—over the next fifteen years, even while he was president of the United States.

Many people were outraged and refused to believe the accusations. "There are such things, after all, as moral impossibilities," Jefferson's granddaughter Ellen would say many years later. His grandson Jeff also repudiated the allegation, explaining the strong resemblance of some young slaves to Thomas Jefferson by claiming that Peter Carr, Jefferson's nephew, was the father.

Jefferson himself steadfastly refused to reply to the accusations. In a letter to a friend written many years later he wrote, "As to federal slanders, I never wished them to be answered, but by the tenor of my life, half a century of which has been a theatre at which the public have been spectators, and competent judges of its merit. Their approbation has taught a lesson, useful to the world, that any man who fears no truths has nothing to fear from lies. I should have fancied myself half guilty had I condescended to put pen to paper in refutation of their falsehoods, or drawn to them respect by any notice from myself."[1]

In the light of recent findings from genetic (DNA) testing, however, that indicate that Eston Hemings was likely the son of Thomas Jefferson and Sally Hemings,[2] it now seems fair to say that Thomas Jefferson may have lived the great paradox of American history. The institution of slavery resonated through his life. Perhaps nowhere was this more powerfully illustrated than in his own home.

# 36

# "The Venerable Corps of Grandfathers"

"I RECEIVE WITH REAL PLEASURE your congratulations on my advancement to the venerable corps of grandfathers, and can assure you with truth that I expect from it more felicity than any other advancement ever gave me. I only wish for the hour when I may go and enjoy it entire."[1]

So Thomas Jefferson had responded to Elizabeth Eppes after the birth of his first grandchild on January 23, 1791. The little girl born to Martha and Tom Randolph was named Anne by her grandfather. This birth ushered in a period of his life that brought him untold joy—as well as deep sorrow.

During his years after the presidency, when he was able, finally, to "go and enjoy it entire," he derived his greatest happiness from his grandchildren. While his natural reserve and his superior intellect may have made him appear withdrawn or intimidating to some adults, he was always at ease with children. His warmth toward them is evident in all their reminiscences about him and in the letters they exchanged with him as soon as they were old enough to read and write.

He thoughtfully responded to all their questions—both serious and trifling—so that they felt comfortable going to him with their problems. He devoted as much time and effort to selecting a new dress or a toy for a young child as he did to outlining a course of study for an older one.

His sense of family was strong. Like his father before him, he cared for the fatherless, and his home was always filled with nieces and nephews as well as with his own children and grandchildren. He even strove, when possible, to keep his slave families together, occasionally buying or selling a slave at the slave's request to keep a marriage or a family intact.

Many members of the Hemings family were often in the house as well. Sally, who had been ladies' maid to Patsy and Polly in France, continued in that position at Monticello. Ultimately, she looked after Jefferson's chamber and wardrobe, cared for Martha Randolph's younger children, and did sewing and other light work. As a young child, she had

Watercolor of Monticello, showing Jefferson's grandchildren, 1826. (Courtesy of Monticello/Thomas Jefferson Foundation, Inc.)

run errands for Martha Jefferson, and she always worked inside the house.

As Jefferson's grandchildren grew older, they often organized week-end dances at Monticello, to which they invited young men from Char-lottesville. They frequently asked Beverly Hemings, Sally's oldest son, to provide the music. He and his brothers, Madison and Eston, had all learned to play the violin and could "call the figures of favorite dances." Eston, the youngest (born on May 21, 1808), was regarded as a "master of the violin." In this as in his looks, his manner of speech, and his gentlemanly bearing, Eston's resemblance to Thomas Jefferson was said to have been remarkable. In fact, it was said that if he were seen at twilight, he might be mistaken for him.

A manuscript survives on which Thomas Jefferson had written out a Scottish dance tune called "Moneymusk." It was very likely a favorite of his, and was played by both him and Eston. Many years later, in the 1840s, when Eston was living in southern Ohio, he was known for playing this tune at dances. Some of the Irishmen who had been hired to work on the reconstruction of Monticello in the early 1800s also played the fiddle, and occasionally slaves, hired workers, and family members made music together on the mountain.[2]

In addition to all the children, there was a constant stream of visitors, and workmen continued to swarm through the as-yet-unfinished house. There could be more than twenty people in the house at one time. An entire beef might be consumed in two days. Frequently there weren't enough beds to sleep in, nor were there stables enough for the horses.

Jefferson described his life at Monticello in a letter to a friend:

> My mornings are devoted to correspondence. From breakfast to dinner I am in my shops, my garden, or on horseback among my farms; from dinner to dark, I give to society and recreation with my neighbors and friends; and from candle-light to early bed-time I read. My health is perfect, and my strength considerably reinforced by the activity of the course I pursue. . . . A part of my occupation, and by no means the least pleasing, is the direction of the studies of such young men as ask it. They . . . have the use of my library and counsel, and make a part of my society.[3]

But it is the reminiscences of his grandchildren, written years later when they were grown men and women, that best depict his life at that time and attest to the place he held in their hearts, and they in his. Ellen Wayles Randolph, the second and possibly the favorite of his granddaughters, described the times the grandchildren spent with him in the garden:

> I remember well, when he first returned to Monticello, how immediately he began to prepare new beds for his flowers . . . with . . . a crowd of younger grandchildren clustering round to see the progress, and inquire anxiously the name of each separate deposit.
>
> Then, when spring returned, how eagerly we watched the first appearance of the shoots above ground. . . . and what joy it was for one of us to discover the tender green breaking through the mould, and run to grandpapa to announce that we really believed Marcus Aurelius [a deep purple tulip] was coming up. . . . With how much pleasure, compounded of our pleasure and his own . . . he would immediately go out to verify the fact, and praise us for our diligent watchfulness.[4]

His granddaughter Virginia remembered that they raced after him delightedly, yet "not one of us, in our wildest moods, ever placed a foot on one of the garden beds, for that would violate one of his rules, and yet I never heard him utter a harsh word to one of us, or speak in a raised tone of voice, or use a threat. He simply said, 'Do,' or 'Do not.'"[5]

Reminiscing about her grandfather on another occasion, Ellen wrote:

> As a child, girl, and woman, I loved and honored him above all earthly beings. And well I might. From him seemed to flow all the pleasures of my life. To him I owed all the small blessings and joyful surprises of my childish and girlish years. . . . Our grandfather seemed to read our hearts, to see our invisible wishes . . . to wave the fairy wand, to brighten our young lives by his goodness and his gifts.[6]

Virginia, five years younger than Ellen, lamented the fact that she was born the year her grandfather was elected president and was therefore too young to correspond with him during his years in Washington. But when he was home, she remembered:

> On winter evenings, when it grew too dark to read, in the half hour which passed before candles came in, as we all sat round the fire, he taught us several childish games, and would play them with us.
>
> When the candles were brought, all was quiet immediately, for he took up his book to read; and we would not speak out of a whisper, lest we should disturb him, and generally we followed his example and took a book. . . . When the snow fell, we would go out, as soon as it stopped, to clear it off the terraces with shovels, that he might have his usual walk on them without treading in snow.[7]

In sharp contrast to these loving reminiscences is Madison Hemings's statement to an Ohio newspaperman in 1873 in which he described the relationship between the Hemings and Jefferson families. "We were the only children of his by a slave woman," he said of himself and his siblings. When he spoke of Thomas Jefferson he portrayed a man "uniformly kind to all about him," but one who "was not in the habit of showing partiality or fatherly affection to us children," although he "was affectionate towards his white grandchildren."[8]

Nonetheless, Sally Hemings's children were relatively happy growing up in the "great house." Perhaps the most significant contribution to this happiness was their knowledge, gleaned from their mother, that they would not be slaves forever. They knew that they would be granted their freedom when they turned twenty-one. Mr. Jefferson had given his word.*

One Jefferson scholar has mused that perhaps the price of this freedom for Sally's children was the denial by Thomas Jefferson of their paternity. In this way he prepared himself for the day when they would walk away from Monticello—and from him—and make their way in the white world.[9]

---

*According to Jefferson's interpretation of the laws of Virginia, Sally's children were white: after three "crossings" with whites, a black person was legally white. And Sally's children could "pass" into the white world as white.

And their mother was well treated. She probably lived in the stone cottage when she first returned from France, and then moved to one of the new log cabins, twelve feet by fourteen feet, that were built farther down Mulberry Row in 1792. Later, after the completion of the dependencies, she may have lived in one of these "servants' rooms" under the south terrace.

When Sally's children were young, they spent some of their time running errands, but they were always permitted to participate in childhood activities and to be with their mother. Their playmates were the many offspring of the extended Hemings family, as well as the Randolph children. Madison and his siblings were growing up at Monticello at about the same time that Martha Randolph and her children came to live there. It was these grandchildren who taught the Hemings children their ABCs. Monticello was very much a black and white household.[10]

Although girls were generally sent to learn to spin and weave at the age of ten, Harriet, Sally's only surviving daughter, did not become a spinner in Jefferson's textile shop until she was fourteen. While most young boys were sent to the fields when they reached sixteen, when Beverly turned twelve and his brothers turned fourteen, they were placed with their uncle John Hemings, the best slave artisan on the plantation, to learn carpentry. In this way, Thomas Jefferson ensured that the three boys would be able to earn a living when they were freed.

John Hemings, born at Monticello in 1775, was Betty Hemings's youngest son. His father was John Nielson, a white Englishman who had begun to work for Jefferson as a carpenter the year before. Thus John was Sally's half brother. As a young boy John had been a field worker, but at the age of fourteen, he became one of a "gang" of what Jefferson called "out-carpenters." They spent their days "out" in the woods, felling trees for firewood, fences, and charcoal and hewing logs for building. When he reached seventeen, he was one of the men who built the log dwellings on Mulberry Row in which his sisters lived.[11]

John—or Johnny, as Jefferson often called him—was trained first by his father and then by James Dinsmore, an unusually fine woodworker who had come from Ireland and whom Jefferson had hired in 1798. John Hemings would become a master craftsman in his own right, finishing much of the decorative interior woodwork in the remodeled Monticello, as well as making beautiful pieces of furniture. He was much loved by all the family. Martha Randolph's children called him "Daddy." His wife, Priscilla, was their nurse, or "Mammy," as they called her. The children would often visit "Daddy" in the joinery on Mulberry Row and plead with him to make them "a box for their flowers or drawings. His reported reply was: 'Yes, yes! My little mistises, but Grandpapa comes first! There are new bookshelves to be made, trellises for the roses, besides farm work to be done.'"[12]

A story told about a visitor to the joinery offers insight into the relationship between Johnny and his master. One hot summer day a very tired carpenter yielded to temptation and sat down on the workbench, then quickly fell asleep. When a slight noise awakened him he saw Mr. Jefferson tiptoeing out and closing the door behind him. "Johnny Hemings had indeed been caught 'napping,' but by one who recognized in it the needed rest of a faithful servant."[13]

It was to this servant that Jefferson entrusted much of the ongoing repair work at Poplar Forest. In 1825, writing about the work he was completing on the roof and windows, Hemings told his master: "I hope by the next to be able to let you know when I shall finish and when to send for me. Dear Sir, I hope you well."

The neat irony—and the humanity—implicit in the slave's informing the master as to the time to order his return, as well as his inquiry concerning Jefferson's health, suggest the subtle complexities of this relationship.[14]

For many years Ellen was the belle and pride of the family. While not as beautiful as Anne, Ellen too had inherited the fair skin and rosy complexion of the Jeffersons. She was intelligent, reflective, and unusually articulate. Her grandfather is reputed to have once said that had she been a man, she would have been a great one. But because she was a woman in the early nineteenth century, and particularly a granddaughter of the president of the United States, her role was sorely limited.

"My dear Ellen," as he called her, remained her grandfather's constant companion during his later years, until her marriage, at the age of twenty-nine, to Joseph Coolidge Jr., in the drawing room at Monticello

Ellen Wayles Coolidge, "my dear Ellen," was Jefferson's favorite granddaughter. Her sisters knew that nobody could fill her place. (Courtesy of Monticello/ Thomas Jefferson Foundation, Inc.)

on May 27, 1825. The story is told that when Ellen married and moved with her husband to Boston, whenever her sisters saw their grandfather looking at her empty chair, one of them hastened to sit in it, although they knew that nobody could fill her place.

Shortly after Ellen and Joseph arrived in Boston, they learned that the ship carrying her baggage had been lost at sea. The loss was a great one. Not only did her luggage contain personal items, wedding gifts, and furniture for her new home, but it included a handsome writing desk that had been a gift from her grandfather and in which she had placed some of her most treasured possessions—letters and other memorabilia she had received from him over the years. The writing desk had been designed and crafted by John Hemings. Ellen was his favorite among the grandchildren, and eager to create something special for her, he had combined several woods in unusual patterns and had produced an exceptionally beautiful piece of furniture.

Jefferson understood the wrenching pain this must have caused the lonely young bride, and as consolation he sent Ellen and Joseph the writing box on which he had written the Declaration of Independence so many years before. "It claims no merit of particular beauty. It is plain, neat, convenient. . . . Its imaginary value will increase with years, and if [Joseph Coolidge] lives . . . another half-century, he may see it carried in the procession of our nation's birthday," he wrote to Ellen.[15]

He wrote out an affidavit attesting to its history and to its link to the "Great Charter of our Independence." The lap desk remained in the Coolidge family until 1880 when, after the deaths of both Ellen and Joseph, their children decided to present it to the nation.

Thomas Jefferson Randolph, the second of Martha's children, was Thomas Jefferson's first grandson. He had been born at Monticello in September of 1792, while Martha was living there and her father was on vacation from his duties as secretary of state. Named for his grandfather, he was an enormous baby and grew to be a huge man, resembling in many ways his great-grandfather Peter Jefferson. He would become an adored and adoring grandson, the mainstay of his grandfather's later life. Jefferson, as his grandfather called him, became his favorite grandchild and ultimately took the place of the son he had never had.

It was to this grandson, just beginning college, that Jefferson wrote a letter that is remarkable for the advice it offered. He had already provided for young Jefferson all the things that he thought a boy going off to college should have, had given him pocket money, and had paid his

Thomas Jefferson Randolph, cherished grandson, whom Jefferson considered "the greatest of the God-sends which Heaven has granted to me." (Courtesy of Monticello/Thomas Jefferson Foundation, Inc.)

tuition. But he was concerned with more than material things. His grandson was only fifteen and alone in Philadelphia for the first time.

> Thrown on a wide world, among entire strangers, without a friend or guardian to advise, so young too and with so little experience of mankind, your dangers are great, and still your safety must rest on yourself. A determination never to do what is wrong, prudence and good humor, will go far towards securing to you the estimation of the world. When I recollect that at fourteen years of age, the whole care and direction of myself was thrown on myself entirely, without a relation or friend qualified to advise or guide me, and recollect the various sorts of bad company with which I associated from time to time, I am astonished I did not turn off with some of them, and become as worthless to society as they were. I had the good fortune to become acquainted very early with some characters of very high standing, and to feel the incessant wish that I could ever become what they were. Under temptation and difficulties, I would ask myself what would Dr. Small, Mr. Wythe, Peyton Randolph do in this situation. . . .
>
> I must not omit the important [rule] of never entering into dispute or argument with another. I never saw an instance of one or two disputants convincing the other by argument.
>
> . . . When I hear another express an opinion which is not mine, I say to myself, he has a right to his opinion, as I to mine; why should I question it? . . . Be a listener only, keep within yourself, and endeavor to establish with yourself the habit of silence, especially on politics.[16]

To this cherished grandson, he wrote near the end of his life, "Yourself particularly, dear Jefferson, I consider as the greatest of the Godsends which heaven has granted to me."[17]

The relationship between Thomas Jefferson and his namesake grew stronger and stronger over the years, and the older man came to rely heavily on the younger. His feelings were evident when, as an old man, he learned late one evening that this grandson had been stabbed—perhaps mortally—by Anne's alcoholic husband, Charles Bankhead. Jefferson immediately had his horse Eagle brought to the door and, although he was too feeble to mount the mare without help, and against the pleas of his family, he struck the animal such a blow that it bounded off down the dark mountain at "full gallop" and got its master the four miles to Charlottesville and his grandson in record time. When he found him "laid on a bale of blankets in the counting room of a store," he knelt at his head and wept.[18]

❧ 37 ❧

# "I Cannot Live without Books"

D URING HIS RETIREMENT, Jefferson gradually came to the conclusion that a collection of books such as his should be in public rather than in private hands. Late in the summer of 1814, something happened in Washington that made him decide to act. The invading British army burned the Capitol during the War of 1812, often referred to as one of the forgotten wars of the United States. It was, in fact, a war that once and for all confirmed American independence. The British army was successfully stopped when it attempted to capture Baltimore and New Orleans, and naval victories in which American vessels proved themselves superior to similarly sized British vessels launched American naval traditions.[1]

When the British burned Washington, the congressional library, housed in the Capitol, was destroyed. Jefferson immediately offered his own magnificent collection of books as a replacement, at any fee deemed appropriate by Congress. His only condition was that the collection be accepted in its entirety. He recognized that the country was at war and in debt and that many congressmen would object to spending money on books, particularly those that did not deal specifically with legislation. His library covered the entire field of human knowledge. It was far superior to the original owned by Congress and, at 6,700 volumes, was more than twice its size.

Jefferson had begun to classify his books in 1783, after his wife died, and he had continued to add titles to the catalog over the next thirty years. Now he carefully revised it and had labels pasted to the spine of each book that corresponded to its listing in the catalog.

Congress deliberated about accepting his offer for four months. Eventually the deliberations became partisan, and some of his political enemies mocked both him and his books. When the resolution finally did pass, it was only by a narrow margin. But in April, when the ten wagons carrying pine boxes filled with books wended their way to Washington, it marked the beginning of a great national library, one of the finest and most accessible in the world. While Thomas Jefferson never claimed that he founded the Library of Congress, certainly the institution that emerged out of the ashes was his creation. He used the money he received from Congress, $23,950 (about half its cost and one-quarter its value) to pay off troubling old debts. Then he immediately began assembling another library at an astonishing rate. "I cannot live without books," he wrote to John Adams.

The friendship between these two venerable patriots had recently been renewed after eleven years of silence between them. In 1812 they began a correspondence that has become a classic in American letters and an unrivaled record of an extraordinary friendship. Their mutual friend Benjamin Rush was responsible for bringing about the reconciliation by repeatedly reminding them of their past comradeship and urging them to renew communication.

When Jefferson learned that John Adams had said, "I always loved Jefferson, and still do," he loosened the tight rein he generally kept on his emotions and declared that he would express his unchanged affection as soon as the right moment presented itself. They had been young rebels together, and Jefferson had never forgotten Adams's support of him in 1776 or his own closeness to the entire Adams family while in France.

"A letter from you calls up recollections very dear to my mind," he wrote. "It carries me back to the times when, beset with difficulties and dangers, we were fellow-laborers in the same cause, struggling for what is most valuable to man, his right of self-government."[2]

It was John Adams who made the first move, but Jefferson responded immediately. Both agreed that they ought not to die before they had explained themselves to one another.

Their correspondence began, appropriately, with an exchange of books, and their letters over the next fourteen years were filled with references to their reading. The letters are memorable for their discussions of politics, history, philosophy, religion, and psychology. And as these two old friends reviewed the past and surveyed the present, their letters revealed the special warmth of feeling they had for one another.

When Thomas Jefferson offered his books to the Library of Congress, he was giving substance to his faith in learning. Throughout his long life he had advocated public education, convinced that freedom and knowledge were inseparable. He had always believed that the common people must be educated. Only then would America be able to retain her freedom. Education was the true agent of change.

When he first set down in the Declaration of Independence his belief in the right to life, liberty, and the pursuit of happiness, he knew that education was the only sure foundation for the preservation of freedom and happiness.

From 1776 until 1779, when he was working with George Wythe on the revision of the laws of Virginia, he also drew up a Bill for the More General Diffusion of Knowledge, which, along with his bills for Amending the Constitution of the College of William and Mary and for Establishing a Public Library, was part of "a systematical plan of general education."[3] The objective of knowledge, he said, was to render the young "useful instruments for the public." Knowledge must be used to instill republican attitudes such as political responsibility, love of liberty, and hatred of tyranny. These bills were accompanied by a detailed plan for a public school system that recommended three stages in the educational process: primary, secondary, and higher. This would become the foundation of modern education.

His hope was that passage of "a bill for general education" would ensure that the people "would be qualified to understand their rights, to maintain them, and to exercise with intelligence their parts in self-government."[4] "Educate and inform the whole mass of people," he had written. "They are the only sure reliance for the preservation of our liberty."

If his bill had been passed by the legislature as he had presented it in

1779, it might have been listed with the Statute for Religious Freedom among his greatest achievements. Unfortunately, it was not passed until almost the end of the century, and then in a much abridged version. Yet "nothing else that he did or proposed during his entire career showed him more clearly to be a major American prophet."[5]

Now, near the end of his life, he found the opportunity to make his dream a reality. In the spring of 1814, when he was seventy-one years old, he was invited to become a member of the board of trustees of a small, unorganized private school known as Albemarle Academy. His first suggestion was that it be transformed into Central College, which became the seed out of which the University of Virginia would develop.

A few months later, in a letter to his nephew Peter Carr, who was also on the board of Central College, Jefferson outlined his views on education. These became his Bill for Establishing a System of Public Education. That bill was sent to the Virginia legislature in October 1817 and passed both houses in February 1818.

Soon Jefferson was appointed to a group organized to recommend a site for a state university. At the meeting of this group he took from his pocket a card cut into the shape of Virginia, with the proposed site of the university indicated by a dot. By balancing the dot on the point of a pencil, he proved that Charlottesville was in fact near the geographic center of the state. Then he produced another cardboard map of Virginia on which he had written, in his precise, minute handwriting, the population of every part of the state. Again, it was clear that Charlottesville was centrally located.

His report to the committee also included his ideas of what a liberal university should be. It remains one of his great educational papers. Characteristically, he then went to work quietly behind the scenes to have the paper adopted, and the University of Virginia was chartered the following year.

Suddenly, he had a new zest for living and a new spring to his step. His mind teemed with ideas and plans that had been simmering for years. He quickly made his old friend James Madison—who had recently retired from the presidency—his right-hand man and swung into action.

Jefferson became the architect of the university at every level. It was

The University of Virginia, Mr. Jefferson's school, was the first university to have no religious affiliation. It was "based on the illimitable freedom of the human mind." (Courtesy of Bill Sublette)

he who chose its site, supplied its bricks, and saw to its construction. It was he who designed its buildings, laid out its paths, and supervised its plantings. He wrote its curriculum and recruited its faculty. And it was he who provided the library with the books he had acquired after selling his first collection to the Library of Congress. Perhaps most important, because of him the University of Virginia became the first university to have no religious affiliation. "This institution will be based on the illimitable freedom of the human mind. For here we are not afraid to follow truth wherever it may lead, nor to tolerate any error so long as reason is left free to combat it."[6]

The university was laid out as a rectangle open at one end to a view of the mountains; at the closed end was the magnificent Rotunda, modeled after the Pantheon in Rome. The dome room in the Rotunda became the library—Jefferson's Temple of Knowledge.

All the pavilions that line the two long sides of the lawn are neoclassical in design, reflecting his great love of classical Greek and Roman architecture, but with different combinations of these elements. This, Jefferson believed, would avoid monotony in the structure. More importantly, the pavilions would serve as examples for professors of architecture to use in their lectures.

Not only did he plan and personally supervise all aspects of the university, he struck the first peg into the ground. Then, using the little ruler he always carried in his pocket, he measured off the ground and marked off the foundation. From that time until the university's completion, Jefferson could always be found at the building site. Early every morning he would mount his horse Eagle and canter down the mountain to Charlottesville. Once there, he used a walking stick of his own invention made of three sticks that, when spread out and covered with a cloth, became a seat. Late afternoons, after dinner back at Monticello, he could continue to watch what was going on at the Charlottesville site through the lens of his telescope set up on the north terrace.

In 1822, when he was seventy-nine, a visitor to the construction site was amazed to see him take a chisel from the hand of an Italian stonecutter and show the craftsman how to model an ornament on a column.

Jefferson separated the functions of the university into distinct buildings, bringing to fruition an ideal of education that had been maturing throughout his life. This plan for what he called an "academical village" created a setting in which learning would be an integral part of living, and it was totally his own. No model has ever been found for it. "By interspersing the student dormitories among the professors' pavilions he hoped to replicate the intellectual camaraderie he had enjoyed with William Small and George Wythe in Williamsburg" so many years before.[7] Both architecturally and intellectually, the creation of the university became the crowning achievement of his life, the culmination of his hopes and dreams for the new nation, his monument to Enlightenment rationality. He referred to it as "the last service I can render my country."[8]

When the school finally opened on March 7, 1825, Mr. Jefferson was its first rector and chairman of the board of trustees. The University of Virginia, which has been called "the lengthened shadow of one man,"[9] made possible a perpetuation of his dream of an educational system that would promote academic excellence in his native Virginia. He had set an example for the state universities that play such an important role in U.S. education today.

Shortly before the official opening of the university, Jefferson learned with joy that his old friend Lafayette was returning to America after thirty-five years and would visit him at Monticello. On a glorious November morning, Lafayette and his colorful entourage entered Albemarle County, where he was met by Jefferson's grandson Jefferson Randolph, who accompanied him the rest of the way up the mountain to Monticello. Crowds lined the way: citizens on one side, Lafayette's brightly plumed cavalrymen on the other.

As they neared the house, Lafayette, now lame and broken in health by a long imprisonment during the French Revolution, caught sight of his old friend waiting on the portico. He gave the order to halt his carriage and stepped out. Each moved forward to greet the other, feebly at first, then quickening to a shuffling run. Tears were shed by both as they embraced, saying, "My dear Jefferson," "My dear Lafayette." This was one of the rare instances in Jefferson's life of a public display of emotion.

Lafayette found Mr. Jefferson "much aged" after thirty-five years but "marvelously well" at eighty-one and "in full possession of all the vigor of his mind and heart."[10]

The following day Lafayette was honored at a dinner in the Rotunda of the university, the first public dinner to be given there.

Israel Gillette (later Israel Gillette Jefferson), a young slave of Jefferson's who was accompanying Jefferson and Lafayette during one of their daily rides, years later recalled a conversation between the two old men that he had never forgotten, and "treasured . . . up in my heart." "The great and good" Lafayette told his host that he had given "his best services to and spent his money in behalf of the Americans freely because he felt that they were fighting for a great and noble principle—the freedom of mankind." But he was grieved to see so many still in bondage. "No man could rightly hold ownership in his brother man," Israel heard Lafayette tell Mr. Jefferson, who replied that he thought "the time would come" when the slaves would be free. When Lafayette indicated that he thought the slaves should be educated, Jefferson agreed that they should be taught to read print but not to write: "to teach them to write would enable them to forge papers, when they could no longer be kept in subjugation."[11]

☙ 38 ☜

# "Thomas Jefferson Still Survives"

T HROUGHOUT HIS LIFE, aside from a few bouts with rheumatism and periodic attacks of migraine headaches, Jefferson had remained remarkably healthy. He rarely, if ever, had a cold. His life was a temperate one, orderly and industrious, and he exercised regularly. From the time he was a tall, lanky, redheaded boy of sixteen, he had always considered walking the best exercise. As an old man he continued to believe that two hours of hard exercise every day was essential. Health, he had always contended, was worth even more than learning.

His financial well-being was another story.

His son-in-law Thomas Mann Randolph had been forced to declare bankruptcy some years before, and the care and support of Martha and all her children had fallen to Jefferson. Then, in 1818, Jefferson, already in dire financial straits himself, had endorsed a note for $20,000 for his friend Wilson Cary Nicholas, ex-governor of Virginia and father of his grandson Jefferson's wife, Jane. When Nicholas went bankrupt a year later, Thomas Jefferson was called on to pay. His loyalty was remarkable. He honored his guarantee and never allowed one word to be uttered against his longtime friend, nor did he ever hint at the disaster in the presence of his granddaughter-in-law.

By now, Jefferson Randolph had assumed the management of his grandfather's farms. He attempted to relieve him of the unpleasantness resulting from the fluctuation in the market price paid for their crops, which was making it increasingly difficult to pay off long-standing debts. In the end, after his grandfather had died, it was young Jefferson who personally saw to it that all these debts were paid.

As Thomas Jefferson's debts, and the accumulated interest on them, continued to mount, his health steadily declined. While debt was the rule rather than the exception in the society in which he lived, he concluded a letter to an overseer with the poignant statement, "To owe what I cannot pay is a constant torment."[1] He tried in vain to find a purchaser for his lands. He worried that his family would lose Monticello. But he refused to accept the offer of an interest-free loan from the U.S. Treasury because, he said, that would cost the taxpayers money.

Early in 1826, he hit upon the idea of holding a lottery to dispose of some of his properties. With the help of his grandson Jeff, he secured permission for the lottery from the Virginia legislature. But when the public protested against this indignity and some voluntary contributions were made, the project was abandoned.

His grandsons and his nephews also rallied around him, offering what support they could. A heartbroken young Francis Eppes wrote to his grandfather from Poplar Forest at the end of February 1826:

> It was with infinite pain My Dr. Grandfather, that I saw your application to the legislature . . . and I write . . . to express, My unfeigned grief [and] to assure you that I return to your funds with the utmost good will, the portion of property [Poplar Forest] which you designed for me. . . . You have been to me ever, an affectionate, and tender Father, and you shall find me ever, a loving, and devoted son . . . I shall remain ever, as deeply indebted, as though your kind intentions had been completely fulfilled. . . . May God bless and long preserve you My dearest Grandfather, my best friend, with most sincere love your grandson, Frans. Eppes.[2]

His grandfather declined the offer.

Haunted by the thought that his debts were so substantial that Martha would be left with nothing, he prevailed upon Jeff to promise that he would never abandon his mother. Thomas Jefferson never knew that Monticello would soon pass out of the hands of his heirs forever, and most of his family of slaves would be sold on the auction block.

In March 1826 Jefferson made out his last will and testament. He left a watch to each of his grandchildren, all his books to the University of Virginia, and all his personal papers—his farm and account books and the treasure of his vast personal correspondence—to his grandson Jeff.

In late 1821 Jefferson had allowed Sally Hemings's oldest son, Beverly, to "run away" to freedom, something Jefferson had never permitted before. Then, early in 1822, when Beverly's sister, Harriet, turned twenty-one, Jefferson saw to it that she was given fifty dollars and put on a stage-coach to freedom. In all likelihood, Beverly had been sent ahead to wait for her arrival in Washington, or to meet her along the way. By the timing of their departures Thomas Jefferson was ensuring that Harriet, a beautiful young woman, would be protected. Both Beverly and Harriet passed into white society and married white spouses.[3]

Now, in his will, Jefferson gave freedom to seven more of his slaves. All were part of the Hemings family. To Burwell Colbert, Betty Hemings's grandson, who for the years of Jefferson's last retirement had held the position of greatest responsibility in the household, Jefferson wrote: "I give to my good, affectionate, and faithful servant Burwell his freedom, and the sum of three hundred Dollars to buy necessaries to commence his trade of painter and glazier, or to use otherwise as he pleases." He was also to be given tenancy of a "comfortable log house" and an acre of land.

As an adult, Burwell was responsible for running the household and for the upkeep of the house itself. He supervised the activities of all the other house servants and was himself head waiter and Jefferson's personal servant. Even as a young boy he had occupied a special place in his master's affections. He had been allowed to do "pretty much as he pleased," and was occasionally given pocket money. When Burwell was in his twenties, Jefferson began to give him an annual gratuity of twenty dollars. At age seventeen, when working in the nailery, he was "absolutely excepted from the whip altogether."[4]

To Burwell's uncle John Hemings, Jefferson bequeathed the tools of his trade, life tenancy of a log house, and an acre of land. Further, John was allowed the "service" of his two apprentices, his nephews Madison and Eston Hemings, until they reached the age of twenty-one, when they too would be freed.* Jefferson then petitioned the Virginia legislature to exempt them from the 1806 law requiring freed slaves to leave the

---

*Madison was already past twenty-one. He became free immediately after Jefferson's death. Eston, although only nineteen, was freed soon after.

state. Sally was not mentioned in the will, but she was "given her time" (informally freed) by Martha. She then went to live with her two sons in a rented house in Charlottesville until she died. All three were listed as white in the census of 1830.[5]

Jefferson could do no more. But he had kept the two promises he had made so long ago. He had promised his wife that he would never marry again, and he had tried to be both mother and father to his daughters. And he had promised Sally that he would free her children. He knew that Martha and Jeff would protect her. In honoring those promises he had given two of the greatest gifts one human being can give to another: he had given unbounded love to one family and freedom to the other. Sally's children were spared the dread of remaining slaves all their lives. They knew they would be freed when they turned twenty-one, and they would have a skilled trade to pursue for their own livelihood. Their mother had had the courage to demand this; their father was a man of his word.[6]

Jefferson had been profoundly troubled all his life by an institution that violated everything he believed in. He had grappled with the problem he could solve neither intellectually nor morally. He had thought he could reform slavery and establish a humane institution, but even by the time he was born, slavery was a firmly established feature in plantation society and was essential to plantation economy. Jefferson's own livelihood depended on its continuation. Unable to abolish or reform slavery, he feared, with his friend John Adams, that "the nation would be wrecked on the shoals of slavery."

When in 1814 Edward Coles, an earnest and idealistic young friend and neighbor, wrote to Jefferson asking him to forcefully denounce slavery and to endorse Coles's plan to take his slaves to Illinois where he could free them, Jefferson counseled him against it. Coles's letter was "a welcome voice" from this generation, Jefferson told him, but he, Jefferson, was too old. "This enterprise is for the young; for those who can follow it up, and bear it through to its consummation. It shall have all my prayers, & these are the only weapons of an old man." But he didn't think the time was right. Coles would be abandoning these people— and abandoning his country (Virginia). He must remain in *his country*, he told him. And he must be patient. "My opinion has ever been that, until we can do more for them, we should endeavor, with those whom fortune has thrown on our hands, to feed and clothe them well, protect them from all ill usage, require such reasonable labor only as is performed voluntarily by freemen, & be led by no repugnancies to abdicate them, and our duties to them."[7]

Jefferson had long ago realized that the abolition of slavery would be a long, painful process, requiring "persuasion, perseverance, and patience." Less than a month before he died he wrote, "The revolution in public opinion which this cause requires, is not to be expected in a day, or perhaps in an age; but time, which outlives all things, will outlive this evil also. My sentiments have been forty years before the public. Had I repeated them forty times, they would only have become the more stale and threadbare. Although I shall not live to see them consummated, they will not die with me; but living or dying, they will ever be in my most fervent prayer."[8]

Jefferson never lost his faith in America. He saw the possibilities for the future and was certain that the United States could build something far better than Europe. "I steer my bark with hope in the head, leaving fear astern," he had said to John Adams.

Now, to James Madison, his dear friend of fifty years, Jefferson left his gold-headed walking stick and a request that he watch over the University of Virginia. A letter from Jefferson to Madison, perhaps better than anything, reveals his heart: "The friendship which has subsisted between us, now half a century, and the harmony of our political principles and pursuits, have been sources of constant happiness to me through that long period." And, he told him, it was a great comfort to him to know that the university would be in his care.

It has also been a great solace to me to believe that you are engaged in vindicating to posterity the course we have pursued for preserving to them, *in all their purity,* the blessings of self-government. . . . If ever the earth has beheld a system of administration conducted with a single and steadfast eye to the general interest and happiness of those committed to it . . . it is that to which our lives have been devoted. To myself you have been a pillar of support through life. Take care of me when dead, and be assured that I shall leave you with my last affections."⁹

It was March of 1826 before Jeff Randolph realized that his grandfather might be seriously ill. Speaking of an event scheduled to take place in midsummer, Thomas Jefferson said that he *might* live until that time. He had been suffering from a severe case of diarrhea for several weeks, and his strength was steadily declining. But he had not revealed this to his family.

He continued to ride Eagle—alone. When his family begged him to allow a servant to accompany him, he reminded them that he had ridden alone since childhood, that he must converse with nature alone, and that he had always "helped himself." He dreaded a dotty old age, he told them.

By early June he was so weak that he could mount the horse only by standing on one of the terraces and lowering himself into the saddle. His crippled wrist had grown worse as he grew older, and he had difficulty holding the reins. Eagle seemed to understand and, although generally a fiery and impatient horse, stood perfectly still while its master mounted, then moved slowly and quietly down the path.

Late in June Jefferson received an invitation to join in the celebration of the fiftieth anniversary of American independence, to be held in Washington. As he thought back to those memorable days, some of the old spirit surged through his body and he found the strength to reply—with an eloquence reminiscent of his Declaration:

It adds sensibly to the sufferings of sickness, to be deprived by it of a personal participation in the rejoicings of that day. . . . I should indeed, with peculiar delight, have met and exchanged there congratulations personally with the small band, the remnant of that host of worthies, who joined with us on that day, in the bold and doubtful election we were to make for our country, between submission or the sword. . . . May it be to the world . . . the signal of arousing men to burst the chains under which monkish ignorance and superstition had persuaded them to bind themselves, and to assume the blessings and security of self-government. . . . All eyes are opened, or opening, to the rights of man. The general spread of the light of science has already laid open to every view the palpable truth, that the mass of mankind has not been born with saddles on their backs, nor a favored few booted and spurred, ready to ride them legitimately, by the grace of God. These are grounds of hope for others. For ourselves, let the annual return of this day, forever refresh our recollections of these rights, and an undiminished devotion to them.[10]

We know how much the celebration meant to him and how much he would have liked to participate in the festivities because some years earlier he had refused to divulge the date of his birthday to a committee intent on designating it a national holiday. He suggested, instead, that they honor him by celebrating the Fourth of July as the nation's birthday.

Soon after he wrote his reply, Jefferson became too weak to leave his bed. Members of his family prevailed upon him to allow them to stay with him, but he would not allow Martha to sit up at night. Jeff Randolph and Nicholas Trist, his granddaughter Virginia's husband and grandson of his old friend Elizabeth Trist, maintained the vigil. He suffered no pain, but grew steadily weaker. Throughout, he remained calm and composed and concerned for his family. He reassured them that he had no fear of dying, that he was "like an old watch, with a pinion worn out here, and a wheel there, until it can go no longer."

On July 2 he called his family to his bedside and spoke to each of them briefly, characteristically offering advice—admonishing them to be good and truthful. He told Jeff that all the bitterness that had been hurled at him over the years by his enemies had in truth not abused him. His enemies, he said, had never known *him.* They had created an imaginary being to whom they had given his name. To Martha he said that in an old pocketbook in a particular drawer she would find something for herself.

That night he lapsed into unconsciousness. He awoke briefly on the evening of July 3, and whispered, "This is the Fourth?" Nicholas Trist, sitting with him, had been constantly turning his eyes from the clock in the corner of the room to his grandfather-in-law's face. Now he couldn't bear to say no. He pretended not to hear.

"This is the Fourth?" he repeated. Although it was not quite eleven o'clock, Nicholas nodded yes.

"Ah, just as I wished," he murmured, and sank back asleep again. Jefferson and Nicholas watched anxiously as the hands of the clock moved slowly around to midnight. "At fifteen minutes before twelve we stood noting the minute hand of the watch, hoping a few minutes of prolonged life." Soon, they knew, he would "see his own glorious Fourth."

At four o'clock in the morning he called out for his servant Burwell in "a clear and strong voice." He did not speak again. At ten o'clock, he "fixed his eyes intently" on Jeff, seeming to ask for something. His grandson did not understand, but his devoted servant Burwell Colbert did. He raised his master higher on his pillows.[11]

"He ceased to breathe, without a struggle, fifty minutes past meridian*—July 4th, 1826. I closed his eyes with my own hands," Jefferson Randolph recalled.[12]

At just that time, bells were ringing and cannons booming in every city and town throughout the country in celebration of the anniversary of his Declaration. He would have liked that.

A few hours later, in Braintree, Massachusetts, a dying John Adams uttered his last words, "Thomas Jefferson still survives."

Jefferson was buried at five o'clock the next day beneath the old oak tree on the side of his mountain, between his beloved wife and daughter and near his dear friend Dabney Carr, without pomp, in a simple graveside ceremony. His gardener Wormley dug the grave. John Hemings had made the coffin from wood he had been saving for just this purpose. No invitations were sent, but Albemarle neighbors and students came in droves, in spite of a soft summer rain.

Martha, too distraught to cry, found her father's parting gift, a little poem he had written for her entitled "A Death-bed Adieu from Th.J to M.R."

> Life's visions are vanished, its dreams are no more;
> Dear friends of my bosom, why bathed in tears?
> I go to my fathers, I welcome the shore

---

*At 12:50 p.m. It was later noted that the Declaration of Independence had been presented to the Congress at approximately that time.

The cemetery at Monticello, near the old oak tree on the side of the mountain. (Courtesy of L. H. Bober)

> Which crowns all my hopes or which buries my cares.
> Then farewell, my dear, my lov'd daughter, adieu!
> The last pang of life is parting from you!
> Two seraphs await me long shrouded in death;*
> I will bear them your love on my last parting breath.

Thomas Jefferson had written to John Adams just three years before he died, telling his friend that he was awaiting death "with more readiness than reluctance." "May we meet there again, in Congress, with our antient [ancient] Colleagues, and receive with them the seal of approbation 'Well done, good and faithful servants.'"[13] And he had long ago revealed to his friend James Madison his desire for "the esteem of the world." This he had earned.

He had truly set himself and his house on a mountaintop. But he strove all his life to lift his fellow human beings to the same lofty heights. Now he could be content that his personal dream had come

---

*His wife, Martha, and daughter Maria.

true: "I am as happy nowhere else, and in no other society, and all my wishes end, where I hope my days will, at Monticello."[14]

Toward the end of his life, Thomas Jefferson had written out, on the torn back of an old letter, specific instructions for a monument to be erected after his death. His family found them among his papers.

He had described a simple stone, then ordered,

> On the face of the obelisk the following inscription and not a word more:
>
> HERE WAS BURIED
>
> THOMAS JEFFERSON
>
> AUTHOR OF THE DECLARATION OF INDEPENDENCE,
>
> OF THE STATUTE OF VIRGINIA FOR RELIGIOUS FREEDOM,
>
> AND FATHER OF THE UNIVERSITY OF VIRGINIA

because by these, as testimonials that I have lived, I wish most to be remembered.

Political achievements had never been important to him. He had accepted his assignments as simply his duty, and he had done his best. He had always championed the rights of the people. Now he recognized that they would be freer because he had lived. He needed no other monument. He had, indeed, been the draftsman of the nation, and his eloquent language resonates still.

# Author's Note

IN 1891 the historian Henry Adams observed about Thomas Jefferson, "Almost every other American statesman might be described in a parenthesis. A few broad strokes of the brush would paint the portraits of all the early presidents with this exception, and a few more strokes would answer for any member of their many cabinets; but Jefferson could be painted only touch by touch, with a fine pencil, and the perfection of the likeness depended upon the shifting and uncertain flicker of its semi-transparent shadows."

Over the past several years much new scholarship has allowed "a few more strokes" to be added to the portrait of Thomas Jefferson "touch by touch."

In June 2000 I attended a five-day symposium at the University of Virginia entitled "Jefferson and Slavery," at which Jefferson scholars attempted to take another look at the available evidence concerning Jefferson's stand on slavery and race, and to put it all into perspective.

There, as my mind slowly began to adjust to the possibility of a different view of Jefferson as a slaveholder, I began to question my—and other scholars'—conclusions. When Robin Gabriel, Director of Education at Monticello, spoke to me of the need for a new book and suggested that I write it, I began to think seriously about the possibility.

Thus, out of that conference emerged my decision to write a new biography of Thomas Jefferson. In June 2002 I was invited to be one of the lecturers at a University of Virginia symposium entitled "Writing the Life of Thomas Jefferson," which gave me the opportunity to articulate my reasons for writing the book and my goals for it. First was my own need as a historian to revisit Jefferson's story in order to better understand and address the controversy raging around him, to reassess his role in history, and to consider his relationship to us today. Second, my determination to undertake the project was reinforced when one of my granddaughters invited me to participate in a discussion of Annette Gordon-Reed's book *Thomas Jefferson and Sally Hemings: An American Controversy* in her college class, and indicated her pride that I would admit—and attempt to correct—my error in overlooking some of the evidence.

The results of DNA testing concerning a possible relationship between Thomas Jefferson and his slave Sally Hemings that appeared in the journal *Nature* in November 1998 had set in motion much new probing. One good effect that may have resulted from this DNA testing is that scholars were stimulated to take another look at *all* the available evidence, and to view that evidence sensitively and carefully—particularly oral history. Black oral history—heretofore ignored—can provide an important perspective on the complex relationship between a slave owner and those he owned.

In the past there had been an unwillingness to accept the story handed down through generations of Hemings family members, that Madison Hemings was the son of Sally Hemings and Thomas Jefferson. Some regarded it as a specious attempt to add luster to the Hemings family lineage. I—and many of my colleagues—were guilty of accepting this view. Further, what had been the core feature of the Jefferson family denial of the Jefferson-Hemings relationship—that Jefferson's nephew Peter Carr was the father of Sally's children—has now been undermined by genetic testing. Indeed, it was precisely this theory that I supported in my book *Thomas Jefferson: Man on a Mountain* (Atheneum, 1988; Aladdin, 1997).

Great people inspire others to search for the greatness within themselves. We all need heroes to inspire us. But what constitutes a hero? Must one be considered perfect in *every* respect before being considered a hero? Might a flawed human being be a hero?

Plato conceived of the human soul as perpetually drawn by two horses, one white and the other black, one pulling the soul up toward the highest in its nature, the other dragging it down to the lowest. A good biographer is one who can see both and can show how someone who has this difficult pair to drive can succeed as well as fail. Indeed, it is the negotiation within a person—between strength and weakness—that ultimately determines the hero.

At the conclusion of Winthrop Jordan's great work of American historical scholarship *White over Black: American Attitudes toward the Negro, 1550–1812,* Jordan affirmed this metaphor for the human soul: "Within every white American who stood confronted by the Negro, there had arisen a perpetual duel between his higher and lower natures" (581). Thomas Jefferson seems a perfect example of this concept, and it is a theme that I explore in this book.

I have placed Jefferson in the context of slavery, on his mountaintop and in his world, and have attempted to bring to life a man who was born into a society in which slavery was ubiquitous and to show how the institution of slavery resonated throughout his life. By 1775 nearly half the population in Virginia were slaves, and slavery had become essential to the plantation economy. Thus, the climate of opinion of the times must become the foundation on which Jefferson's story rests.

I have tried to examine the issue of slavery in general, as well as to provide an in-depth look at slave life at Monticello. I hope my readers will see Monticello as a real place—a working plantation—and that they will see Jefferson's world as he saw it, and to the extent that it is possible, as his slaves saw it.

Thomas Jefferson's often contradictory ideas and actions on slavery and race relations are causing much concern about how to look at him. In 1874 the eminent biographer James Parton said, "If Jefferson was wrong, America is wrong. If America is right, Jefferson was right." Is this still true? Personally, I find that almost twenty years after my first biography of Thomas Jefferson was published I am still addressing these questions and attempting to enrich my understanding of the man.

Jefferson's most enduring legacy has been a particular understanding of personal freedom—a philosophy of fundamental human rights as he expressed it in the Declaration of Independence. In fact, it is his incandescent writing in the Declaration that gives us his sharpest self-portrait.

But reference to the Declaration invariably brings up the question of how its author could have written such ringing words about equality and freedom yet remain a slaveholder. That his life was a paradox is notorious. But can we—indeed dare we—ignore the words that flowed from what John Adams called his "masterly pen" expressing the most potent idea of modern history, that all men are created equal?

Preservation of the republic was, for Jefferson, the highest moral imperative. While he knew that slavery was immoral, he feared that if he took a single action toward freeing the slaves, he would lose the ability to lead the fragile new nation. Despite his lyrical denunciations of slavery, his brilliant mind seemed unable to find a solution.

Yet he never abandoned the hope that the unfinished business of the Revolution would still be accomplished. He never abandoned his conviction that slavery should be abolished. "It ought never to be despaired of," he wrote less than a year before he died. "Every plan should be adopted, every experiment tried, which may do something toward the ultimate object."

I would hope that as Jefferson calls to us across the ages, my readers will come to know a perennial optimist who once told John Adams that he "steered his bark with hope in the head, leaving fear astern"; a man to whom subtlety and understatement were a way of life; and a man who believed in the illimitable freedom of the human mind. He was a rare blend of prophet and practical statesman, a reluctant rebel who saw the possibilities of the times in which he lived yet recognized the importance of the past.

The most important thing to remember about Thomas Jefferson is that he taught us the power of the word. He taught us that ideas matter—that words beautifully shaped can reshape lives. Jefferson distilled into one remarkable sentence the essence of our creed: "We hold these truths to be self-evident; that all men are created equal; that they are endowed by their Creator with certain unalienable rights; that among these are life, liberty, and the pursuit of happiness. . . ." Indeed, in the words he wrote he changed the shape of our country and became one of the most notable champions of freedom and enlightenment in recorded history. He had a vision of what the world *should* be.

Jefferson speaks not only to Americans today but to people the world over—particularly in the emerging democracies of Europe. In a sense, his words are responsible for the most liberal reforms, including the eventual end of slavery, the civil rights movement, and the suffrage of women.

Even before his death, the language of the Declaration was appropriated by new claimants—freed Blacks, abolitionists, early advocates of women's rights—until it received decisive transformation by Abraham Lincoln at Gettysburg, when he said: "We are a nation dedicated to the proposition that all men are created equal." Thomas Jefferson wrote that proposition.

Freeing the human spirit was Jefferson's lifelong crusade. He never wavered in his belief that "the people are the only sure reliance for the preservation of liberty." It is essential that we not lose faith in Jefferson as a hero, but we cannot, indeed we must not, hide the (arguably) wrong choices he made.

History is an argument without end. That is its fascination. We will never all agree on Jefferson, but the recent focus on race and slavery has enriched our understanding of him. While we have not validated one or another opinion on Jefferson, we know more now than we ever knew. But much of it does not have to do with Sally Hemings. The question of a possible sexual relationship is not important in itself. As John Hope Franklin said so eloquently, "The fact that he owned her is."

We must situate Jefferson in a series of horizons—in his world, on his mountaintop plantation, as a Virginian, as a nationalist, and as a man of the entire world, a man of the Enlightenment, a man of his time. We must consider carefully what it meant to be a man of his time. Now I ask my readers to consider carefully the challenge that faces all of us today and decide: Have we learned from Jefferson how to take up that challenge—here and around the globe—and break down the barriers between the races?

# Acknowledgments

REVISITING THE LIFE of someone you thought you understood more than twenty years ago to search for new material and consider different interpretations of the old can be a daunting task. It requires the help of extraordinary mentors to aid in the journey back to times and places already visited, to open new doors, and to help you view those aspects of the life through a different lens. I am blessed to have had that guidance.

Daniel P. Jordan, President of the Thomas Jefferson Foundation, has graciously extended his hospitality to my husband and me since we first began visiting Monticello in the mid-1980s. He continues to make us feel warm and welcome. His extraordinary leadership of Monticello is an inspiration to all who know him. And Andrew O'Shaughnessy, Director of the International Center for Jefferson Studies, which granted me a generous fellowship to live and to study in the Jefferson environment—an invaluable asset—has been most supportive.

It was Robin Gabriel, Director of the Monticello Education Department, who first suggested that I rethink my interpretation of Thomas Jefferson to reflect all the new material that has come to light about him over the past years. After planting the seed, she then went on to nourish its growth by discussing Jefferson with me, offering suggestions, recommending books, and then reading parts of the manuscript with a finely tuned critical eye toward its particular readership. She has always championed my work, offering encouragement all along the way, and for this I am grateful. But it is her friendship that I treasure the most.

Peter Onuf, distinguished Thomas Jefferson Foundation Professor of History at the University of Virginia, has given unstintingly of his time, perhaps most importantly during an extended conversation on the lawn at Oxford University in the spring of 2003. It was then that he helped me set the focus of this book and validated for me my need to write it. Many more long discussions over the years, in addition to two symposia he conducted at the University of Virginia that focused on Thomas Jefferson, and his close reading of the manuscript at various stages along the way, have been invaluable. I owe him a tremendous debt of gratitude.

Cinder Stanton, Shannon Senior Research Historian at Monticello, was never too busy to talk to me, generously sharing her research and her wealth of knowledge about the slave families at Monticello and helping me to see things from a different perspective.

Susan Stein, Curator of Monticello, taught me how to "read" Monticello—how to see it as a work of art as well as a busy plantation, and as the quintessential autobiographical house. More than that, her hospitality during our stays in Charlottesville added a much-appreciated warm touch.

William Beiswanger, Monticello's Director of Restoration, shared documents—and explanations—offering me yet another window into the mind of Thomas Jefferson.

Others at Monticello to whom I express my gratitude are Peter Hatch, Elizabeth Chew, Gaye Wilson, Kim Curtis; and at the International Center for Jefferson Studies, Jack Robertson, Foundation Librarian, and his able assistant, Leah Stearns; Anna Berkes, Research Librarian; Jeff Looney, Editor of the Papers of Thomas Jefferson, Retirement Series, who shared so many stories of Jefferson with me and offered additional insights; Katherine Knisely, who made things move smoothly during my fellowship; and Endrina Tay, who offered much-needed technical support.

Members of the staff at Jefferson's Poplar Forest were always gracious and most helpful.

I owe a special debt of gratitude to Jan Lewis, who first spoke to me of Jefferson's "shadow family," and who shared with me much to ponder.

I am grateful, also, to Allen Terdiman, with whom I shared long conversations during the early stages of this book, and who forced me to take a deeper look into my own feelings about Thomas Jefferson.

Andrew Burstein read several drafts of the manuscript and made wise and insightful suggestions for its improvement.

Annette Gordon-Reed's thoughtful assessment of my original proposal and later of several drafts of the manuscript, her own brilliant work on the subject of Thomas Jefferson and slavery—which made a profound impact on my thinking—her lectures that I was privileged to hear at the University of Virginia, and her full responses to my queries, have given me the courage to pursue this topic. Her daughter, Susan Reed, brought her unique perspective to bear on my telling of Jefferson's story, and in so doing, made some fine suggestions.

Chip Stokes, Chairman of the Jefferson Legacy Foundation, welcomed us to his own splendid "Monticello" atop a mountain in Ripton, Vermont, and made his amazing private library of Jefferson books available to me. He read an early draft of the manuscript carefully, bringing to it his remarkable knowledge and insight.

Ann Samson, extraordinary teacher, shared her eleventh-grade honors class in American history with me, and afforded me an opportunity to learn from her students.

Jesse Freedman, at the start of what promises to be a brilliant career as a historian, fueled my interest in the Enlightenment and kept me supplied with much to read on the topic.

Fran Post offered treasured friendship and warm hospitality in Williamsburg, Virginia, as well as excellent research skills as she worked with me at the Rockefeller Library there, and later helped with picture research.

Marcia Marshall, my longtime editor and friend, somehow managed to accomplish her wizardry even from Minneapolis. This is a better book because of her.

My agent, Liza Voges, believed in this book from the start, and has worked diligently on my behalf.

Over the years that I have been involved in this project, many other people have helped in ways too numerous to describe: Jean Yarbrough, Professor of Social Sciences at Bowdoin College; dear friend Wally Green; Ann Willis, Bill Barker, and Bob Hill of Colonial Williamsburg; and Donna Brooks.

At the University of Virginia Press, Dick Holway had faith in my project from the very beginning, and quietly offered support all along the way. Ellen Satrom, with Dick's able assistant, Angie Hogan, patiently guided me through the intricacies of publishing with a university press. And copy editor Ruth Melville paid meticulous attention to detail in the final stages of the manuscript and reference notes.

My daughter, Betsy Bober Polivy, whose vision, editing skills, and constant encouragement, not to mention plethora of books, books, books, has been a tremendous support and an inspiration throughout.

My grandson, Evan Polivy, put his outstanding artistic talents to work to suggest ideas for the jacket design.

Two of my granddaughters, Melanie Lukens-Bober and Joelle Bober Polivy, have provided unusual support. They posed questions I needed to hear and to address. They saw the contradictions in Jefferson's attitude toward slavery, but recognized his extraordinary contribution to freedom even when they were very young students. Their thoughtful appraisals of Jefferson validated my need to attempt to reassess his role in history. Joelle's help in the early stages—organizing files, locating books and pictures—set me on my way. In the final stages Melanie's help with reference notes became for me a lee port in a storm. Their careful and critical readings of the manuscript throughout were invaluable. It is their support and their love that have kept me writing.

My husband, Larry, whose infinite patience, understanding, and encouragement seem inexhaustible, has for many years borne the burden of a wife who was living in the eighteenth century. But he has done so with grace, willingly undertaking any twenty-first century task that would allow me the freedom to write. Accompanying me on research trips and on numerous sojourns to Charlottesville, all the while taking his magnificent photographs, has multiplied the joy. His sharing and his love make it all possible.

# *Notes*

## SHORT TITLES AND ABBREVIATIONS

Boyd — *The Papers of Thomas Jefferson*, ed. Julian P. Boyd

*Family Letters* — *The Family Letters of Thomas Jefferson*, ed. Edwin Morris Betts and James A. Bear Jr.

Foner — *The Basic Writings of Thomas Jefferson*, ed. Philip S. Foner

Ford — *The Writings of Thomas Jefferson*, ed. Paul Leicester Ford

L & B — *The Writings of Thomas Jefferson*, ed. A. A. Lipscomb and A. E. Bergh

Malone — Dumas Malone, *Jefferson and His Time*

Randolph — Sarah N. Randolph, *The Domestic Life of Thomas Jefferson*

*Republic of Letters* — Thomas Jefferson and James Madison: *The Republic of Letters: The Correspondence*

Peterson — *Thomas Jefferson: Writings*, ed. Merrill D. Peterson

*Reference Biography* — Merrill D. Peterson, ed., *Thomas Jefferson: A Reference Biography*

UVA — Alderman Library, University of Virginia

## I. ON THE EDGE OF THE WILDERNESS

1. Stanton, *Free Some Day*, 19–20.
2. Bailey and Kennedy, *American Pageant*, 1:12–13.
3. Wilkins, *Jefferson's Pillow*, 18; *Encyclopedia of the North American Colonies*, 56–57.
4. Randolph, 22.
5. Parton, *Life of Thomas Jefferson*, 9–10.
6. Ibid.
7. Burstein, *Inner Jefferson*, 13.
8. H. S. Randall, *Life of Jefferson*, 1:23.

9. TJ, *Literary Commonplace Book,* 19, quotation from Nicholas Rowe's *Tamerlane.*
10. H. S. Randall, *Life of Jefferson,* 1:21–24.
11. TJ to John Harvie, Jan. 14, 1760, L & B, 4:268–69.

### 2. DISCOVERING DEVILSBURG

1. TJ, *Notes on the State of Virginia* (ed. Shuffleton), 158.
2. Stanton, *Free Some Day,* 20.

### 3. "BOLD IN THE PURSUIT OF KNOWLEDGE"

1. TJ to Dr. Benjamin Rush, Aug. 17, 1811, Foner, 693.
2. *Virginia Historical Register,* July 1850, quoted in Malone 1:58.
3. John Burk, early Virginia historian, to L. H. Girardin, Jan. 15, 1815, L & B, 14:231: "the ornament & delight of VA."
4. TJ, *Autobiography,* Peterson, 4.
5. Black, *Eighteenth-Century Britain,* 145–46.
6. J. C. Miller, *Origins of the American Revolution,* 170, 492.
7. Locke, *Two Treatises,* 289.
8. TJ, *Literary Commonplace Book,* 11.
9. TJ to Francis Eppes, Jan. 19, 1821, Peterson, 1451; TJ, *Literary Commonplace Book,* 155–57.
10. Peterson, *Thomas Jefferson and the New Nation,* 13.
11. TJ to Thomas Cooper, Feb. 10, 1814, L & B, 14:85.
12. TJ to John Page, Dec. 25, 1762, Foner, 488.
13. M. Kimball, *Jefferson: Road to Glory,* 78–79.
14. TJ to John Page, Oct. 7, 1763, Foner, 495.

### 4. RHETORIC OF REVOLUTION

1. Nash, *Unknown American Revolution,* 59.
2. Burk, *History of Virginia,* 3:299.
3. Wirt, *Life of Patrick Henry,* 83.
4. Quoted in Nash, *Unknown American Revolution,* 117–18.

### 5. THE SPIRIT OF THE LAW

1. From Euripides' *Orestes,* 1155.
2. TJ to John Page, June 25, 1804, Foner, 666.

3. TJ to Joseph Priestley, Jan. 27, 1800, Peterson, 1072.
4. Ketcham, *Presidents above Party*, 100; TJ to Peter Carr, 1787, Peterson, 900–902. For Hutcheson quotation, see http://cepa.newschool.edu/het/profiles/hutches.htm.
5. *Reference Biography*, 50.
6. As quoted in TJ, *Literary Commonplace Book*, 259.
7. Montesquieu, *Esprit des lois*, bk. 8, chap. 3.

### 6. ZEAL TO IMPROVE THE WORLD

1. TJ, *Garden Book*, 8.
2. TJ, *Notes on the State of Virginia* (ed. Shuffleton), Query VI, note on 71.
3. Malone, 2:93.
4. *Reference Biography*, 233–38.
5. TJ, *Autobiography*, Foner, 412.

### 7. FIRST ASSIGNMENT, FIRST FAILURE

1. TJ, *Autobiography*, Peterson, 6.
2. *Journals of the House of Burgesses*, 1766–69, Mar. 21, 1768.
3. Ibid., Apr. 14, 1768, 174.
4. Ibid., May 17, 1769, 214.
5. Bober, *Countdown to Independence*, 127.
6. Ibid., 121–28.

### 8. ESSAY IN ARCHITECTURE

1. TJ, Aug. 3, 1767, *Garden Book*, 6.
2. TJ, May 15, 1768, ibid., 12–13.
3. Ibid., 14.
4. TJ to James Ogilvie, Feb. 20, 1771, Ford, 1:390–91.
5. TJ to Benjamin Henry Latrobe, Oct. 10, 1809, quoted in Cheuk, *Thomas Jefferson's Monticello*, 2.

### 9. ALL MEN ARE BORN FREE

1. Malone 1:125–26.
2. TJ to John Page, Feb. 21, 1770, Foner, 503–5.
3. See W. S. Randall, *Thomas Jefferson: A Life*, 133–34.

4. TJ to Robert Walsh, Apr. 5, 1823, UVA, in Malone, 1:127; Wills, *Inventing America,* 167.

5. Thomas Nelson Jr. to TJ, Mar. 6, 1770, Coolidge Collection, Massachusetts Historical Society; and Thomas Nelson Sr. to TJ, ibid.

6. George Wythe to TJ, Mar. 9, 1770, *Garden Book,* 20. See also Malone 1: 126–27.

7. TJ, *Howell vs. Netherland,* April 1770, *Reports of Cases Determined in the General Court,* 90–96.

8. Locke, *Two Treatises,* 287.

### 10. "WORTHY OF THE LADY"

1. Milton, *Paradise Lost,* 4.337, quoted in TJ, *Literary Commonplace Book,* 95.

2. TJ to John Page, Feb. 21, 1770, Foner, 503–5.

3. Stanton, *Free Some Day,* 18.

4. See Randolph, 43–44; W. S. Randall: *Jefferson: A Life,* 156; Malone 1:156–59, app. I, D, 432–33.

5. TJ to Thomas Adams, June 1, 1777, Foner, 505–6.

### 11. "YOUNG HOT-HEADS"

1. Bober, *Countdown to Independence,* 175.

2. TJ, *Autobiography,* Peterson, 7.

3. Parton, *Life of Jefferson,* 125.

4. TJ, *Autobiography,* Peterson, 6–8.

5. Ibid., 8–9.

### 12. THE RIGHTS OF BRITISH AMERICA

1. *Massachusetts Spy,* June 30, 1774.

2. Chinard, *Thomas Jefferson, Apostle of Americanism,* 31.

3. Jayne, *Jefferson's Declaration of Independence,* 52–54.

4. TJ, *Summary View,* Peterson, 105–6.

5. Ibid., 106.

6. Ibid., 121, 122.

7. Ibid., 121.

8. Ibid., 115–16.

9. TJ, *Autobiography,* Peterson, 11; Edmund Randolph, "Essay on the Revolutionary History of Virginia," 216.

10. TJ, *Autobiography*, Peterson, 414–15.
11. Maier, *American Scripture*, 112.

### 13. A MASTERLY PEN

1. Jefferson, *Autobiography*, Peterson, 5.
2. Stanton, *Free Some Day*, 103, and "Those Who Labor for My Happiness," in *Jeffersonian Legacies*, ed. Onuf, 152.
3. TJ, *Autobiography*, Ford, 1:82; TJ to John Bernard, in Padover, *Thomas Jefferson*, 25.
4. TJ to Thomas Mann Randolph Jr., L & B, 6:167.
5. See Onuf, "Scholars' Jefferson," esp. 687.
6. W. S. Randall, *Jefferson: A Life*, 95–96.
7. Wirt, *Patrick Henry*, 138–41.
8. E. Randolph, "Essay," 223.
9. TJ, *Autobiography*, Ford, 9:340.
10. TJ to William Wirt, Aug. 14–15, 1814, in Wirt, *Patrick Henry*, 143.
11. *Journals of the House of Burgesses*, 1773–76, July 31, 1775, 17.
12. TJ to William Small, May 7, 1775, Ford, 1:453–54.
13. Quotation from E. Randolph, "Essay," 223. For a full discussion, see Bober, *Countdown to Independence*, chap. 27, 245–62.
14. Account Book, Spring, 1775. See TJ, *Garden Book*.
15. Boyd, 1:675–76, part of note on *Summary View*.
16. John Adams to Timothy Pickering, Aug. 6, 1822, *Works*, 2:512–14 note.
17. Drafted in 1775; approved July 6, *Journals of Congress*, 1777, 7:147–48.
18. Whitney, *Colonial Williamsburg Interpreter*, 16.
19. Ibid.
20. Bobrick, *Angel in the Whirlwind*, 162.

### 14. "AN EXPRESSION OF THE AMERICAN MIND"

1. Thomas Paine, *Common Sense*, in Paine, *Writings*, 1:84. See also Beloff, *Jefferson and American Democracy*, 245, 253.
2. Stanton, *Free Some Day*, 20, 18.
3. John Adams to James Warren, May 26, 1776, Adams, *Works*, 9:374.
4. TJ to Thomas Nelson, May 16, 1776, L & B, 4:253–56.
5. TJ to Samuel Kercheval, July 20, 1816, Ford, 12:4–7.
6. Tomlins and Mann, *Many Legalities*, 115.
7. Wilkins, *Jefferson's Pillow*, 30.

8. *Journals of the House of Burgesses*, 1773–76, June 7, 1776.
9. Jefferson, *Autobiography*, Foner, 421.
10. Ibid.
11. John Adams, *Works*, 2:512.

### 15. A REVOLUTIONARY DOCUMENT

1. Jayne, *Jefferson's Declaration*, 22.
2. Ibid., 53.
3. TJ to Henry Lee, May 8, 1825, Peterson, 1501.
4. Jayne, *Jefferson's Declaration*, 53; Commager, *Jefferson, Nationalism*, 81.
5. Commager, *Jefferson, Nationalism*, 83.
6. John Adams, *Diary and Autobiography*, quoted in J. Ellis, *American Sphinx* (1998 ed.), 44.
7. *Reference Biography*, 147.
8. Rakove, "Our Jefferson"; Onuf, "Scholars' Jefferson," 681; Becker, *Declaration of Independence*, 196.
9. *Reference Biography*, 34–36.
10. Beloff, *Jefferson and American Democracy*, 69; Maier, *American Scripture*, 206–8.
11. Commager, *Jefferson, Nationalism*, 87–88; Jayne, *Jefferson's Declaration*, 122–26; Maier, *American Scripture*, 136.
12. Wood, *Radicalism of the American Revolution*, 232–33.
13. Commager, *Jefferson, Nationalism*, 84–87; see also Onuf, *Jefferson's Empire*, 3–17.
14. Wilkins, *Jefferson's Pillow*, 29–30.
15. John Adams, *Works*, 4:193.
16. Quoted in Commager, *Jefferson, Nationalism*, 93–94.
17. Chinard, *Thomas Jefferson, Apostle of Americanism*, 75–76.
18. Onuf, "Scholars' Jefferson," 681.
19. TJ to John Page, July 20, 1776, L & B, *Writings*, 4:268.
20. Beloff, *Jefferson and American Democracy*, 67; Becker, *Declaration of Independence*, 136–41.
21. TJ, Ford, 10:327 (footnote to letter to James Monroe).
22. John Adams to Abigail Adams, July 3, 1776, in Adams and Adams, *Book of Abigail and John*, 139–42.
23. Story recounted by TJ in Ford, 10:120 (written in 1818).
24. Original Draft, before edited by Congress. See Wills, *Inventing America*, 378.
25. John Adams, *Works*, 2:514.

26. TJ, notes taken during the debate on the Declaration, in Becker, *Declaration of Independence,* 171–72.
27. Maier, *American Scripture,* 146.
28. Wills, *Genius of Liberty,* 18.
29. Richard Henry Lee to TJ, July 21, 1776, *Letters of Richard Henry Lee,* 1:210.
30. John Page to TJ, July 20, 1776, *New England Historical and Genealogical Register,* 56:210.
31. Parton, *Life of Jefferson,* 192.

## 16. LEGAL REFORM IN VIRGINIA

1. TJ to Richard Henry Lee, July 8, 1776, L & B, 3:34.
2. Richard Henry Lee to TJ, Sept. 27, 1776, ibid.
3. TJ to John Hancock, Oct. 11, 1776, Ford, 2:91–92.

## 17. RELIGIOUS LIBERTY

1. Boyd, 2:305.
2. Ibid., 306.
3. John Adams to TJ, May 26, 1777, *Adams–Jefferson Letters,* 5–6.
4. TJ, *Autobiography,* Peterson, 44.
5. TJ, *Notes on the State of Virginia,* Query VII, Peterson, 285.
6. TJ, *Autobiography,* Peterson, 34.
7. Ibid.
8. TJ to Samuel Kercheval, Jan. 19, 1810, Peterson, 1213–14.
9. TJ, *Notes on the State of Virginia,* Query VII, Peterson, 285; Malone, 1:275.
10. Ferling, *Setting the World Ablaze,* 158–59.
11. See Malone, 1:275–80; and Peterson and Vaughan, *Virginia Statute,* vii–x.
12. TJ, *Notes on the State of Virginia,* Query VII, Peterson, 285–86.
13. Peterson and Vaughan, *Virginia Statute,* viii.
14. Peterson, *Thomas Jefferson and the American Revolution,* 36.
15. Bowers, *Young Jefferson,* 210–12; Jayne, *Jefferson's Declaration,* 156–57.
16. Marty, preface to Sheridan.
17. Mapp, *Faiths of Our Fathers,* 3–15.
18. Allen Jayne, in talks at the Summer Salon, Board of Trustees of the Jefferson Legacy Foundation, Ripton, VT, Aug. 19, 2004.
19. Mapp, *Faiths of Our Fathers,* 5.
20. Peterson and Vaughan, *Virginia Statute,* 1–3; Winifred E. Garrison, quoted in ibid., 1–2; Marty, preface to Sheridan.

21. Bailyn, *Begin the World Anew*, 40.
22. Quoted in Peterson and Vaughan, *Virginia Statute*, xi.

### 18. "PUBLIC SERVICE AND PRIVATE MISERY"

1. TJ to Richard Henry Lee, June 17, 1779, Ford, 2:192.
2. Peterson, *Jefferson and the Revolution*, 42.
3. John Adams to Abigail Adams, June 26, 1776, *Book of Abigail and John*, 137.
4. William Fleming to TJ, June 1779, Jefferson Papers, Library of Congress.
5. Monroe quoted in Bowers, *Young Jefferson*, 256.
6. TJ to James Monroe, May 20, 1782, Peterson, 777–80.
7. B. E. Davis, *Monticello Scrapbook*, 40.
8. Ibid.
9. Stanton, *Free Some Day*, 21.
10. TJ to Dr. William Gordon, July 16, 1788, Ford, 5:39.

### 19. "ONE FATAL STAIN"

1. TJ, *Autobiography*, Peterson, 55.
2. Commager, *Jefferson, Nationalism*, 36.
3. TJ, *Notes on the State of Virginia* (ed. Shuffleton), Query VI.
4. Ibid., esp. 63–71.
5. Commager, *Jefferson, Nationalism*, 33–41.
6. Shuffleton, introduction to *Notes on the State of Virginia*, xxii–xxv.
7. TJ, *Notes on the State of Virginia*, Query II, Peterson, 131.
8. Shuffleton, introduction to *Notes on the State of Virginia*, xxii–xxv; see also Jordan, *White over Black*, 477.
9. Shuffleton, introduction to *Notes on the State of Virginia*, xxvi.
10. Onuf, "Scholars' Jefferson," 682–84.
11. Rakove, "Our Jefferson," 220.
12. TJ to John Adams, Jan. 22, 1821, *Adams–Jefferson Letters*, 570.
13. TJ, *Autobiography*, Peterson, 44.
14. TJ, *Notes on the State of Virginia*, Peterson, 270.
15. Hume quoted in Popkin, "Philosophical Basis of Eighteenth-Century Racism," 245.
16. Wilkins, *Jefferson's Pillow*, 29.
17. Popkin, "Eighteenth-Century Racism," 246–47.
18. Ibid., 246.
19. See Popkin, "Eighteenth-Century Racism"; and Jordan, *White over Black*, chap. 5.

20. J. C. Miller, *Wolf by the Ears*, 52; Jordan, *White over Black*, 429–30.
21. Rakove, "Our Jefferson," 223; and John Chester Miller, "Slavery," in *Reference Biography*, 426.
22. TJ, *Notes on the State of Virginia*, Query XVIII, Peterson, 288–89.
23. For a full discussion, see Jordan, *Black over White*, 429–40.
24. Ellen Randolph Coolidge to TJ, Aug. 1, 1825, *Family Letters*, 454.
25. TJ to Ellen Randolph Coolidge, Aug. 27, 1825, ibid., 457.
26. John Adams to TJ, May 22, 1785, *Adams–Jefferson Letters*, 21.


20. "THAT ETERNAL SEPARATION"

1. Chastellux, *Voyages*, 2:41–42.
2. Ibid.; McLaughlin, *Jefferson and Monticello*, 202.
3. Chastellux, *Voyages*, 2:41–42.
4. TJ to James Monroe, May 20, 1782, Peterson, 780.
5. Quoted in Randolph, 62–63.
6. Ibid., 63.
7. Ibid.
8. TJ to Elizabeth Eppes, Oct. 3, 1782, Boyd, 6:198.
9. TJ to Chastellux, Nov. 26, 1782, Randolph, 68.
10. James Madison to Edmund Randolph, June 28, 1782, quoted in W. H. Adams, *Paris Years*, 34.
11. TJ to Samuel Henley, Nov. 27, 1785, ibid.


21. A NEW DOOR OPENS

1. TJ, *Autobiography*, Peterson, 46.
2. D. Wilson, *Jefferson's Books*, 34–42.
3. Jefferson to Marbois, Dec. 5, 1783, Malone, 1:405.
4. Malone, 2:404–5.
5. TJ to Martha (Patsy), Nov. 28, 1783, Boyd, 6:359.
6. Washington's Farewell Address to Congress, Boyd, 6:411–12.
7. TJ to Patsy, Dec. 22, 1783, Boyd, 6:359.
8. TJ to G. K. von Hogendorp, n.d. (probably summer 1784), in M. Kimball, *Jefferson: War and Peace*, 328.
9. TJ to Jean Nicholas Demeunier, June 1786, Boyd, 10:58.
10. Madonia, ed., *Facing the Past*, 30; "Monticello Report: Thomas Jefferson and William Short," R. Bowman, Monticello Research Department, Sept. 29, 1997, http://www.monticello.org/reports/people/short.html.
11. TJ to William Short, Apr. 30, 1784, Boyd, 7:149.

12. Burstein, *Inner Jefferson,* 148. For a thoughtful and enlightening discussion of what friendship meant to Jefferson, see ibid., 131–70.
13. TJ to James Madison, May 8, 1784, *Republic of Letters,* 316.
14. TJ to James Madison, Feb. 20, 1784, ibid., 297.

### 22. "BEHOLD ME ON THE VAUNTED SCENE OF EUROPE"

1. Martha (Patsy) to Elizabeth Trist, ca. Aug. 1784, Edgehill Randolph Collection, UVA.
2. TJ to Nathaniel Greene, Jan. 12, 1785, Ford, 4:25.
3. Abigail Adams, *Letters,* 216.
4. TJ to Dr. James Currie, ca. Feb. 1785, Malone, 2:12.
5. TJ to Francis Eppes, Feb. 5, 1785, Boyd, 7:635–36.
6. Elizabeth Eppes to TJ, Oct. 31, 1784, ibid., 441.
7. Beloff, *Jefferson and American Democracy,* 102.
8. TJ to James Madison, June 20, 1787, *Republic of Letters,* 481.
9. Abigail Adams, *Letters,* 87.
10. Ibid., 240–41.
11. D. Wilson, "Evolution of Jefferson's *Notes.*"
12. TJ to James Madison, May 1785, Ford, 4:46–47.
13. TJ to James Monroe, June 17, 1785, Peterson, 804–5.
14. J. C. Miller, *Wolf by the Ears,* 88.
15. TJ to Brissot de Warville, Feb. 11, 1788, quoted in J. Ellis, *American Sphinx,* 88.
16. Goodman, "Enlightenment Salons."
17. TJ to Elizabeth Eppes, Sept. 22, 1785, Randolph, 105.
18. W. H. Adams, *Paris Years,* 20.
19. Abigail Adams, *Letters,* 191.
20. Ibid., 207.
21. TJ to James Monroe, June 17, 1785, Peterson, 805.
22. TJ to Thomas Turpin, Feb. 5, 1769, ibid., 739.
23. TJ to Charles Bellini, Sept. 30, 1785, ibid., 833.
24. Benjamin Harrison to TJ, July 20, 1784, Boyd, 7:374–78.
25. TJ to James Madison, Dec. 16, 1786, Foner, 545–46.

### 23. DIALOGUE BETWEEN THE HEAD AND THE HEART

1. TJ to David Humphreys, Aug. 14, 1787, Boyd, 12:32, quoted in W. H. Adams, *Paris Years,* 59.
2. G. Wilson and Chew, "Fashioning an American Diplomat."
3. TJ to Angelica Schuyler Church, Sept. 21, 1788, Boyd, 13:623.

4. TJ to Anne Bingham, May 11, 1788, Ford, 5:8–10.
5. Anne Bingham to TJ, June 1, 1787, Boyd, 11:392–93.
6. TJ to Madame de Tessé, Jan. 30, 1803.
7. Trumbull, *Autobiography*, 92–93; also quoted in W. H. Adams, *Paris Years*, 91.
8. W. H. Adams, *Paris Years*, 91.
9. M. Kimball, *Jefferson: Scene of Europe*, 118.
10. Quoted in Bullock, *My Head and My Heart*, 14.
11. TJ to Maria Cosway, Oct. 12, 1786, ibid., 31–32.
12. Trumbull, *Autobiography*, 101–2.
13. Maria Cosway to TJ, ca. Sept. 20, 1786, Randolph, 85.
14. TJ to Maria Cosway, probably Sept. 21, 1786, Butterfield and Rice, "Jefferson's Earliest Note," 31–32.
15. Maria Cosway to TJ, n.d., Randolph, 86.
16. TJ to Maria Cosway, Oct. 12, 1786, ibid., 87.
17. TJ to S. Smith, Oct. 22, 1786, Ford, 4:325.
18. Malone, 2:76.
19. Bullock, *My Head and My Heart*, 30, 41–42.
20. TJ to Maria Cosway, Dec. 25, 1786, UVA.
21. Quoted in Corzine, *The French Revolution*, 27.
22. TJ to James Madison, Jan. 30, 1787, Peterson, 882.
23. TJ to Abigail Adams, Feb. 22, 1787, ibid., 889–90.
24. See Malone 2:xvii–xx, 165–66.

## 24. CHANGING THE SHAPE OF HIS COUNTRY

1. TJ to Lafayette, Apr. 11, 1787, Peterson, 895.
2. See F. Kimball, "Thomas Jefferson and the First Monument," 13; also in M. Kimball, 76.
3. TJ to Madame de Tessé, Mar. 20, 1787, Boyd, 13:226.
4. TJ to James Madison, Sept. 20, 1785, Peterson, 828–30.
5. Stanton, introduction to Moore and Moore, *Thomas Jefferson's Journey*, 13.
6. Beloff, *Jefferson and American Democracy*, 105; Nock, *Mr. Jefferson*, 103.
7. TJ to Martha (Patsy), Mar. 28, 1787, *Family Letters*, 34.
8. Martha (Patsy) to TJ, Apr. 9, 1787, ibid., 37–38.
9. TJ to Martha (Patsy), May 5, 1787, ibid., 40.
10. TJ to Maria Cosway, July 1, 1787, in M. Kimball, *Jefferson: Scene of Europe*, 177.
11. Maria Cosway to TJ, Dec. 1787, and TJ to Maria Cosway, Jan. 1788, Coolidge Collection, Massachusetts Historical Society.

12. TJ to Maria Cosway, Sept. 26, 1788, UVA.
13. Ibid.

### 25. "SHE MUST COME"

1. TJ to Francis Eppes, Aug. 30, 1785, in M. Kimball, *Jefferson: Scene of Europe,* 304.
2. TJ to Elizabeth Eppes, Sept. 22, 1785, ibid.
3. TJ to Polly, Sept. 20, 1785, *Family Letters,* 29.
4. Polly to TJ, Sept. 13, 1785, ibid.
5. TJ to Elizabeth Eppes, Jan. or Feb. 1786, Randolph, 107.
6. Elizabeth Eppes to TJ, Mar. 1787, ibid., 124.
7. See Gordon-Reed, *Thomas Jefferson and Sally Hemings,* chap. 5, esp. 160ff.

### 26. "CRUSADE AGAINST IGNORANCE"

1. TJ to James Madison, Dec. 20, 1787, Foner, 563–64.
2. *Republic of Letters,* 3–4.
3. TJ to the Danbury Baptists, Jan. 1, 1802, Dreisbach, *Thomas Jefferson and the Wall of Separation,* 148.
4. TJ to M. l'Abbé Arnoux, Paris, July 19, 1789, L & B, 7:422.
5. See Commager, *Jefferson, Nationalism,* 67.
6. TJ to George Wythe, Aug. 13, 1786, Peterson, 859.
7. TJ to Thomas Mann Randolph Jr., L & B, 6:165.

### 27. A SUMMER OF VIOLENCE

1. TJ to George Washington, L & B, 7:349–50.
2. TJ to Francis Hopkinson, ibid., 301–2.
3. See Bailyn, *Faces of Revolution,* 30.
4. TJ to John Jay, Nov. 1788, Hall, *Mr. Jefferson's Ladies,* 99.
5. TJ to George Washington, spring 1789, L & B, 7:349–50.
6. J. Ellis, *American Sphinx,* 116.
7. W. H. Adams, *Paris Years,* 23.
8. "Memoirs of Madison Hemings," in Gordon-Reed, *Jefferson and Hemings,* 245–48.
9. Ibid., 246.
10. Abigail Adams to TJ, June 27, 1787, *Adams–Jefferson Letters,* 179.
11. Gordon-Reed, *Jefferson and Hemings,* 164.
12. Ibid., 166, 179.
13. For a full and thoughtful discussion of this issue, see ibid., chap. 5, 158–209.

14. TJ to James Maurice, Sept. 16, 1789, Boyd, 15:433, quoted in Gordon-Reed, *Jefferson and Hemings*, 180.
15. Quoted in Merrill Peterson, "Thomas Jefferson: A Brief Life," in Weymouth, *Thomas Jefferson*, 24.
16. TJ to James Monroe, Apr. 15, 1785.
17. Printed in the *Gazette of the United States*, Dec. 16, 1789, quoted in Malone, 2:244.
18. TJ to George Washington, Dec. 15, 1789, Foner, 592–93.
19. Patsy quoted in Randolph, 152.

### 28. CONFLICT IN THE CABINET

1. Quoted in Stanton, *Free Some Day*, 22; see 19–27 for a full discussion of Jupiter and Philip.
2. TJ, Ford, 9:273.
3. Quoted in Christman, *"The Spirit of Party,"* 23.
4. TJ to Martha, Apr. 4, 1790, *Family Letters*, 50–51.
5. Martha to TJ, Apr. 25, 1790, ibid., 52–53.
6. TJ to Maria, May 8, 1791, Boyd, 20:380–81.
7. TJ to Maria, May 30, 1791, *Family Letters*, 83.
8. Maria to TJ, July 10, 1791, ibid., 87.
9. TJ to Martha, July 7, 1793, ibid., 121–22.
10. Benjamin Banneker to TJ, Aug. 19, 1791, in Bedini, *Life of Benjamin Banneker*, 152.
11. Quoted in Franklin and Moss, *From Slavery to Freedom*, 88–89.
12. Benjamin Banneker to TJ, Aug. 19, 1791, and TJ to Banneker, Aug. 30, 1791, in Bedini, *Life of Banneker*, 152–61.
13. TJ to L'Enfant, 1791, quoted by Meyer Reinhold, "The Classical World," in *Reference Biography*, 143.
14. Latrobe quoted in ibid., 139.

### 29. "OUR OWN DEAR MONTICELLO"

1. TJ to James Madison, June 9, 1793, Peterson, 1010.
2. TJ to Angelica Schuyler Church, Nov. 27, 1793, ibid., 1013.
3. TJ to Horatio Gates, Feb. 3, 1794, Library of Congress, #16747.
4. William L. Beiswanger, "Essay in Architecture," in Cheuk, *Thomas Jefferson's Monticello*, 5.
5. TJ to Maria Cosway, Oct. 12, 1786, in Bullock, *My Head and My Heart*, 31–32.
6. Conversation with Susan Stein, June 2002.
7. E. S. Morgan, *Meaning of Independence*, 78.

8. McLaughlin, *Jefferson and Monticello*, 93.

9. Thomas Mann Randolph to TJ, Aug. 14, 1793, in Stanton, *Free Some Day*, 19–22.

10. TJ to Benjamin Austin, Jan. 9, 1816, Peterson, 1369–72.

11. Duc de La Rochefoucauld-Liancourt, "A Frenchman Views Jefferson the Farmer," in Peterson, *Visitors to Monticello*, 28.

12. Lucia Stanton, "Mulberry Row," in Cheuk, *Thomas Jefferson's Monticello*, 192.

13. See www.monticello.org/jefferson/dayinlife/plantation/home.html (accessed June 2006).

14. McLaughlin, *Jefferson and Monticello*, 110–11.

15. Stanton, *Slavery at Monticello*, 23, 27; and *Free Some Day*, 47.

16. TJ to Thomas Mann Randolph, Jan. 23, 1801, quoted in Schwarz, *Slave Laws in Virginia*, 51.

17. Quoted in Stanton, *Slavery at Monticello*, 24.

18. Ibid., 27.

19. "Memoirs of a Monticello Slave," in Bear, *Jefferson at Monticello*, 23.

20. Ibid., 15–16.

21. Stanton, *Slavery at Monticello*, 29.

22. Stanton, *Free Some Day*, 28–29.

23. Ibid., 29–30.

### 30. "I HAVE NO AMBITION TO GOVERN MEN"

1. Bailey and Kennedy, *American Pageant*, 151; Corzine, *The French Revolution*, 8–9, 82–83.

2. *Republic of Letters*, 881–83.

3. Quoted in Nock, *Mr. Jefferson*, 130–31.

4. Peterson, *Adams and Jefferson*, 64; TJ to James Madison, Sept. 21, 1795, in ibid., 64–65.

5. TJ to James Madison, Apr. 27, 1795, *Republic of Letters*, 877.

6. TJ to James Madison, Jan. 1, 1797, ibid., 952–54.

7. TJ to John Adams, Dec. 28, 1796, ibid., 954–55.

8. TJ to James Madison, Jan. 1, 1797, ibid., 944, 953.

9. Quoted in Bowen, *Miracle at Philadelphia*, 95.

10. Ohline, "Republicanism and Slavery," 563–84.

11. Hamilton quoted in Bowen, *Miracle at Philadelphia*, 201; Ohline, "Republicanism and Slavery," 564.

12. Ohline, "Republicanism and Slavery," 584; Michael A. Bellesiles, "Soaked with Blood," in *Revolution of 1800*, ed. Horn, Lewis, and Onuf, 77.

13. Bober, *Abigail Adams*, 187–89.

14. Beloff, *Jefferson and American Democracy*, 176–77.

15. Bailey and Kennedy, *American Pageant*, 156–60.
16. Quoted in Padover, *Thomas Jefferson*, 258.
17. TJ to Carrington, Jan. 16, 1787, Ford, 4:359.
18. TJ to Martha, June 8, 1797, *Family Letters*, 145–47.
19. TJ to Maria, Jan. 7, 1798, ibid., 151–53.
20. TJ to Martha, Mar. 27, 1797, ibid., 142.
21. TJ to Maria, July 13, 1798, and July 14, 1798, ibid., 166–67, 167–68.

31. "WE ARE ALL REPUBLICANS, WE ARE ALL FEDERALISTS"

1. TJ to John Adams, fall 1800, quoted in Simon, *What Kind of Nation*, 118.
2. TJ to Benjamin Rush, Sept. 23, 1800, Peterson, 1080–82.
3. Van der Linden, *Turning Point*, 158–62.
4. John Adams to Eldridge Gerry, Dec. 30, 1800, Adams, *Works*, 9:577–78.
5. TJ to Martha, Jan. 26, 1801, Simon, *What Kind of Nation*, 135.
6. TJ to James Monroe, Feb. 15, 1801, ibid., 136.
7. James A. Bayard to Richard Bassett, Feb. 17, 1801, quoted in Van der Linden, *Turning Point*, 313.
8. Simon, *What Kind of Nation*, 135–36.
9. See W. S. Randall, *Jefferson: A Life*, 547; Chinard, *Thomas Jefferson, Apostle of Americanism*, 369–75; Van der Linden, *Turning Point*, 308–14; Beran, *Jefferson's Demons*, 145.
10. Wills, *Negro President*, 89.
11. TJ to Lafayette, Mar. 6, 1801, L & B, 10:214.
12. TJ to Spencer Roane, Sept. 6, 1819, L & B, 15:212.
13. Wills, *Negro President*, 87.
14. TJ to Thomas Lomax, Feb. 25, 1801, quoted in Chinard, *Apostle of Americanism*, 379.
15. Cunningham, *In Pursuit of Reason*, 238; Simon, *What Kind of Nation*, 141.
16. Cunningham, *In Pursuit of Reason*, 23–24; H. Adams, *History of the United States*, 137–47; Van der Linden, *Turning Point*, 318–20.
17. Margaret Bayard Smith to Susan Smith, Mar. 4, 1801, Samuel Harrison Smith Papers, Library of Congress, 6:66, 921–22.
18. Van der Linden, *Turning Point*, 320–21.
19. H. Adams, *History of the United States*, 146.
20. Beran, *Jefferson's Demons*, 152. In 1799 Jefferson had written to a student at William and Mary: "As long as we may think as we will, and speak as we think, the condition of man will proceed in improvement." It was an important conviction of his.
21. See Beloff, *Jefferson and American Democracy*, 190–92; Chinard, *Apostle of Americanism*, 380.

22. TJ, "First Inaugural Address," Peterson, 492–96.
23. Benjamin Rush to TJ, Mar. 12, 1801, quoted in Malone, 4:32.
24. Simon, *What Kind of Nation*, 141.
25. M. B. Smith, *First Forty Years*.
26. Ibid.

## 32. ARCHITECT OF AMERICAN EXPANSION

1. J. Ellis, *American Sphinx*, 190.
2. Douglas Brinkley, quoted in *Smithsonian*, Apr. 2003, 104.
3. TJ to Robert Livingston, Apr. 18, 1802, Peterson, 1104–7, quotation on 1105.
4. TJ to James Monroe, Jan. 13, 1803, ibid., 1111–13.
5. TJ to Robert Livingston, Apr. 18, 1802, ibid., 1105.
6. For a full discussion, see Beloff, *Jefferson and American Democracy*, 201–11; and G. Wilson, "Jefferson's Big Deal."
7. Horn, Lewis, and Onuf, introduction to *Revolution of 1800*, xiv.
8. Instructions to Captain Lewis, June 20, 1803, in Peterson, 1126–29; and W. S. Randall, *Jefferson: A Life*, 567–69.
9. TJ to Maria, Oct. 26, 1801, *Family Letters*, 210–11.
10. TJ to Maria, Feb. 12, 1800, ibid., 185–86.
11. Stanton, *Free Some Day*, 27.
12. H. S. Randall, *Life of Jefferson*, 3:510; Randolph, 321–22; Stanton, *Free Some Day*, 25–26.
13. TJ to Maria, Feb. 26, 1804, *Family Letters*, 258.
14. TJ to Maria, Mar. 3, 1804, ibid.
15. TJ to James Madison, Apr. 9, 1804, *Republic of Letters*, 1303–4.
16. TJ to James Madison, Apr. 23, 1804, ibid., 1322–23.
17. TJ to John Page, June 25, 1804, Foner, 665–66.
18. Abigail Adams to TJ, May 20, 1804, Randolph, 304–5.
19. J. Ellis, *American Sphinx*, 192–93.
20. TJ to P. S. Dupont de Nemours, Mar. 2, 1809, Peterson, 1203–4.
21. TJ's reply, Mar. 4, 1809, Malone, 5:667–68, and *Republic of Letters*, 1563.
22. Malone, 5:666.

## 33. OCTAGONAL RETREAT

1. TJ to Charles Willson Peale, Aug. 20, 1811, Peterson, 1249.
2. Ellen Randolph Coolidge to Henry S. Randall, Feb. 18, 1856, Randall, *Life of Jefferson*, 3:342.
3. TJ to Joel Yancey, Nov. 10, 1818, TJ, *Farm Book*, 41.
4. Hannah to TJ, Nov. 15, 1818, ibid., 42.

### 34. "A FIRE BELL IN THE NIGHT"

1. TJ to Hugh Nelson, Mar. 12, 1820, quoted in *Jefferson Cyclopedia,* 564.
2. TJ to John Adams, Dec. 1819, and Adams to TJ, Dec. 21, 1819, *Adams–Jefferson Letters,* 548–49, 551.
3. John Chester Miller, "Slavery," in *Reference Biography,* 431.
4. TJ to John Holmes, Apr. 22, 1820, Peterson, 1433–35.

### 35. SCANDAL

1. TJ to Dr. George Logan, June 20, 1816, Ford, 10:27.
2. See Foster et al., "Jefferson Fostered Child"; and my preface, above.

### 36. "THE VENERABLE CORPS OF GRANDFATHERS"

1. TJ to Elizabeth Eppes, May 15, 1791, Randolph, 201.
2. Stanton, *Free Some Day,* 101.
3. TJ to Thaddeus Kosciusko, Feb. 26, 1810, in Randolph, 331–32.
4. Ellen Randolph Coolidge to Henry S. Randall, about 1850, ibid., 340–43.
5. Virginia J. Trist to Henry S. Randall, May 26, 1839, ibid., 345–46.
6. Ellen Randolph Coolidge to Henry S. Randall, about 1850, ibid., 344.
7. Virginia J. Trist to Henry S. Randall, May 26, 1839, ibid.
8. "Life among the Lowly, No. 1," *Pike County (Ohio) Republican,* Mar. 13, 1873, in Gordon-Reed, *Jefferson and Hemings,* 245–48.
9. Onuf, "Every Generation," 169.
10. See Sobel, *World They Made Together,* 139–42.
11. Stanton, *Free Some Day,* 135–36.
12. Ibid., 138.
13. Ellen Randolph Coolidge, quoted in Bear, "The Hemings Family," 87.
14. *American Heritage Magazine,* Apr. 1993, 109.
15. TJ to Ellen Randolph Coolidge, Nov. 14, 1825, Coolidge Collection, Massachusetts Historical Society.
16. TJ to Thomas Jefferson Randolph, Nov. 24, 1808, *Family Letters,* 362–65.
17. TJ to Thomas Jefferson Randolph, Feb. 8, 1826, ibid., 469–70.
18. Thomas Jefferson Randolph Recollections, UVA, accession #1397.

### 37. "I CANNOT LIVE WITHOUT BOOKS"

1. See http://www.historycentral.com/1812/Index.html.
2. TJ to John Adams, early in 1812, Randolph, 354–55.
3. TJ, *Autobiography,* Peterson, 42.

4. Ibid., 44.
5. Malone, 1:280.
6. TJ to William Roscoe, Dec. 27, 1820, L & B, 15:303.
7. Addis, *Jefferson's Vision for Education,* 94–95.
8. TJ to José Correa, Oct. 24, 1820, *Garden Book,* 590.
9. See Bruce, *History of the University of Virginia; the Lengthened Shadow of One Man.* The phrase comes from Emerson, "An institution is the lengthened shadow of one man," in his essay "Self-Reliance."
10. From Lafayette's memoirs, Nov. 8, 1824, quoted in Chinard, *Apostle of Americanism,* 531.
11. "Memoirs of Israel Jefferson," in Gordon-Reed, *Jefferson and Hemings,* 252.

38. "THOMAS JEFFERSON STILL SURVIVES"

1. TJ to Joel Yancey, May 25, 1818, quoted in Chambers, *Jefferson's Poplar Forest.*
2. Francis Eppes to TJ, Feb. 23, 1826, *Family Letters,* 470–72.
3. Gordon-Reed, *Jefferson and Hemings,* 31–33.
4. Stanton, *Free Some Day,* 120–21.
5. Gordon-Reed, *Jefferson and Hemings,* 26–34; Stanton, "Other End of the Telescope."
6. I gratefully acknowledge my indebtedness to Jan Ellen Lewis for the illuminating conversations we had on this topic at the International Center for Jefferson Studies.
7. TJ to Edward Coles, Aug. 25, 1814, Peterson, 1343–46.
8. TJ to James Heaton, May 20, 1826, ibid., 1516.
9. TJ to James Madison, Feb. 17, 1826, *Republic of Letters,* 1964–67.
10. TJ to Roger C. Weightman, June 24, 1826, Peterson, 1516–17.
11. Stanton, *Free Some Day,* 125.
12. H. S. Randall, *Life of Jefferson,* 3:543–48.
13. TJ to John Adams, Apr. 11, 1823, *Adams–Jefferson Letters,* 594.
14. TJ to George Gilmer, Aug. 12, 1787, Boyd, 12:26.

# Bibliography

## ORIGINAL SOURCES

Albemarle County Will Book, No. 2. UVA.

Carr and Cary Papers, 1785–1839. Special Collections Department, UVA.

*Catalogue of the Library of Thomas Jefferson.* Compiled with annotations by E. Millicent Sowerby. Washington, D.C.: Library of Congress, 1952.

*The Collected Papers to Commemorate Fifty Years of the Monticello Association of the Descendants of Thomas Jefferson.* Ed. George Green Shackelford. Published by the Monticello Association. Princeton: Princeton University Press, 1965.

The Coolidge Collection. Massachusetts Historical Society.

The Edgehill Randolph Collection. UVA.

The Jefferson Papers. Library of Congress.

*Journals of Congress.*

*Journals of the House of Burgesses.*

The New England Historical and Genealogical Register.

Olive Branch Petition, July 8, 1775. Facsimile. From the original in H.M. Public Record Office, London.

Report of the Committee of Revisers [Jefferson, George Wythe, and Edward Pendleton]. Appointed by the General Assembly of Virginia in 1776. Richmond, 1784.

*Reports of Cases Determined in the General Court of Virginia from 1768 to 1772.* Charlottesville: published by the legatee of Jefferson's manuscript papers, 1829. (This work contains a few of his own cases.)

*The Virginia Gazette.*

*Virginia Historical Register,* vol. 3.

## WRITINGS OF THOMAS JEFFERSON

*The Basic Writings of Thomas Jefferson.* Ed. Philip S. Foner. New York: Wiley, 1944.

*The Commonplace Book of Thomas Jefferson: A Repertory of His Ideas on Government.* Introduction and Notes by Gilbert Chinard. Baltimore: Johns Hopkins Press, 1926.

*The Complete Anas of Thomas Jefferson.* Ed. Franklin B. Sawvel. New York: Round Table Press, 1903.

*The Family Letters of Thomas Jefferson.* Ed. Edwin M. Betts and James A. Bear Jr. Columbia: University of Missouri Press, 1966.

*The Founding Fathers: Thomas Jefferson: A Biography in His Own Words.* Introduction by Joseph L. Gardner. New York: Newsweek, 1974.

*The Jefferson Cyclopedia: A Comprehensive Collection of the Views of Thomas Jefferson, Classified and Arranged in Alphabetical Order.* Ed. J. P. Foley. New York and London: Funk & Wagnalls, 1900.

*A Jefferson Profile as Revealed in His Letters.* Ed. Saul K. Padover. New York: John Day, 1956.

*Jefferson's Literary Commonplace Book.* Ed. Douglas Wilson. Princeton: Princeton University Press, 1989.

*The Literary Bible of Thomas Jefferson: His Commonplace Book of Philosophers and Poets.* Introduction by Gilbert Chinard. Baltimore: Johns Hopkins Press, 1928.

*The Papers of Thomas Jefferson.* Ed. Julian P. Boyd. 20 vols. Vol. 21, Index, ed. Charles Cullen. Princeton: Princeton University Press, 1953.

*The Papers of Thomas Jefferson, Retirement Series,* vol. 1. Ed. J. Jefferson Looney. Princeton: Princeton University Press, 2004.

*Thomas Jefferson: Writings.* Ed. Merrill D. Peterson. New York: Library of America, 1984.

*Thomas Jefferson's Architectural Drawings.* With commentary and a checklist by Frederick Doveton Nichols. Charlottesville: Thomas Jefferson Memorial Foundation and University Press of Virginia, 1961.

*Thomas Jefferson's Farm Book.* Ed. Edwin Morris Betts. Charlottesville: Thomas Jefferson Memorial Foundation, 1999.

*Thomas Jefferson's Farm Book, with Commentary and Relevant Extracts from Other Writings.* Ed. Edwin Morris Betts. Charlottesville: University Press of Virginia, 1976. (Originally owned by the Massachusetts Historical Society.)

*Thomas Jefferson's Garden Book.* Annotated by Edwin Morris Betts. Philadelphia: American Philosophical Society, 1981.

*Thomas Jefferson's Notes on the State of Virginia.* Ed. Frank Shuffleton. New York: Penguin Books, 1999.

*To the Girls and Boys: Being the Delightful, Little-Known Letters of Thomas*

*Jefferson to and from His Children and Grandchildren.* Selected, with histori-
cal notes, by Edward Boykin. New York: Funk & Wagnalls, 1964.
*The Writings of Thomas Jefferson.* Ed. Paul Leicester Ford. 10 vols. New York:
G. P. Putnam's Sons, 1892–99.
*The Writings of Thomas Jefferson.* Ed. A. A. Lipscomb and A. E. Bergh. 20
vols. Washington, D.C.: Thomas Jefferson Memorial Association, 1903.

### WRITINGS OF JEFFERSON'S CONTEMPORARIES

Adams, Abigail. *Letters of Mrs. Adams.* Ed. Charles Francis Adams. Boston,
1848.
Adams, Abigail, and John Adams. *The Book of Abigail and John: Selected Letters
of the Adams Family, 1762–1784.* Ed. L. H. Butterfield, Marc Friedlander,
and Mary-Jo Kline. Cambridge, Mass.: Harvard University Press, 1975.
Adams, John. *Works.* Ed. Charles Francis Adams. 10 vols. Boston, 1856.
Adams, John, and Thomas Jefferson. *The Adams–Jefferson Letters.* Ed. Lester
Cappon. Chapel Hill: University of North Carolina Press, 1988.
Biddle, Nicholas. "Eulogium on Thomas Jefferson." Delivered before the
American Philosophical Society, on April, 11, 1827. Philadelphia:
Robert H. Small, 1827.
Burk, John. *The History of Virginia from Its First Settlement to the Present Day.*
4 vols. Petersburg, Va.: Dickenson & Pescud, 1804–16.
Jefferson, Thomas, and James Madison. *The Republic of Letters: The Corre-
spondence between Thomas Jefferson and James Madison, 1776–1826.*
Ed. James Morton Smith. 3 vols. New York: Norton, 1995.
Lafayette, Marquis de, and Thomas Jefferson. *Letters of Lafayette and Jeffer-
son.* Ed. Gilbert Chinard. Baltimore: Johns Hopkins Press, 1929.
Lee, Richard Henry. *The Letters of Richard Henry Lee.* Ed. James Curtis
Ballagh. 2 vols. New York: Macmillan, 1911–14.
Madison, James. *Papers of James Madison.* Library of Congress.
———. *The Writings of James Madison, . . .* Ed. Gaillard Hunt. 9 vols. New
York: G. P. Putnam's Sons, 1900–1910.
Mazzei, Philip. *Memoirs, 1730–1816.* Trans. Howard R. Marraro. New York:
Columbia University Press, 1942.
Paine, Thomas. *The Writings of Thomas Paine.* Ed. Moncure Daniel Conway.
Vol. 1, 1774–1779. New York and London: Knickerbocker Press, 1894.
Trumbull, John. *Autobiography, Reminiscences and Letters.* New York, 1841.
Washington, George. *Writings.* Ed. J. C. Fitzpatrick. 39 vols. Washington,
D.C.: Government Printing Office, 1931–41.

SECONDARY SOURCES

Abernethy, Thomas Perkins. *Historical Sketch of the University of Virginia.* Richmond: Dietz Press, 1948.

Adair, Douglas. *Fame and the Founding Fathers.* New York: W. W. Norton, 1974.

Adams, Henry. *History of the United States of America during the Administration of Thomas Jefferson.* New York: A and C. Boni, 1930.

Adams, William Howard, ed. *The Eye of Thomas Jefferson.* Washington, D.C.: National Gallery of Art, 1976.

———. *Jefferson's Monticello.* New York: Abbeville Press, 1983.

———. *The Paris Years of Thomas Jefferson.* New Haven: Yale University Press, 1997.

Addis, Cameron. *Jefferson's Vision for Education, 1760–1845.* New York: Peter Lang, 2003.

Appleby, Joyce. *Thomas Jefferson.* New York: Henry Holt, 2003.

Ashley, Maurice. *England in the Seventeenth Century (1603–1714).* Middlesex, England: Penguin Books, 1958.

Bailey, Thomas A., and David M. Kennedy. *The American Pageant: A History of the Republic.* 6th ed. 2 vols. Lexington, Mass.: D. C. Heath, 1979.

Bailyn, Bernard. "Considering the Slave Trade: History and Memory." *William and Mary Quarterly,* 3rd ser., 58, no. 1 (Jan. 2001): 245–52.

———. *Faces of Revolution: Personalities and Themes in the Struggle for American Independence.* New York: Knopf, 1990.

———. *To Begin the World Anew: The Genius and Ambiguities of the American Founders.* New York: Alfred A. Knopf, 2003.

Barrett, Clifton Waller. *The Struggle to Create a University.* University of Virginia Founder's Day Address. Charlottesville: Thomas Jefferson Memorial Foundation, 1973.

Bear, James A., Jr. "The Hemings Family of Monticello." *Virginia Cavalcade* 29, no. 2 (Autumn 1979): 78–87.

———, ed. *Jefferson at Monticello: Recollections of a Monticello Slave and of a Monticello Overseer.* Charlottesville: University Press of Virginia, 1967.

Becker, Carl. *The Declaration of Independence: A Study in the History of Political Ideas.* New York: Vintage Books, 1958.

Bedini, Silvio A. *Declaration of Independence Desk: Relic of Revolution.* Washington, D.C.: Smithsonian Institution Press, 1981.

———. *The Life of Benjamin Banneker.* New York: Charles Scribner's Sons, 1972.

Beloff, Max. *Thomas Jefferson and American Democracy.* London: English Universities Press, 1948.

Beran, Michael Knox. *Jefferson's Demons: Portrait of a Restless Mind.* New York: Free Press, 2003.

Berlin, Ira. *Many Thousands Gone: The First Two Centuries of Slavery in North America.* Cambridge, Mass.: Belknap Press of Harvard University, 1998.

Bernier, Olivier. *The World in 1800.* New York: John Wiley, 2000.

Bernstein, R. B. *Thomas Jefferson.* New York: Oxford University Press, 2003.

Betts, Edwin M., and Hazlehurst Bolton Perkins. *Thomas Jefferson's Flower Garden at Monticello.* Richmond: Dietz Press, 1941.

Bierne, Francis F. "A Visit to Shadwell." Baltimore *Evening Sun,* Apr. 13, 1943.

Binger, Carl. *Thomas Jefferson: A Well-Tempered Mind.* New York: W. W. Norton, 1970.

Black, Jeremy. *Eighteenth-Century Britain, 1688–1783.* New York: Palgrave, 2001.

Bober, Natalie. *Abigail Adams: Witness to a Revolution.* New York: Atheneum Books for Young Readers, 1995.

———. *Countdown to Independence.* New York: Atheneum Books for Young Readers, 2001.

———. *Thomas Jefferson: Man on a Mountain.* New York: Atheneum Books for Young Readers, 1988.

Bobrick, Benson. *Angel in the Whirlwind: The Triumph of the American Revolution.* New York: Simon & Schuster, 1997.

Boorstin, Daniel J. *The Lost World of Thomas Jefferson.* Boston: Beacon Press, 1948.

Bowen, Catherine Drinker. *John Adams and the American Revolution.* Boston: Little, Brown, 1950.

———. *Miracle at Philadelphia: The Story of the Constitutional Convention, May to September, 1787.* Boston: Little, Brown, 1966.

Bowers, Claude G. *Making Democracy a Reality: Jefferson, Jackson, and Pope.* Memphis: Memphis State College Press, 1954.

———. *The Young Jefferson, 1743–1789.* Cambridge, Mass.: Riverside Press, 1945.

Bowling, Kenneth R. "Dinner at Jefferson's: A Note on Jacob E. Cooke's 'The Compromise of 1790.'" *William and Mary Quarterly,* 3rd ser., 28, no. 4 (Oct. 1971): 629–48.

Boyd, Julian P. *The Declaration of Independence: The Evolution of the Text.* Ed. Gerard W. Gawalt. Rev. ed. Washington, D.C.: Library of Congress, 1999.

———. *The Declaration of Independence: The Evolution of the Text as Shown by*

*Facsimiles of Various Drafts by Its Author, Thomas Jefferson.* Princeton: Princeton University Press, 1945.

——. "New Light on Jefferson and His Great Task." *New York Times Magazine*, Apr. 13, 1947.

——. *Number 7: Alexander Hamilton's Secret Attempts to Control American Foreign Policy.* Princeton: Princeton University Press, 1964.

——. *The Spirit of Christmas at Monticello.* New York: Oxford University Press, 1964.

Brodie, Fawn M. *Thomas Jefferson: An Intimate History.* New York: W. W. Norton, 1974.

Brookhiser, Richard. *Founding Father: Rediscovering George Washington.* New York: Free Press, 1996.

——. *What Would the Founders Do?* New York: Basic Books, 2006.

Brown, Margaret W. *Story of the Declaration of Independence Desk and How It Came to the National Museum.* Washington, D.C.: Smithsonian Institute, 1954.

Bruce, Philip Alexander. *History of the University of Virginia, 1819–1919; the Lengthened Shadow of One Man.* Vol. 1. New York: Macmillan, 1920.

Bullock, Helen Duprey. *My Head and My Heart, a Little History of Thomas Jefferson and Maria Cosway.* New York: G. P. Putnam's Sons, 1945.

Burnett, Edmund Cody. *The Continental Congress.* New York: Macmillan, 1941.

Burstein, Andrew. *The Inner Jefferson: Portrait of a Grieving Optimist.* Charlottesville: University Press of Virginia, 1995.

——. *Jefferson's Secrets: Death and Desire at Monticello.* New York: Basic Books, 2005.

——. *Letters from the Head and Heart: Writings of Thomas Jefferson.* Charlottesville: Thomas Jefferson Foundation, 2002.

——. *Sentimental Democracy: The Evolution of America's Romantic Self-Image.* New York: Hill and Wang, 1999.

Bush, Alfred L. *The Life Portraits of Thomas Jefferson.* Princeton: Princeton University Press, 1962.

Butterfield, L. H., and H. C. Rice Jr. "Jefferson's Earliest Note to Maria Cosway with Some New Facts and Conjectures on His Broken Wrist." *William and Mary Quarterly,* 3rd ser., 5, no. 1 (Jan. 1948): 31–32.

Chambers, J. Allen, Jr. *Poplar Forest and Thomas Jefferson.* Forest, Va.: Published for the Corporation for Jefferson's Poplar Forest, 1993.

Chastellux, Marquis de. *Voyages dans l'Amérique.* 2 vols. Paris, 1786.

Cheuk, Beth, ed. *Thomas Jefferson's Monticello.* Charlottesville: Thomas Jefferson Foundation, distributed by University of North Carolina Press, 1998.

Chinard, Gilbert. "Thomas Jefferson as Classical Scholar." *Johns Hopkins Alumni Magazine* 18 (1930): 291–303.

———. *Thomas Jefferson, the Apostle of Americanism.* Boston: Little, Brown, 1929.

Christman, Margaret C. S., ed. *"The Spirit of Party": Hamilton and Jefferson at Odds.* Washington, D.C.: National Portrait Gallery, Smithsonian Institution, 1992.

Coates, Eyler Robert. *The Jefferson–Hemings Myth: An American Travesty.* Presented by the Thomas Jefferson Heritage Society. Charlottesville: Jefferson Editions, 2001.

Commager, Henry Steele. *Jefferson, Nationalism, and the Enlightenment.* New York: George Braziller, 1975.

Conway, Moncure Daniel. *Omitted Chapters of History Disclosed in the Life and Papers of Edmund Randolph.* New York and London: Putnam's, 1888.

Cooke, Jacob Ernest, ed. *Encyclopedia of the North American Colonies.* New York: Charles Scribner's Sons, 1993.

Corzine, Phyllis. *The French Revolution.* San Diego: Lucent Books, 1995.

Crafts, Hannah. *The Bondwoman's Narrative.* Ed. Henry Louis Gates Jr. New York: Warner Books, 2002.

"The Creation of the American Republic, 1776–1787: A Symposium of Views and Reviews." Forum in *William and Mary Quarterly,* 3rd ser., 44, no. 3 (July 1987): 549–640.

Cripe, Helen. *Thomas Jefferson and Music.* Charlottesville: University Press of Virginia, 1974.

Cunningham, Nobel E., Jr. *In Pursuit of Reason: The Life of Thomas Jefferson.* Baton Rouge: Louisiana State University Press, 1987.

Dabney, Virginius. *The Jefferson Scandals: A Rebuttal.* New York: Dodd, Mead, 1981.

———. *Mr. Jefferson's University: A History.* Charlottesville: University Press of Virginia, 1981.

Davis, Betty Elise. *Monticello Scrapbook.* Charlottesville: Michie Co., 1939.

Davis, David Brion. *The Problem of Slavery in the Age of Revolution, 1770–1823.* New York: Oxford University Press, 1999.

———. *Slavery in the Colonial Chesapeake.* Williamsburg, Va.: Colonial Williamsburg Foundation, 1986.

Davis, David Brion, and Robert P. Forbes. Foreword to *William and Mary Quarterly,* 3rd ser., 58, no. 1 (Jan. 2001): 7–8.

Donovan, Frank. *The Thomas Jefferson Papers.* New York: Dodd, Mead, 1963.

Dos Passos, John. *The Head and Heart of Thomas Jefferson.* Garden City, N.Y.: Doubleday, 1954.

Dreisbach, Daniel L. *Thomas Jefferson and the Wall of Separation between Church and State.* New York: New York University Press, 2002.

Eliot, Charles W., ed. *American Historical Documents: 1000–1904.* New York: P. F. Collier, 1938.

Ellis, Edward S. "Thomas Jefferson, a Character Sketch." *The Patriot* (The University Association, Chicago) 1, no. 1 (Apr. 1898).

Ellis, Joseph J. *American Sphinx: The Character of Thomas Jefferson.* New York: Alfred A. Knopf, 1997; Vintage ed. 1998.

———. *Founding Brothers: The Revolutionary Generation.* New York: Alfred A. Knopf, 2000.

———. *His Excellency: George Washington.* New York: Alfred A. Knopf, 2004.

———, ed. *What Did the Declaration Declare?* Boston: Bedford/St. Martin's, 1999.

Ferling, John. *A Leap in the Dark: The Struggle to Create the American Republic.* New York: Oxford University Press, 2003.

———. *Setting the World Ablaze: Washington, Adams, Jefferson, and the American Revolution.* Oxford: Oxford University Press, 2000.

Fleming, Thomas. *The Man from Monticello.* New York: William Morrow, 1969.

Fliegelman, Jay. *Declaring Independence: Jefferson, Natural Language, and the Culture of Performance.* Stanford: Stanford University Press, 1993.

Foster, Eugene, et al. "Jefferson Fathered Slave's Last Child." *Nature Magazine,* Nov. 5, 1998, 27–28.

Fowler, William M., Jr. *The Baron of Beacon Hill: A Biography of John Hancock.* Boston: Houghton Mifflin, 1980.

Franklin, John Hope. *Mirror to America.* New York: Farrar, Straus and Giroux, 2005.

Franklin, John Hope, and Alfred A. Moss Jr. *From Slavery to Freedom: A History of Negro Americans.* New York: McGraw-Hill, 1988.

Freehling, William W. *The Road to Disunion,* vol. 1: *Secessionists at Bay, 1776–1854.* New York: Oxford University Press, 1990.

Freeman, Joanne B. *Affairs of Honor: National Politics in the New Republic.* New Haven: Yale University Press, 2001.

Freudenberg, Anne. *Malone and Jefferson.* Charlottesville: University of Virginia Library, 1981.

Gates, Henry Louis, Jr. Preface to *William and Mary Quarterly,* 3rd ser., 58, no. 1 (Jan. 2001): 3–5.

Goodman, Dena. "Enlightenment Salons: The Convergence of Female and Philosophic Ambitions." *Eighteenth-Century Studies* 22 (1989): 329–50.

Gordon-Reed, Annette. *Thomas Jefferson and Sally Hemings: An American Controversy*. Charlottesville: University Press of Virginia, 1997.

Green, Jack P., and J. R. Pole, eds. *The Blackwell Encyclopedia of the American Revolution*. Cambridge, Mass.: Blackwell Reference, 1991.

Grizzard, Frank. "Joinery at Jefferson's Monticello." Unpublished manuscript, 1989, Jefferson Library, Monticello.

Hall, Gordon Langley. *Mr. Jefferson's Ladies*. Boston: Beacon Press, 1966.

Halliday, E. M. *Understanding Thomas Jefferson*. New York: HarperCollins, 2001.

Hamowy, Ronald. "Jefferson and the Scottish Enlightenment: A Critique of Garry Wills's *Inventing America. . . .*" *William and Mary Quarterly* 36 (1979): 503–23.

Heath, Barbara J. *Hidden Lives: The Archaeology of Slave Life at Thomas Jefferson's Poplar Forest*. Charlottesville: University Press of Virginia, 1999.

Heath, James A. "Thomas Jefferson: Architect of American Public Education." Ph.D. diss., Pepperdine University, 1998.

Hochman, Steven Harold. "Thomas Jefferson: A Personal Financial Biography." Ph.D. diss., University of Virginia, 1987.

Horn, James, Jan Ellen Lewis, and Peter Onuf, eds. *The Revolution of 1800: Democracy, Race, and the New Republic*. Charlottesville: University of Virginia Press, 2002.

*In Search of Early America:* William and Mary Quarterly, *1943–1993*. Williamsburg, Va.: Institute of Early American History and Culture, 1993.

Jayne, Allen. *Jefferson's Declaration of Independence: Origins, Philosophy, and Theology*. Lexington: University Press of Kentucky, 1998.

Jordan, Winthrop D. *White over Black: American Attitudes toward the Negro, 1550–1812*. Chapel Hill: Published for the Omohundro Institute of Early American History and Culture at Williamsburg, Va., by the University of North Carolina Press, 1968.

Kelso, William M. "Digging on Jefferson's Mountain." *World Book Encyclopedia—1985 Yearbook*, 100–117. Chicago: World Book, 1985.

Kennedy, Roger G. *Mr. Jefferson's Lost Cause: Land, Farmers, Slavery, and the Louisiana Purchase*. New York: Oxford University Press, 2003.

Ketcham, Ralph. *Presidents above Party: The First American Presidency, 1789–1829*. Chapel Hill: University of North Carolina Press, 1984.

Kimball, Fiske. *Life Portraits of Thomas Jefferson*. Charlottesville: Thomas Jefferson Memorial Foundation, 1962.

———. "Thomas Jefferson and the First Monument of the Classical Revival in America." *Journal of the American Institute of Architects* III, no. 9 (Sept. 1915).

Kimball, Marie. "The Epicure of the White House." *Virginia Quarterly Review* 9 (Jan. 1933): 71–81.

———. "In Search of Jefferson's Birthplace." *Virginia Magazine of History and Biography* 51 (Oct. 1943): 313–25.

———. *Jefferson: The Road to Glory.* Westport, Conn.: Greenwood Press, 1977.

———. *Jefferson: The Scene of Europe.* New York: Coward McCann, 1950.

———. *Jefferson: War and Peace.* New York: Coward McCann, 1947.

———. "Jefferson, Patron of the Arts." *Antiques* 43, no. 4 (Apr. 1943): 164–67.

Koch, Adrienne, ed. *The American Enlightenment: The Shaping of the American Experiment and a Free Society.* New York: George Braziller, 1965.

———. *The Philosophy of Thomas Jefferson.* New York: Columbia University Press, 1943.

Kolchin, Peter. *American Slavery, 1619–1877.* New York: Hill and Wang, 2003.

Langhorne, Elizabeth. "Black Music and Tales from Jefferson's Monticello." *Folklore and Folklife in Virginia* 1 (1979).

———. *Monticello: A Family Story.* Chapel Hill: Algonquin Books, 1989.

Lanier, Shannon, and Jane Feldman. *Jefferson's Children: The Story of One American Family.* New York: Random House, 2000.

Lester, Julius, comp. *To Be a Slave.* New York: Scholastic, 1968.

Levy, Andrew. "The Anti-Jefferson." *American Scholar* 70 (Spring 2001): 15–35.

Lewis, Jan. *The Pursuit of Happiness: Family and Values in Jefferson's Virginia.* Cambridge: Cambridge University Press, 1983.

Lewis, Jan, and Peter Onuf, eds. *Sally Hemings and Thomas Jefferson: History, Memory, and Civic Culture.* Charlottesville: University Press of Virginia, 1999.

Locke, John. *John Locke: Two Treatises of Government.* Ed. Peter Laslett. London: Cambridge University Press, 1960.

Lyons, Mary E. *Letters from a Slave Girl: The Story of Harriet Jacobs.* New York: Aladdin Paperbacks, 1996.

Madonia, Ann C., ed. *Facing the Past: Portraits from the Permanent Collection.* Catalog of an exhibition held at the Muscarelle Museum of Art, Williamsburg, Va., March 20–August 15, 1999.

Maier, Pauline. *American Scripture: Making of the Declaration of Independence.* New York: Random House, 1998.

Malone, Dumas. *Jefferson and His Time.* 6 vols. Boston: Little, Brown, 1948–81.

Vol. 1, *Jefferson the Virginian* (1948).

Vol. 2, *Jefferson and the Rights of Man* (1951).

Vol. 3, *Jefferson and the Ordeal of Liberty* (1962).

Vol. 4, *Jefferson the President: First Term, 1801–1805* (1970).

Vol. 5, *Jefferson the President: Second Term, 1805–1809* (1974).

Vol. 6, *The Sage of Monticello* (1981).

———. "Jefferson Goes to School in Williamsburg." *Virginia Quarterly Review* 33, no. 4 (Autumn 1957).

———. "Mr. Jefferson's Private Life." *Proceedings of the American Antiquarian Society* 84 (1974).

———. "Polly Jefferson and Her Father." *Virginia Quarterly Review* 7 (Jan. 1931): 81–95.

Malone, Dumas, and William H. B. Thomas. *A Miracle of Virginia—the School for Statesmen.* Charlottesville: Ben Franklin Publishing, 1984.

Mapp, Alf J., Jr. *The Faiths of Our Fathers: What America's Founders Really Believed.* Lanham, Md.: Rowman & Littlefield, 2003.

———. *Thomas Jefferson: A Strange Case of Mistaken Identity.* New York: Madison Books, 1987.

Marty, Martin E. Preface to *Jefferson and Religion,* by Eugene R. Sheridan. Charlottesville: Thomas Jefferson Memorial Foundation, 1998.

Mayo, Bernard. *Another Peppercorn for Mr. Jefferson.* Charlottesville: Thomas Jefferson Memorial Foundation, 1977.

McColley, Robert. *Slavery and Jeffersonian Virginia.* Urbana: University of Illinois Press, 1973.

McCoy, Drew R. *The Last of the Fathers: James Madison and the Republican Legacy.* Cambridge: Cambridge University Press, 1989.

McLaughlin, Jack. *Jefferson and Monticello: The Biography of a Builder.* New York: Henry Holt, 1988.

Mellon, Matthew T. *Early American Views on Negro Slavery.* New York: Bergman, 1969.

Miller, Charles A. *Jefferson and Nature: An Interpretation.* Baltimore: Johns Hopkins University Press, 1988.

Miller, John Chester. *Origins of the American Revolution.* Boston: Little, Brown, 1943.

———. *The Wolf by the Ears: Thomas Jefferson and Slavery.* Charlottesville: University Press of Virginia, with the Thomas Jefferson Memorial Foundation, 1991.

Miroff, Bruce. *Icons of Democracy: American Leaders as Heroes, Aristocrats, Dissenters, and Democrats.* New York: Basic Books, 1993.

Moore, Roy, and Alma Moore. *Thomas Jefferson's Journey to the South of France.* Introduction by Lucia Stanton. New York: Stewart, Tabori & Chang, 1999.

Morgan, Edmund S. *American Slavery, American Freedom: The Ordeal of Colonial Virginia.* New York: Norton, 1975.

————. *The Meaning of Independence.* Charlottesville: University Press of Virginia, 1976.

Morgan, Philip. *Slave Counterpoint: Black Culture in the Eighteenth-Century Chesapeake and Lowcountry.* Chapel Hill: Published for the Omohundro Institute of Early American History and Culture, Williamsburg, Va., by the University of North Carolina Press, 1998.

Moscow, Henry, with Dumas Malone. *Thomas Jefferson and His World.* New York: American Heritage, 1960.

Munves, James. *Thomas Jefferson and the Declaration of Independence.* New York: Charles Scribner's Sons, 1978.

Nash, Gary B. *The Unknown American Revolution: The Unruly Birth of Democracy and the Struggle to Create America.* New York: Viking Penguin, 2005.

Nichols, Frederick D., and James A. Bear Jr. *Monticello: A Guidebook.* Monticello: Thomas Jefferson Memorial Foundation, 1982.

Nock, Albert Jay. *Mr. Jefferson.* Tampa: Hallberg, 1983.

Nutting, Wallace. *Virginia Beautiful.* New York: Garden City, 1935.

Ohline, Howard A. "Republicanism and Slavery: Origins of the Three-Fifths Clause in the United States Constitution." *William and Mary Quarterly,* 3rd ser., 28, no. 4 (Oct. 1971): 563–84.

Onuf, Peter. "Every Generation Is an 'Independant Nation': Colonialization, Miscegenation, and the Fate of Jefferson's Children." *William and Mary Quarterly,* 3rd ser., 57, no. 1 (Jan. 2000): 153–70.

————, ed. *Jeffersonian Legacies.* Charlottesville: University Press of Virginia, 1993.

————. *Jefferson's Empire: The Language of American Nationhood.* Charlottesville: University Press of Virginia, 2000.

————. "The Scholars' Jefferson." *William and Mary Quarterly,* 3rd ser., 50, no. 4 (Oct. 1993): 671–99.

Padover, Saul K. *Thomas Jefferson.* New York: Harcourt, Brace, 1942.

Parton, James. *Life of Thomas Jefferson.* Boston: James R. Osgood, 1874. Reprint, New York: Da Capo Press, 1971.

Penrice, Daniel. "Jeffersonian Architecture." *Bostonian Magazine* (Boston University) 59, no. 4 (July/Aug. 1985).

Peterson, Merrill D. *Adams and Jefferson: A Revolutionary Dialogue.* New York: Oxford University Press, 1976.

————. *The Jefferson Image in the American Mind.* New York: Oxford University Press, 1960.

————, ed. *Thomas Jefferson: A Reference Biography.* New York: Charles Scribner's Sons, 1986.

————. *Thomas Jefferson and the American Revolution.* Williamsburg: Virginia Independence Bicentennial Commission, 1976.

————. *Thomas Jefferson and the New Nation: A Biography.* New York: Oxford University Press, 1970.

————, ed. *Visitors to Monticello.* Charlottesville: University Press of Virginia, 2000.

Peterson, Merrill D., and Robert C. Vaughan, eds. *The Virginia Statute for Religious Freedom: Its Evolution and Consequences in American History.* Cambridge: Cambridge University Press, 1988.

Pierson, Rev. Hamilton W. *Jefferson at Monticello: The Private Life of Thomas Jefferson.* New York: C. Scribner, 1862.

Pinkney, Andrea Davis. *Dear Benjamin Banneker.* New York: Harcourt Brace, 1994.

Popkin, Richard H. "The Philosophical Basis of Eighteenth-Century Racism." In *Racism in the Eighteenth Century,* ed. Harold E. Pagliaro, 245–62. Cleveland: The Press of Case Western University, 1973.

Rakove, Jack N. "Our Jefferson." In *Sally Hemings and Thomas Jefferson: History, Memory, and Civic Culture,* ed. Jan Lewis and Peter Onuf, 217–24. Charlottesville: University Press of Virginia, 1999.

Randall, Henry S. *The Life of Thomas Jefferson.* 3 vols. 1857. Freeport, N.Y.: Books for Libraries Press, 1970.

Randall, Willard Sterne. *Thomas Jefferson: A Life.* New York: Henry Holt, 1993.

Randolph, Edmund. "Edmund Randolph's Essay on the Revolutionary History of Virginia (1774–1782)." *Virginia Magazine of History and Biography* 43, no. 2 (Apr. 1935).

Randolph, Sarah N. *The Domestic Life of Thomas Jefferson.* New York: Frederick Ungar, 1958.

Rawlings, Mary. *The Albemarle of Other Days.* Charlottesville: Michie Co., 1925.

Rose, Willie Lee. *Slavery and Freedom.* Ed. William W. Freehling. New York: Oxford University Press, 1982.

Rosenberger, Francis Coleman, ed. *Jefferson Reader: A Treasury of Writings about Thomas Jefferson.* New York: E. P. Dutton, 1953.

Rowse, A. L. "The Other Jefferson House." *New York Times,* Travel sec., July 6, 1986.

Russell, Phillips. *Jefferson, Champion of the Free Mind.* New York: Dodd, Mead, 1956.

Rutland, Robert A. *George Mason: Reluctant Statesman.* Baton Rouge: Louisiana State University Press, 1989.

Sanford, Charles B. *Thomas Jefferson and His Library.* Hamden, Conn.: Archon Books, 1977.

Schwarz, Philip J. *Slave Laws in Virginia.* Athens: University of Georgia Press, 1996.

————, ed. *Slavery at the Home of George Washington.* Mt. Vernon, Va.: Mount Vernon Ladies' Association, 2001.

————. *Twice Condemned: Slaves and the Criminal Laws of Virginia, 1705–1865.* Baton Rouge: Louisiana State University Press, 1988.

Sheridan, Eugene R. *Jefferson and Religion.* Monticello Monograph Series. Charlottesville: Thomas Jefferson Memorial Foundation, 2000.

Simon, James F. *What Kind of Nation: Thomas Jefferson, John Marshall, and the Epic Struggle to Create a United States.* New York: Simon & Schuster, 2002.

Sloan, Herbert E. *Principle and Interest: Thomas Jefferson and the Problem of Debt.* Charlottesville: University of Virginia Press, 2001.

Smith, Margaret Bayard. *The First Forty Years of Washington Society.* Ed. Gaillard Hunt. New York: Charles Scribner's Sons, 1906.

Smith, Vern E. "Debating the Wages of Slavery." *Newsweek,* August 27, 2001, 20–25.

Sobel, Mechal. *The World They Made Together: Black and White Values in Eighteenth-Century Virginia.* Princeton: Princeton University Press, 1987.

Stanton, Lucia. *Free Some Day: The African-American Families of Monticello.* Monticello Monograph Series. Charlottesville: Thomas Jefferson Foundation, 2000.

————. "The Other End of the Telescope." *William and Mary Quarterly,* 3rd ser., 57, no. 1 (Jan. 2000): 140–43.

————. *Slavery at Monticello.* Monticello Monograph Series. Charlottesville: University Press of Virginia, 1993; Charlottesville: Thomas Jefferson Memorial Foundation, 1996.

Stanton, Lucia, and Dianne Swann-Wright. *Getting Word: The Monticello African-American Oral History Project.* Charlottesville: Thomas Jefferson Foundation, 2002.

Sydnor, Charles S. *American Revolutionaries in the Making.* New York: Free Press, 1965.

Takaki, Ronald. *A Different Mirror: A History of Multicultural America.* Boston: Little, Brown, 1993.

"Thomas Jefferson and Sally Hemings Redux." Forum in *William and Mary Quarterly,* 3rd ser., 57, no. 1 (Jan. 2000): 121–210.

*Time,* July 4, 1976. Special 1776 issue.

Tomlins, Christopher L., and Bruce H. Mann, eds. *The Many Legalities of Early America.* Chapel Hill: University of North Carolina Press, 2001.

Tripp, Valerie. *An Introduction to Williamsburg.* Wisconsin: Pleasantry Press, in cooperation with the Colonial Williamsburg Foundation, 1985.

Van der Linden, Frank. *The Turning Point: Jefferson's Battle for the Presidency.* Golden, Col.: Fulcrum, 2000.

Webster, Donald, Jr. "The Day Jefferson Got Plastered." *American Heritage* 14, no. 4 (June 1963).

Weymouth, Lally, ed. *Thomas Jefferson: The Man, His World, His Influence.* New York: G. P. Putnam's Sons, 1973.

Whitehill, Walter Muir. "The Many Faces of Monticello." Address at Monticello, April 13, 1964. Charlottesville: Thomas Jefferson Memorial Foundation, 1965.

Whitney, Jeanne, ed. *The Colonial Williamsburg Interpreter Handbook.* Williamsburg, Va.: Department of Interpretive Education, 1985.

Wilkins, Roger. *Jefferson's Pillow.* Boston: Beacon Press, 2001.

Wills, Garry. *Henry Adams and the Making of America.* New York: Houghton Mifflin, 2005.

———. *Inventing America: Jefferson's Declaration of Independence.* Garden City, N.Y.: Doubleday, 1978.

———. *Lincoln at Gettysburg: The Words That Remade America.* New York: Simon & Schuster, 1992.

———. *Mr. Jefferson's University.* Washington, D.C: National Geographic Society, 2002.

———. *Negro President: Jefferson and the Slave Power.* New York: Houghton Mifflin, 2003.

———, ed. *Thomas Jefferson: Genius of Liberty.* New York: Viking Studio, in association with the Library of Congress, 2000.

———. "Uncle Thomas's Cabin." Review of *Thomas Jefferson: An Intimate History,* by Fawn M. Brodie. *New York Review of Books,* Apr. 18, 1974.

Wilson, Douglas. "Evolution of Jefferson's *Notes on the State of Virginia,*" *Virginia Magazine of History and Biography* 112, no. 2 (2004): 111–12.

———. *Jefferson's Books.* Monticello Monograph Series. Charlottesville: Thomas Jefferson Memorial Foundation, 1996.

Wilson, Gaye. "Jefferson's Big Deal: The Louisiana Purchase," *Monticello* 14, no. 1 (Spring 2003).

Wilson, Gaye, and Elizabeth V. Chew. "Fashioning an American Diplomat." *Dress* 29 (2002): 19–25.

Wilstach, Paul. *Jefferson and Monticello.* New York: Doubleday, Doran, 1939.

Wirt, William. *The Life of Patrick Henry.* New York: McElrath & Bangs, 1831.

Wood, Gordon S. *The Creation of the American Republic, 1776–1787.* Chapel Hill: University of North Carolina Press, 1998.

————. *The Radicalism of the American Revolution.* New York: Alfred A. Knopf, 1992.

————. *Revolutionary Characters: What Made the Founders Different.* New York: Penguin, 2006.

Woodfin, Maude. "Contemporary Opinion in Virginia of Thomas Jefferson." In *Essays in Honor of William E. Dodd,* ed. Avery Craven. Chicago: University of Chicago Press, 1935.

*The World of Franklin and Jefferson.* Catalog for an exhibition designed by the office of Charles and Ray Eames, with the cooperation of the Metropolitan Museum of Art. New York: Metropolitan Museum of Art, 1976.

Yarbrough, Jean M. *American Virtues: Thomas Jefferson on the Character of a Free People.* Lawrence: University Press of Kansas, 1998.

————. "Race and the Moral Foundation of the American Republic: Another Look at the Declaration and the Notes on Virginia." *Journal of Politics* 53, no. 1 (Feb. 1991).

Yetman, Norman R. *Voices from Slavery.* New York: Holt, Rinehart, and Winston, 1970.

### FILMS

*The Eye of Thomas Jefferson.* National Gallery of Art, 1976.

*Thomas Jefferson.* Directed by Ken Burns. PBS Home Video, 1997.

*Williamsburg—the Story of a Patriot.* Colonial Williamsburg Foundation, 1957.

### WEB SITES

Association for Preservation of Virginia Antiquities, Preservation Virginia, two dozen sites (including Jamestown): http://www.apva.org

Colonial Williamsburg, colonial and revolutionary Virginia: http://www.history.org

Family Letters Project, the correspondence of Thomas Jefferson's family members: http://familyletters.dataformat.com/default.aspx

Journey through Hallowed Ground, historic sites between Charlottesville and Gettysburg: http://www.hallowedground.org/index.php

Monticello, the home of Thomas Jefferson: http://www.monticello.org/index.html

Monticello Archaeology, including the Digital Archaeological Archive of Comparative Slavery: http://www.monticello.org/archaeology/index.html

Monticello Explorer, virtual tour of the house and grounds: http://explorer.monticello.org/index.html

Thomas Jefferson Digital Archive, compiled at the University of Virginia: http://etext.virginia.edu/jefferson

Thomas Jefferson Portal online catalog, information relevant to his life, times, and legacy: http://tjportal.monticello.org

Thomas Jefferson's Poplar Forest: http://www.poplarforest.org

Thomas Jefferson Papers, an electronic archive of materials at the Massachusetts Historical Society: http://www.thomasjeffersonpapers.org

# Index